Intimate
Letters
of
England's
Kings

MARGARET
SANDERS

AMBERLEY

First Published 1959

This edition first published 2014

Amberley Publishing
The Hill, Stroud
Gloucestershire, GL5 4EP

www.amberley-books.com

British Library Cataloguing in Publication Data.
A catalogue record for this book is available from the British Library.

ISBN 978 1 4456 3810 2 (paperback)   .
ISBN 978 1 4456 2026 8 (ebook)

Typeset in 10pt on 12pt Sabon.
Typesetting and Origination by Fakenham Prepress Solutions.
Printed in the UK.

Contents

Preface

'Nothing is so capable of giving a true account of *History*', wrote Dean Swift, 'as *Letters* are; which describe actions while they are *alive* and *breathing*, whereas all *other* relations are of actions *past* and *dead*'.

Nevertheless, few readers – however interested in their country's history – could be expected to have the inclination, still less the time these days, to pore over old tomes and documents in the hope of coming across some diverting letters, or illuminating first-hand information relating to famous persons or events of bygone centuries. Yet there is to be found in historical archives much material which if presented imaginatively and in a defined pattern – an aim here humbly attempted – can convey a clear conception of 'the renowned dead' as individuals.

While this selection of *Intimate Letters of England's Kings* has been compiled as an independent work and is complete in itself, at the same time it serves as a companion volume to *Intimate Letters of England's Queens*, and covers the identical period in history from the Tudor Dynasty to the House of Hanover. There are, of course, numerous letters extant written by Kings of England prior to the Tudor period, but to have included even a percentage of these would have made too copious a collection. It was therefore considered best to confine the scope of this compilation to the three dynasties most familiar to the general reader, as was done in the case of the queens' correspondence.

The object of this book is the same as that of the previous volume: to present for the general reader's interest and entertainment, through the medium of specially selected letters, aspects of each sovereign's personal character and circumstances perhaps not commonly known, and these royal scribes' feelings and reactions – vital or ephemeral – regarding happenings in their private or public lives.

It should be emphasised that the compilation is in no way concerned with the kings' abilities as rulers or in statecraft: for, as will be appreciated, it does not necessarily follow that a monarch virtuous in his domestic life is by that fact a correspondingly good ruler, or a dissolute king a bad ruler.

The spelling generally has been made conformable with modern usage, except in the case of the letters of Henry VII, where the ancient words and quaint phraseology have been retained in order not to destroy the character of the originals. Although this first Tudor monarch's correspondence could not be termed intimate, it is concerned with matters directly personal to himself, and is noteworthy in that it provides contemporary information regarding the impostors – Lambert Simnel and Perkin Warbeck – who sought to rob him of his throne. In certain other instances, too, letters have been introduced into this collection which while not being strictly intimate throw light on important happenings affecting the particular king's individual attitudes and affairs.

Brief details of each sovereign's personal history have been included in the text to refresh the reader's memory, and to be of assistance in following the circumstances pertaining at the time that the letter was written.

Margaret Sanders
Scotsgrove
Near Thame
Oxon

1

Henry VII (1457–1509)

Henry VII, son of Edmund, Earl of Richmond, and Margaret Beaufort, only child of John, Duke of Somerset, was born – reputedly at Pembroke Castle in Wales – on 26 June 1457. 'It was on this day of St Anne', records his mother in one of her letters, 'that I did bring into the world my good and gracious prince, and only beloved son'. The little countess was in her fourteenth year when she became a mother, and within a few months of her son's birth she was left a widow.

Owing to Margaret Beaufort's extraction – she was a great-granddaughter of John of Gaunt, fourth son of Edward III – her son became of no small political importance during the Wars of the Roses, as alleged heir to the House of Lancaster, of which John of Gaunt had been the root. As a consequence, with the ascendancy of the House of York, Henry of Richmond was to know adversities and endure exile for over a quarter of a century before, without means or title, he assumed the Crown of England at the age of twenty-eight.

He was acclaimed king in 1485 after his victory over Richard III on Bosworth Field, and by his politic marriage with Elizabeth of York – the eldest daughter of Edward IV and Elizabeth Woodville and the direct claimant to the succession – the Royal Houses of York and Lancaster were united. Thus was established the House of Tudor, so named after Henry's paternal grandfather, Owen Tudor.

This first Tudor monarch, however, was to find himself faced with no easy task in maintaining his kingship. The long and furious civil wars were not at an end, and he was forced to keep a vigilant eye on the insubordinate nobility, while abroad he had the reputation of being a mere adventurer. He had won the Crown by conquest in one battle only. It was considered he might just as easily forfeit it again by defeat in a future affray.

The new king in no way smoothed his own path by his attitude towards his consort, due to jealousy of her influence and her superior claim. His harsh treatment of Elizabeth of York, combined with his refusal at first to her right to a coronation, increased the enmity of the partisans of the House of York. Further, the birth of his son Arthur occasioned additional antagonism, as it threatened to perpetuate the Crown in the family of one who was regarded by the Yorkist faction as a usurper.

One of Henry's deadliest opponents was Margaret, sister of Edward IV and widow of Charles 'the Bold', Duke of Burgundy. Eager for the restoration of the House of York, she was so active in engineering plots against Henry VII that she was known as Henry's 'Juno', because she was to him 'as Juno was to Æneas, stirring both heaven and hell to do him mischief'.

With her nephew, the Earl of Lincoln, she was determined to create internal strife against the new sovereign. It was unquestionably due to her intrigues that within two years of Henry's ascending the throne the Lambert Simnel rebellion broke out. The instigators had conceived a fantastic plot by which Simnel – a young and handsome offspring of a joiner at Oxford – was persuaded to impersonate Edward Plantagenet, orphan son of the Duke of Clarence, a younger brother of Edward IV. Edward Plantagenet was under guard in the Tower at the time, Henry VII having sensed there might be trouble from that quarter. It is assumed that the plotters, not wishing to endanger the real Edward's life, produced

Simnel as a counterfeit with the intention that if the rebellion succeeded they would free Edward Plantagenet and declare him king, as a true Warwick.

When the disturbing news of this challenge to his sovereignty reached Henry VII, he sent out a call to arms, and prudently decided to bring the real Edward of Warwick from the Tower. He had him presented before the populace at St Paul's before sending him into confinement at the royal palace at Sheen.

Shortly afterwards the insurgents, headed by Lincoln with an army supplied by Margaret of Burgundy, suffered defeat at Stoke, in Nottinghamshire, at the hands of the king's forces. Lincoln and other leaders of the rebellion were found dead on the field. The fifteen-year-old Lambert Simnel, however, was taken prisoner. He was fortunate in not losing his life on the gallows. Simnel had no worse fate, as every schoolchild knows, than being made a turnspit in the king's kitchens, but nevertheless a depressing contrast of fortune for one who had been ceremoniously crowned in Dublin as Edward VI, King of England and France, and Lord of Ireland not so very long before.

As a result of this insurrection Henry VII realised that he would be well advised to propitiate the House of York by recognising his wife's regal status. He hastily issued instructions for her coronation, and made ample provision for her maintenance as his queen. From that time, instead of being kept determinedly in the background, Elizabeth of York enjoyed the same consideration as former queens of England.

Nevertheless, six years later occurred another and more serious attempt by the House of York to wrest the Crown from Henry VII. The impostor on this occasion was Perkin Warbeck, a native of Tournay in Picardy. Twenty years of age, of handsome appearance and courtly manners, the pretender to the throne announced himself as Richard, second son of Edward IV, who had been supposed murdered in the Tower with his brother, Edward V, ten years earlier.

The youth's claim was, for a time, supported by Charles VIII of France, and he was publicly acclaimed by Margaret of Burgundy, who dubbed him 'The White Rose of England', and appointed him a special guard of halberdiers. How he explained his escape from the Tower, and where he had been living in the interim, is not recorded. In any event, his story satisfied the king's enemies that he was indeed Richard, Duke of York. It was supposed that Margaret of Burgundy had tutored him for the part he was to play, and that he was actually a natural son of Edward IV. James IV of Scotland also looked favourably upon Perkin Warbeck's claim, and gave him in marriage a near relation, Lady Catherine Gordon, daughter of the Earl of Huntly.

To Sir Gilbert Talbot, 1493

The news of Warbeck's advent flung Henry VII into a state of turmoil and anxiety once more. In the following letter to Sir Gilbert Talbot – a valued servant who had distinguished himself on Bosworth Field, on which occasion he had been created knight banneret by Henry VII – the king is outlining his instructions in a call to arms to meet this fresh threat to his kingdom.

Trusty and well-beloved, We greet you well: And not forgetting the great malice that the Lady Margaret of Burgundy beareth continually against us – as she showed lately in sending hither of a feigned boy, surmising him to have been the son of the Duke of Clarence, and caused him to be accompanied with the Earl of Lincoln, the Lord Lovel[1] and with great multitude of Irishmen and of Almains[2] whose end, blessed be God! was as ye know well: And forseeing now the perseverance of the same her malice, by the untrue contriving eftsoon[3] of another feigned lad called Perkin Warbeck, born of Tournay in Picardy (which at first [coming] into Ireland called himself the bastard son of King Richard; and after that the son of the said Duke of Clarence; and now the second son of our father [-in-law], King Edward the IVth, whom God assoil): Wherethrough she intendeth, by promising unto the Flemings and other of the archduke's obeissaunce[4] – to whom she laboureth daily to take her way – and by her promise to certain aliens, captains of strange nations, to have [as reward] duchies, counties, baronies, and other lands within this our realm, to induce them thereby to land here to the destruction and disinheritance of the noblemen and other of our subjects the inhabitants of the same, and finally to the subversion of this our realm: In case she attaine to her malicious purpose – that God defend! – we therefore, and to the intent that we may be alway purveied[5] and in readiness to resist her malice, write unto you at this time, and will and desire you that, preparing on horseback, defensibly arrayed, four score persons, whereof we desire you to make as many spears, with their custrells[6] and demi-lances, well-horsed as ye can furnish, and the remainder to be archers and bills,[7] ye be thoroughly appointed and ready to come upon a day's warning for to do us service of war in this case.

And ye shall have for every horseman well and defensibly arrayed, that is to say, for a spear and his custrel twelvepence; a demi-lance ninepence; and an archer, or bill, on horseback, eightpence by the day, from the time of your coming out unto the time of your return to your home again. And thus doing, ye shall have such thanks of us for your loving, and true acquittal in that behalf as shall be to your weal and honour for time to come. We pray you herein ye will make such diligence as that ye be ready with your said number to come unto us upon any our sudden warning.

Given under our signet at our castle of Kenilworth,[8] the twentieth day of July, 1493.

To our trusty and well-beloved knight and councillor, Sir Gilbert Talbot.

To the mayor and citizens of Waterford, 1497

Perkin Warbeck's grave threat to Henry's crown was not to be easily repelled. In fact, the activities of the pretender and his supporters were to trouble the king and the nation for nearly seven years. Henry was almost in despair of subduing the insurrectionists, until the Battle of Blackheath in 1497 terminated in a decisive victory for the king, and the arrest of Perkin Warbeck. He was taken to London, where he remained a close prisoner for six months.

Warbeck succeeded, however, in making good his escape, but the coast was so vigilantly guarded that he was compelled to surrender himself to the prior of the monastery at Beaulieu, as mentioned by Henry in the following letter to the Mayor of Waterford, on which city Warbeck had made unsuccessful siege a year or so earlier.

Trusty and well-beloved, We greet you well: And whereas Perkin Warbeck, lately accompanied by divers and many our rebels of Cornwall, advanced themselves to our city of Exeter, which was denied unto them, and so they came to the town of Taunton: at which town as soon as they had knowledge that our chamberlain, our steward of house-hold, Sir John Chynie[9] and other of our loving subjects with them, were coming so far forth towards the said Perkin as to our monastery of Glastonbury – the same Perkin took with him John Heron, Edward Skelton, and Nicholas Ashley, and stole away from his said company about midnight, and fled with all the haste they could make. We had well provided beforehand for the sea-coasts, that, if he had attempted that way (as he thought indeed to have done) he should have been put from his purpose, as it is coming to pass. For, when they perceived they might not get to the sea, and that they were had in a quick chase and pursuit, they were compelled to address themselves unto our monastery of Beaulieu;[10] to the which, of chance and of fortune, it happened some of our menial servants to repair, and some we sent thither purposely.

The said Perkin, Heron, Skelton and Ashley, seeing our said servants there – and remembering that all the country was warned to make watch and give attendance, that they should not avoid nor escape by sea – made instances unto our servants to sue unto us for them, the said Perkin desiring to be sure of his life and he would come unto us, and show what he is; and, over that, do unto us such service as should content us. And so by agreement between our said servants and them, they [were encouraged] to depart from Beaulieu, and to put themselves in our grace and pity.

The abbot and convent hearing thereof demanded of them why and for what cause they would depart. Whereunto they gave answer in the presence of the said abbot and convent, and of many other, that, without any manner of constraint, they would come unto us of their free wills, in trust of our grace and pardon aforesaid. And so, the said Perkin came unto us to the town of Taunton, from whence he [had] fled; and immediately after his first coming, humbly submitting himself unto us, hath of his free will openly showed, in the presence of all the council here with us, and of other nobles, his name to be *Piers Osbeck*, (whereas he hath been named Perkin Warbeck), and to be none Englishman born, but born of Tournay, and son of John Osbeck, and sometime while he lived comptroller of the said Tournay; with many other circumstances too long to write, declaring by whose means he took upon him this presumption and folly.[11]

And so, now this great abusion[12] which hath long continued, is now openly known by his own confession: We write this news unto you, for we be undoubtedly sure, that calling to mind the great abusion that divers folks have been in, by reason of the said Perkin, and the great business and charges that we and our realm have been put unto in that behalf, you would be glad to hear the certainty of the same, which we affirm unto you for assured truth.

Sithence the writing of these premises, we be ascertained that Perkin's wife is in good surety for us, and trust that she shall shortly come unto us to this our city of Exeter, as she is in dole[13] ...

And sithence our coming to this our city of Exeter for the punition[14] of this great rebellion, and for so to order the parts of Cornwall, as the people may live in their due obeisances[15] to us and in good restfulness unto themselves for time to come; the commons of this shire of Devon come daily before us in great multitudes in their shirts, the foremost of them having halters about their necks, and full humbly with lamentable cries for our grace and remission, submit themselves unto us; whereupon doing, first, the chief stirrers and misdoers [among them having been tried out] for to abide their corrections according, we grant to the residue our said grace and pardon. And our commissioners, the Earl of Devon, our chamberlain, and our steward of household, have done and do daily in likewise in our county of Cornwall.

Yeven under our signet at our said city of Exeter, the 17th day of October.

To our trusty and well-beloved, the Mayor and his brethren of our city of Waterford.

The subsequent history of the pretender may here briefly be related. He was confined to the Tower, but being detected in conjunction with the Earl of Warwick in plotting against the Government and forming new plans of escape, he was hanged at Tyburn in 1499, after Henry VII had spared his life for upwards of two years. Warwick – last of the Plantagenet princes – was beheaded on Tower Hill shortly after Perkin Warbeck's death.

To his mother, Margaret Beaufort, *c.* 1498

The fame of the high-born Margaret Beaufort, Countess of Richmond – one of the wealthiest and most cultured women of her day – is due more to her benevolence and encouragement of learning than to the fact that she was the mother of Henry VII. She was a patroness of England's first printer and book-seller, Caxton, and founded St John's and Christ's colleges at Cambridge, as well as chairs of divinity there and at Oxford.

After being twice widowed, she took as her third husband Lord Thomas Stanley, later created Earl of Derby. It was at this time that Margaret Beaufort acted as State governess to Elizabeth of York, and it was she herself who had suggested to her son, Henry, after the murder of the little princes in the Tower (whether at the instigation of their uncle, Richard III, or Henry VII is debatable) that he should marry their sister, the direct heir to the Crown.

Henry VII had a deep regard for his mother, as is evidenced by the following excerpts from a letter he wrote to her. Although the communication is undated, it was obviously written prior to 1501, in which year the 'Maister Fisher' mentioned by Henry was appointed chancellor of Cambridge University.

Madame, my most entirely Well-beloved Lady and Mother,

I recommend me unto you in the most humble and lowly wise that I can, beseeching you of your daily and continual blessings.

By your confessor, the bearer, I have received your good and most loving writing ... I shall be as glad to please you as your heart can desire it, and I know well that I am as much bounden so to do as any creature living, for the great and singular motherly love and affection that it hath pleased you at all times to bear towards me. Wherefore, mine own most loving Mother, in my most hearty manner I thank you, beseeching you of your good continuance of the same.

And, madame, your said confessor hath moreover shown unto me, on your behalf, that ye, of your goodness and kind disposition, have given and granted unto me such title and interest as ye have – or ought to have – in such debts and duties which are owing and due unto you in France by the French king[16] and others: wherefore, madame, in my most hearty and humble wise, I thank you. Howbeit, I verily think it will be right hard to recover it [the title] without it being driven by compulsion and force – rather than by any true justice – which is not yet, as we think, any convenient time to be put into execution …

And verily, madame, and I might recover it at this time, or any other, ye be sure ye should have your pleasure therein, as I – and all that God has given me – am, and ever shall be, at your will and commandment, as I have instructed Master Fisher[17] more largely herein, as I doubt not he will declare unto you. And I beseech you to send me your mind and pleasure in the same, which I shall be full glad to follow, with God's grace, the which send and give unto you the full accomplishment of all your noble and virtuous desires.

Written at Greenwich,[18] the 17th day of July, with the hand of your most humble and loving son,

H.R.

… Madame, I have encumbered you now with this long writing, but think that I can do no less, considering that it is so seldom that I do write, wherefore I beseech you to pardon me: for verily, madame, my sight is nothing so perfect as it has been, and I know well it will appayre[19] daily, wherefore I trust that you will not be displeased, though I write not so often with mine own hand, for on my faith I have been three days or I could make an end of this letter.

To My Lady

At the comparatively early age of fifty-two, worn out in mind and body in his determined efforts to stabilise his position and his kingdom, Henry VII died in the spring of 1509 at his palace at Richmond. Originally known as Sheen Palace, the old manor had belonged to the Crown since 1320, but had been destroyed by fire during Henry's reign. He had had the palace rebuilt on a grand scale, and changed its name to Richmond in honour of his own title as Earl of Richmond.

Despite the continuous rebellions that troubled his reign of twenty-four years, Henry VII proved a merciful monarch, sparing bloodshed wherever possible. His main concern was the acquisition of treasure for his coffers, where probably he estimated that his greatest power lay. He died 'the wealthiest prince in Christendom' as a consequence.

The king was buried in the chapel that he founded, and that bears his name, in Westminster Abbey, in the same tomb as his queen, Elizabeth of York, who had predeceased him by six years. Margaret Beaufort died shortly after her son, having acted as regent until Henry VIII's coronation, and was buried in the same chapel.

2

Henry VIII (1491–1547)

Henry VII's second son – born at Greenwich Palace on 28 June 1491 – proved to be the first monarch for centuries to succeed his father without opposition. Happily for Henry VIII he possessed the advantage of uniting in his own person, through his parentage, the line of 'The White Rose' of Lancaster and 'The Red Rose' of York. This strong fusion in blood was responsible for bringing to an end any further broils between those two houses.

When the youthful Henry ascended the throne at the age of eighteen he could claim all the attributes in a monarch guaranteed to delight his subjects. He was handsome, he was spirited, had splendid physique, enjoyed magnificent attire and display, and was skilled in 'all manly sports and pastimes'. In this connection, the Venetian ambassador, in the course of describing the new king's attractions, struck a surprisingly modern note when he wrote to his court, 'He [the king] is extreme fond of tennis, which game it is the prettiest thing in the world to see him play, his fair skin glowing through a shirt of the finest texture.' Nature had done a great deal for Henry. Fortune, materially, had also bestowed gifts upon him. Being easy and generous, Henry VIII was more than ready to squander the treasure which his father had taken such trouble to amass. He had more serious interests, all the same, and endeared himself to men of learning by his appreciation of letters. He was also a good linguist, and no mean musician.

Apart from a series of relatively unimportant amours, the king lived for a number of years in more or less harmonious relationship with his first consort, Catherine of Aragon, his elder brother's widow. Prince Arthur had died at Ludlow Castle in 1502, a victim of what was known as *Sudor Anglicus* – 'English Sweat'. Even before his accession Henry VIII had declared that he desired Catherine 'above all women; above all he loved her, and longed to wed her'.

The turning point in his life can be said to date from the time of his meeting with the femme fatale in the person of Anne Boleyn. This intense and over-mastering passion was to disclose the latent vicious tendencies in Henry VIII's character to the full, spelling disaster for those who loved or sought to serve him. In the early years of his reign, however, despite his obviously rapacious and arbitrary temperament, he maintained high popularity as a sovereign.

To Cardinal Wolsey, *c.* 1515

Although it bears no date, the following letter from the king to Thomas Wolsey must have been written towards the close of the year 1515, as Wolsey was not named cardinal until September of that year. The expected child was therefore Princess Mary, who was born on 18 February 1516 – likewise at Greenwich Palace – and to whom the cardinal acted as godfather.

In view of the fact that Catherine of Aragon had already lost two children shortly after their births, Henry VIII's anxiety regarding his wife's condition, as disclosed in this hasty and somewhat vague missive, can be appreciated. In the normal course he was a clear-headed, if unscrupulous, correspondent, and could write with expression and conviction, and also with charm when he chose.

My Lord Cardinal,[1]

I recommend unto you as heartily as I can, and I am right glad to hear of your good health, which I pray God may long continue. So it is that I have received your letters, to the which (by cause they ask long writing) I have made answer by my secretary.

Two things there be which be so secret that they cause me at this time to write to you myself. The one is that I trust the Queen my wife to be with child; the other is chief cause why I am loth to repair Londonward, by cause about this time is partly of her dangerous times, and by cause of that, I would remove her as little as I may now.

My lord, I write this unto you, not as an ensured thing, but as a thing wherein I have great hope and likelihood, and by cause I do well know that this thing will be comfortable to you to understand: therefore I do write it unto you at this time ...

Written with the hand of your loving prince,

Henry R.

The accompanying interesting series of love letters from Henry VIII to Anne Boleyn calls for a brief explanation. According to certain historical records the letters were stolen from Anne Boleyn's desk towards the end of the year 1528, at which time contention regarding the king's proposed separation from Catherine of Aragon was reaching its peak. The correspondence was conveyed to Rome, in all probability owing to the intrigues of Cardinal Wolsey, who, while initially approving of the annulment of the king's marriage, disapproved of Henry VIII's intention to marry Anne Boleyn.

Suspicion as to who had been responsible for confiscating the letters, however, fell at the time on the papal legate, Campeggio, who had come over from Rome to adjudicate with Wolsey on the validity of the marriage of the king to his brother's widow. As a result of his being suspect, on his departure for Rome the papal legate had to submit to the indignity of having his baggage searched on the pretence that he was conveying some of Wolsey's treasure out of England. No letters, however, were found in his possession and it was assumed that he had had them smuggled abroad by secret agency. If it was Campeggio who had secured this incriminating correspondence it was doubtless done with Wolsey's full connivance.

When the success of the French in Italy, under Bonaparte, in 1796–7 compelled the Pope to sue for peace, among the trophies demanded by the republican general were five hundred manuscripts to be selected by the French commissioners. The letters of Henry VIII formed part of this booty. How they had originally found their way into the archives of the Vatican is not disclosed. They were transferred at this period to the Bibliothèque du Roi in Paris. There they remained until the stipulations of the general peace of 1815 obliged France to disgorge the treasures of art and literature of which she had plundered the nations of Europe.

During the time of their retention in Paris these letters had been copied with scrupulous accuracy, so we are informed, by a responsible member of the manuscript department of the Bibliothèque du Roi. Since none of them bore any date, however, it is impossible to ascertain their true chronological order, and their arrangement can only be a matter of opinion. They are given here in what would seem their probable sequence.

The factual data in the précis matter to each letter is from information obtained from Strickland's *Lives of the Queens of England*. Albeit conjectural in relation to the substance of the letters, the précis can be accepted by the reader as reasonably accurate in view of authenticated events in Anne Boleyn's personal history.

Incidentally, Voltaire's witty if superficial remark – 'England separated herself from the Pope because Henry VIII fell in love' – is not without significance in the light of the letters that follow.

To the Lady Anne Boleyn

Records of the early life of the woman who was to cause such an astounding upheaval not only in the history of the royal family but in that of the whole nation are unfortunately contradictory and obscure. It is for this reason that it is impossible to establish the exact year of Anne Boleyn's birth. The earliest year assigned is 1501, the latest 1507, but neither of these dates rests on satisfactory authority. All things considered, however, the first would appear to accord better with the early circumstances of this ill-starred queen's career.

While still in her early teens, Anne Boleyn was one of the English suite chosen by Louis XII to serve in attendance on his youthful bride, Mary – Henry VIII's younger sister, whom Anne accompanied to France in 1514. Anne did not return to this country with the widowed Mary, whose ageing husband had died in 1515, but entered the court of Claude, queen of Francis I, and was absent from England for the next seven years. She made her fateful appearance in the household of Catherine of Aragon in 1522, and swiftly embarked on a romantic love affair with Lord Henry Percy, eldest son of the Earl of Northumberland. Although at this time she was not interested, apparently, in the king's attraction to herself, Henry VIII's jealousy caused him to find means of forcing the lovers to break off their engagement. Anne's resentment was deep, and it seems to have been for this reason that she chose to absent herself from court.

The following letter from her pertinacious royal lover was obviously written to Anne owing to her attitude to the king's behaviour. Henry had privately instructed Wolsey to put an end to Anne's engagement to Percy, so that no blame should fall on him, but Anne had doubtless guessed the truth.

To My Mistress

    As the time seems very long since I heard from you, or concerning your health, the great love I have for you constrains me to send this bearer, to be better informed both of your health and pleasure, particularly because, since my last parting with you, I have been told that you have entirely changed the mind in which I left you, and that you neither mean to come to court with your mother,[2] nor any other way; which report, if true, I cannot enough marvel at, being persuaded in my own mind that I have never committed any offence against you.

And it seems hard, in return for the great love I bear you, to be kept at a distance from the person and presence of the woman in the world that I value the most; and if you loved with as much affection as I hope you do, I am sure that the distance of our two persons would be equally irksome to you – though this does not belong so much to the mistress as to the servant.

Consider well, my mistress, how greatly your absence afflicts me. I hope it is not your will that it should be so. But if I heard for certain that you yourself desire it, I could but mourn my ill fortune, and strive by degrees to abate of my folly. And so, for lack of time, I make an end of this rude letter, beseeching you to give the bearer credence in all he will tell you from me.

Written by the hand of your entire servant,

H.R.

To the Lady Anne Boleyn

From the following letter that Henry VIII wrote to Anne Boleyn at this juncture in their relationship it is obvious that her replies were proving far from satisfactory to her ardent suitor. Her experience at the court of France would have amply qualified Anne in the art of finesse where the game of hearts was concerned, and for some years she was to play her cards with skill.

By revolving in my mind the contents of your last letters, I have put myself into great agony, not knowing how to interpret them – whether to my disadvantage (as I understand some of them) or not. I beseech you earnestly to let me know your real mind as to the love between us two. It is needful for me to obtain this answer, having been for a whole year wounded with the dart of love, and not yet assured whether I shall succeed in finding a place in your heart and affection.

This uncertainty has hindered me of late from declaring you my mistress, lest it should prove that you only entertain for me an ordinary regard. But if you please to do the duty of a true and loyal mistress, and give up yourself heart and body to me, who will be, as I have been, your most loyal servant (if your rigour does not forbid me), I promise you that not only the name shall be given you, but, also that I will take you for my mistress, casting off all others that are in competition with you out of my thoughts and affections, and serving you only.

I beg you to give an entire answer to this my rude letter; that I may know on what and how far I may depend; but if it does not please you to answer me in writing, let me know some place where I may have it by word of mouth, and I will go thither with all my heart.

No more, for fear of tiring you.

Written by the hand of him who would willingly remain

Yours,

H. Rex

To the Lady Anne Boleyn, 1528

From all accounts Anne continued to remain aloof for some time. She would not, of course, have been unaware of the king's ruthless treatment of his previous mistresses, and evidently had no intention of becoming an easy prey to his desires. Eventually, however – probably owing to her father's urgent persuasions, on whose family Henry VIII had begun to shower honours – Anne Boleyn returned to Catherine of Aragon's court.

The king's obsession was before long obvious to everyone, and painfully so to the queen herself. Although she fiercely upbraided Henry VIII in private, Catherine of Aragon never condescended to discuss the matter with his mistress, whose influence at court was increasing beyond measure. It must have been a galling situation for this princess of the ancient and noble Spanish House of Aragon and Castile, but to the very end Catherine of Aragon was to maintain her regal dignity.

The 'book' mentioned by the royal theologian in this letter to Anne was a treatise which he was preparing on the unlawfulness of his marriage to Catherine, which dates the communication as having been written in 1528.

Anne would seem to have made another of her occasional tantalising withdrawals from court to her home at Hever Castle, in Kent. This may have been done to incite the king's ardour, and thereby cause him to toil laboriously at his 'Book of Divorcement' during her absence.

Mine Own Sweetheart,

This shall be to advertise you of the great elengeness[3] that I find here since your departing, for I assure you me thinketh the time longer now since your departing last than I was wont to do a whole fortnight. I think your kindness and my fervency of love causeth it; for, otherwise, I would not have thought it possible that for so little a while it should have grieved me.

But now that I am coming towards you, methinketh my pains be half removed; for also I am right well comforted in so much that my book maketh substantially for my matter[4], in attending to which I have spent above four hours this day, which causes me now to write the shorter letter to you at this time, because of some pain in my head.

Wishing myself (especially an evening) in my sweetheart's arms, whose pretty dukkys I trust shortly to kiss.

Written with the hand of him that was, is, and shall be yours by his own will.

To the Lady Anne Boleyn, 1528

The design of the costly jewel presented by Anne Boleyn to the king, and mentioned by him in the following letter, is of interest. It suggests that she entertained serious doubts and misgivings at times as to her royal lover's stability of affection, and the real nature of his intentions where she was concerned.

Henry VIII reassures her, however, declaring he will outdo her 'in loyalty of heart'. Yet Anne's instinct was not at fault.

For a present so valuable, that nothing could be more (considering the whole of it), I return to you my most hearty thanks, not only on account of the costly diamond, and the ship in which the solitary damsel is tossed about, but chiefly for the fine interpretation and the too humble submission which your goodness hath made to me; for I think it would be very difficult for me to find an occasion to deserve it, if it were not assisted by your great humanity and favour, which I have always sought to seek, and will always seek to preserve by all the services in my power; and this is my firm intention and hope, according to the motto, *Aut illic aut nullibi.*[5]

The demonstrations of your affections are such, the fine thoughts of your letter so cordially expressed, that they oblige me for ever to honour, love, and serve you sincerely, beseeching you to continue in the same and constant purpose; and assuring you that, on, my part, I will not only make you a suitable return, but outdo you in loyalty of heart, if it be possible.

I desire, also, that if at any time before this I have in any way offended you, that you would give me the same absolution that you ask, assuring you that hereafter my heart shall be dedicated to you alone. I wish my person was too. God can do it, if He pleases, to whom I pray once a day for that end, hoping that at length my prayers will be heard. Written by the hand of that secretary, who, in heart, body, and will is

> *Votre royal et plus assure serviteur,*
> *Hy. autre A. B., ne cherche.* Rex.[6]

To the Lady Anne Boleyn, 1528

The epidemic known as 'sweating sickness' made its first appearance in England in 1485. It began in the army with which Henry VIII's father, when Earl of Richmond, landed at Milford Haven (from France, where he had spent his years of exile), and soon spread to London. At given intervals it returned. On the fourth appearance of the 'sweating sickness' in 1517 it carried off a great number of the nobility, and in some towns half the inhabitants.

The outbreak to which Henry VIII is referring in the following letter occurred in 1528 – thus establishing the year in which the letter was written – many courtiers dying of the disease, which generally proved fatal within six hours. Du Bellai, French ambassador at the English court, furnishes interesting particulars of the epidemic in a letter written at this time, in the course of which he remarks, 'One of the *filles de chambre* of Mademoiselle de Boulen [*sic*] was attacked on Tuesday by the sweating sickness. The king left in great haste, and went a dozen miles off, but it is denied that the lady Anne de Boulen was sent away, as suspected, to her brother, the Viscount [George Boleyn, Viscount Rochford, who was later to be beheaded as one of Anne's alleged lovers], who is in Kent. This disease which broke out here four days ago is the easiest in the world to die of. You have a slight pain in the head, and at the heart; all at once you begin to sweat. There is no need for a physician: for if you uncover yourself the least in the world, or cover yourself a little too much, you are taken off without languishing. It is true that if you merely put your hand out of bed during the twenty-four-hours, you instantly become stiff as a peacock ... The king has removed further than he was, and hopes that he shall not have the complaint. Still, he keeps on his guard, confesses every day, receives the sacrament on all holy days, and likewise the queen, who is with him.'

The main subject of the king's letter to Anne Boleyn, however, relates to their joint concern as to the morals of certain inmates of a nunnery. The convent in question – Wilton Abbey in Wiltshire – was according to tradition originally founded in the ninth century by Alfred the Great. Members of the order of the black Benedictine nuns were attired in coarse black serge, interwoven with horsehair, and wore a thick black veil. From the little to be gathered from Henry VIII's letter, it would appear that this unattractive garb was not having the desired chastening effect on that community.

Since your last letters, mine own darling, Walter Welsh, Master Brown, John Clare, Brion of Brearton, and John Cork, the apothecary, be fallen of the sweat in this house, and thanked be God, all well recovered, so that as yet the plague is not fully ceased here, but I trust shortly it shall. By the mercy of God, the rest of us yet be well, and I trust shall pass it, either not to have it, or, at the least, not as easily as the rest have done.

As touching the matter of Wilton [Abbey], my lord Cardinal hath had the nuns before him, and examined them, Mr Bell being present. They have certified me that, for a truth, she – which we would have had abbess – has confessed herself to have had two children by two sundry priests; and further, that she has since been kept by a servant of the Lord Broke[7] that was, and that not long ago. Wherefore, I would not for all the gold in the world clog your conscience nor mine to make her ruler of a house which is of so ungodly demeanour. Nor, I trust, you would not that neither for brother nor sister I should so disdain mine honour or conscience.

And as touching the prioress, and Dame Eleanor's eldest sister, though there is not any evident case proved against them – and that the prioress is so old that for many years she could not be as she was named – yet notwithstanding, to do you pleasure I have decided that neither of them shall have it,[8] but that some other good and well-disposed woman shall have it, whereby the house shall be better reformed, whereof, I assure you, it hath much need, and God much the better served.

As touching your abode at Hever, do therein as best shall like you, for you know best what air doth best suit you.[9] But I would it were come thereto – if it pleased God – that neither of us need care for that, for I assure you I think it long.

Suche is fallen sick of the sweat, and therefore I send you this bearer, because I think you long to hear tidings from us, as we do likewise from you.

Written with the hand *de votre seul*,

H.R.

To the Lady Anne Boleyn, 1528

The 'sweating sickness' finally broke out seriously at the court, and Anne departed to Hever. The king himself, in great personal fear of infection, having already attempted reconciliation with his consort, hurriedly removed himself and the queen as far as possible from London. They retired to Ampthill Palace in Bedfordshire.

There the alarmed monarch went into quarantine, and occupied his time – when not at devotions – compounding medicines, and mixing ointments and lotions to alleviate the sickness. In these practices he was aided by one of his physicians, Dr Butts. Between them they concocted a remedy, as they claimed, known as 'The king's Own Plaister', the royal prescription being made public for the benefit of those enforced to remain in the infected areas.

The following letter has been published many times as a sample of the king's love letters to Anne. It was written while the regal medico was at Ampthill. In spite of his dread of death from the plague, the epistle indicates that the king's ardour 'for a brown girl, with a wen on her throat, and an extra finger'[10] had in no way cooled.

My Mistress and My Friend,

My heart and I surrender ourselves into your hands, and we supplicate to be commended to your good graces, and that by absence your affections may not be diminished to us. For that would be to augment our pain, which would be a great pity, since absence gives enough and more than I ever thought could be felt. This brings to my mind a fact in astronomy, which is, that the further the poles are from the sun, nothwithstanding, the more scorching is his heat. Thus it is with our love; absence has placed distance between us, nevertheless fervour increases – at least on my part. I hope the same from you, assuring you that in my case the anguish of absence is so great, that it would be intolerable were it not for the firm hope I have of your indissoluble affection towards me.

In order to remind you of it, and because I cannot in person be in your presence, I send you the thing which comes nearest that is possible; that is to say, my picture, and the whole device, which you already know of, set in bracelets, wishing myself in their place when it pleaseth you. This is from the hand of

Your servant and friend,

H.R.

To the Lady Anne Boleyn, 1528

Anxiety over the health of his absent mistress continued to agitate and 'frighten' the infatuated monarch, as he makes apparent in the letter that follows.

One of the first victims of the epidemic had been William Carey, Anne's brother-in-law and a gentleman of the king's bedchamber. Carey's death left Anne's sister, Mary, with two children and in reduced circumstances. In the last paragraph Henry is replying to an appeal made by Anne on behalf of her sister, there evidently having been trouble with their stepmother. The latter had been strongly opposed to Mary's love-match with Carey, and was of the opinion that as she had brought pecuniary troubles on herself, Mary should not expect her father to provide for her in her extremity. While the king displays no particular sympathy for Mary – who had been one of his earlier mistresses – it is clear that he is satisfied that his 'mandate' will serve to intimidate Anne's stepmother.

The uneasiness my doubts about your health gave me, disturbed and frightened me exceedingly, and I should not have had any quiet without hearing certain tidings. But now since you have as yet felt nothing, I hope it is with you as it is with us. For when we were at Walton, two ushers, two *valets-de-chambre*, and your brother fell ill, but are now quite well; and since we have returned to your house at Hundsdon[11] we have been perfectly well, God be praised, and have not, at present, one sick person in the family. And I think if you would retire from the Surrey side, as we did, you would escape all danger.

There is another thing which may comfort you, which is, that in truth, in this distemper, few or no women have been taken ill; and besides no person of our court.[12] and few elsewhere, have died of it. For which reason I beg you, my entirely beloved, not to frighten yourself, or to be too uneasy at our absence, for wherever I am, I am yours. And yet we must sometimes submit to our misfortunes, for whoever will struggle against fate is generally but so much the further from gaining his end. Wherefore comfort yourself and take courage, and make this misfortune as easy to you as you can, for I hope shortly to make you sing '*le renvoye*'.[13]

In regard to your sister's matter, I have caused Walter Welche[14] to write to my lord[15] my mind thereon, whereby I trust that Eve shall not deceive Adam; for surely, whatever is said, it cannot stand with his honour but that he must needs take her, his natural daughter,[16] now in her extreme necessity. No more to you at this time, mine own darling, but for a short time I would we were together an evening.

With the hand of yours,

H.R.

To the Lady Anne Boleyn, 1528

All the same, in spite of the king's reassurances in the foregoing letter, both Anne and her father fell victims of the epidemic within a very short space of time. The upsetting news of Anne's illness was conveyed to the king by express messenger at midnight, and he at once dispatched the physician with whom he had been busy concocting lotions. Anne was seriously ill, but was not fated to die on a bed of sickness. Under Dr Butts's care – or maybe due to faith in 'The king's Own Plaister' – she and her father made good recovery.

The most displeasing news that could occur came to me suddenly at night. On three accounts I must lament it. One, to hear of the illness of my mistress, whom I esteem more than all the world, and whose health I desire as I do mine own: I would willingly bear half of what you suffer to cure you. The second, from the fear that I shall have to endure my wearisome absence much longer, which has hitherto given me all the vexation that was possible. The third, because my physician (in whom I have most confidence) is absent at the very time when he could have given me the greatest pleasure. But I hope, by him and his means, to obtain one of my chief joys on earth; that is, the cure of my mistress. Yet, from the want of him, I send you my second.[17] and hope that he will soon make you well. I shall then love him more than ever. I beseech you to be guided by his advice in your illness. By your doing this, I hope soon to see you again, which will be to me a greater comfort than all the precious jewels in the world.

Written by that secretary who is, and for ever will be, your loyal and most assured servant,

H.R.

To the Lady Anne Boleyn, 1528

In due course, fears regarding the epidemic having been allayed, Anne Boleyn hastened back to court. The French ambassador, du Bellai, who had predicted that her influence would be totally eclipsed by absence, was now compelled to report to his government that the contrary was the case. 'I believe the king to be so infatuated with her', he wrote, 'that God alone could abate his madness'. In fact, the pens of all the foreign envoys were scratching away busily during the Boleyn scandal. 'Madame Anne', wrote the Venetian ambassador, who was evidently not impressed by the king's mistress, 'is not one of the handsomest women in the world. She is of middling stature, swarthy complexion, long neck, wide mouth, bosom not much raised, and has in fact nothing but the king's great appetite and her eyes, which are black and beautiful.'

Public opinion, too, became so strong against Anne that eventually the king considered it wiser for her to return to Hever Castle for a while, more especially as Campeggio, the papal legate, was expected shortly to arrive from Rome. Anne retired in great dudgeon, declaring that she would return to court no more. The perplexed king, troubled by her perversity, attempted every means of conciliation, and continued to write Anne tender epistles in the following strain.

Although, my mistress, it has not pleased you to remember the promise you made me when I was last with you; that is, to hear good news from you, and to have an answer to my last letter, yet it seems to me that it belongs to a true servant (seeing that otherwise he can know nothing) to inquire the health of his mistress; and to acquit myself of the duty of a true servant, I send you this letter, beseeching you to apprise me of your welfare. I pray this may continue as long as I desire mine own.

And to cause you yet oftener to remember me, I send you, by the bearer of this, a buck killed last evening very late, by mine own hand – hoping, that when you eat it, you may think of the hunter. From want of room, I must end my letter. Written by the hand of your servant, who very often wishes for you instead of your brother.

H.R.

To the Lady Anne Boleyn, 1528

The legate referred to in the following letter from the king to Anne Boleyn was Campeggio. He was finally to arrive in England in the autumn of 1528 to hold the council of enquiry on the validity of Henry VIII's marriage to his brother's widow.

The reasonable request in your last letter, with the pleasure also that I take to know them true, causes me to send you these news. The legate whom we most desire arrived at Paris on Sunday or Monday last, so that I trust by the next Monday to hear of his arrival at Calais. And then I trust within a while after to enjoy that which I have so longed for, to God's pleasure, and both our comforts.

No more to you at this present, mine own darling, for lack of time. But I would that you were in my arms, or I in yours – for I think it long since I kissed you.

Written after the killing of a hart, at eleven of the clock;
purposing with God's grace, tomorrow, mighty timely, to kill
another, by the hand which, I trust, shortly shall be yours.

Henry R.

Eventually the sympathies of Campeggio and Wolsey were
won over to the queen's cause, after a private conference they
had with her. From that time Wolsey's downfall was inevitable.
'I have been to visit the Cardinal in his distress', wrote the
French ambassador a short while later, 'and have witnessed
the most striking change of fortune. He explained to me his
hard case in the worst rhetoric that was ever heard. Both his
tongue and his heart failed him. He recommended himself
to the pity of the king and madame [Francis I of France and
his mother, Louise, Duchess of Angoulême] with sighs and
tears, and at last left me without having said anything near so
moving as his appearance. His face is dwindled to one-half its
natural size.'

It was during this crisis that Henry VIII was driven to
frenzy by the discovery that his love letters to Anne had
mysteriously disappeared from her desk. She had evidently
been careless with her keys. As already mentioned, the
king issued instructions for Campeggio's baggage to be
searched at Dover. The papal legate was highly indignant. He
protested strongly at the rifling of his trunks. After receiving a
meaningless apology he was permitted to set sail for Italy.

To the Lady Anne Boleyn, 1528

Having absented herself from court for some time, Anne,
in response to the king's entreaties, consented to return.
She made a condition, however. She must be given more
commodious accommodation than that offered at Durham
House. This residence on the banks of the Thames in the

Strand had been a gift to her from Henry VIII. It had been the London residence of Catherine of Aragon when she was Princess of Wales.

The king was delighted to meet the demands of his adored mistress, especially as her request would serve better his own wishes. Using the disgraced and unhappy Wolsey as his agent he secured for Anne the palatial Suffolk House that adjoined the cardinal's own palace – known as York House. At the same time Henry took the opportunity of 'borrowing' York House from the cardinal for his own use, as it provided better facilities for him to visit Anne Boleyn without the knowledge of curious observers. In fact, the king found the cardinal's mansion so convenient that he never returned the 'loan' to the ecclesiastical commissioners on Wolsey's death in 1529. It formed the nucleus of his palace at Whitehall.[18]

In the following hasty letter Henry VIII is announcing that he has obtained a more sumptuous residence according to Anne's request, and that matters affecting the annulment of his marriage are receiving earnest attention.

Darling,

Though I have scant leisure, yet, remembering my promise, I thought it convenient to certify you briefly in what case our affairs stand.

As touching a lodging for you,[19] we have got one by my lord cardinal's means, the like or hire of which could not have been found hereabouts for all causes, as this bearer shall more show you.

As touching our other affairs, I assure you there can be no more done, nor more diligence used, nor all manner of dangers both foreseen and provided for, so that I trust it shall be hereafter to both our comforts, the specialities whereof were both too long to be written, and hardly by messenger to be declared. Wherefore, till your repair hither, I keep something in store, trusting it shall not be long; for I have caused my lord, your father, to make his provisions with speed; and thus, for lack of time, darling, I make an end of my letter, written with the hand of him which I would were yours.

H.R.

To the Lady Anne Boleyn, 1528

While the arrangements for acquiring Suffolk House were in course of completion, the king was caused no little annoyance by discovering that the information he had been sending in confidence to Anne was publicly known in London within twenty-four hours. It would seem that Anne was a tittle-tattler, and in her vanity could not refrain from boasting to all around her of the arrangements the king was making to have easy, if private, access to her presence.

The following reproving letter that he wrote to her is couched in gentle terms, which shows how greatly Henry VIII indulged Anne at this romantic stage in their association.

Darling,

I heartily commend me to you, acquainting you that I am a little perplexed with such things as your brother shall, on my part, declare unto you, to whom I pray you will give full credit, for it were too long to write. In my last letters, I writ to you that I trusted shortly to see you; this is better known in London than anything that is about me, whereof I not a little marvel, but *lack* of *discreet* handling must needs be the cause.

No more to you at this time, but that I trust shortly our meeting shall not depend upon other men's light handling, but upon your own. Writ with the hand of him that longs to be yours.

H.R.

To the Lady Anne Boleyn, 1528

This love letter would appear to have been written when the king was expecting Anne's early return to London and Suffolk House. She took possession of her stately mansion in December, 1528, for on the 9th of that month the French ambassador reported, 'Madamoiselle de Boulan has arrived, and the king has placed her in very fine lodgings immediately adjoining his own: and there, every day, more court is paid to her than *she* ever paid the queen.'

Suffolk House, in fact, became the court. There Anne Boleyn held daily levies, with all the pomp and ceremony of royalty, having her ladies-in-waiting, train bearers and chaplains, and receiving the homage due to Henry VIII's queen.

The approach of the time for which I have so long waited rejoices me so much, that it seems almost to have come already. However, the entire accomplishment cannot be till the two persons meet, which meeting is more desired by me than any thing in this world. For what joy can be greater upon earth than to have the company of her who is dearest to me, knowing likewise that she does the same on her part, the thought of which gives me the greatest pleasure.

Judge what an effect the presence of that person must have on me, whose absence has grieved my heart more than either words or writing can express, and which nothing can cure, save but by begging you, my mistress, to tell your father from me, that I desire him to hasten the time appointed[20] by two days, that he may be at court before the old term or, at farthest, on the day prefixed. For otherwise I shall think he will not do the lover's turn, as he said he would, nor answer my expectation.

No more at present for lack of time; hoping shortly that by word of mouth I shall tell you the rest of the sufferings endured by me from your absence.

Written by the hand of the secretary, who wishes himself at

this moment privately with you, and who is, and always will be,

    Your loyal and most assured servant,

                Hy. autre A.B *ne cherche.* Rex.

The marriage between Henry VIII and Catherine of Aragon was annulled after twenty-four years in 1533 on the grounds that, since Catherine had been the widow of Henry's brother, it had been an 'incestuous intercourse according to the laws of God'.

The magnificent coronation of Queen Anne followed immediately. She was drawn through London's streets in 'a white chariot. There she sat, dressed in white tissue robes, her hair flowing loose over her shoulders, and her temples circled with a light coronet of gold and diamonds – most beautiful, most favoured, as she seemed at that hour, of all England's daughters.'

To Grace, Lady Bedingfeld, 1536

Within four years of the annulment of her marriage, Catherine of Aragon died at Kimbolton Castle in Bedfordshire, where she had been placed in the custody of Sir Edmund Bedingfeld and his wife. Her constitution had been gradually weakened by the mental suffering she had undergone and the climate of the damp fen district, unsuited to one of her warm Spanish blood.

Particulars as to her funeral are mainly to be gathered from the following letter that the king sent at the time to Lady Bedingfeld.

Henry Rex, To our right dear and well-beloved Lady Bedingfeld.

    Forasmuch as it hath pleased Almighty God to call to His mercy out of this transitory life the right excellent princess, our dearest sister, the lady Katharine, relict of our natural brother prince Arthur, of famous memory, deceased, and that we intend to have her body interred according to her honour and estate; at the interment whereof (and for other ceremonies to be done at her funeral, and in conveyance of her corpse from Kimbolton, where it now lieth, to Peterborough, where the same is to be buried) it is requisite to have the presence of a good many ladies of honour.

You shall understand, that we have appointed you to be there one of the principal mourners; and therefore desire you to be in readiness at Kimbolton on the 25th of this month [January], and so to attend on the said corpse till the same shall be buried. Letting you further wit, that for the mourning apparel of your own person we send you by this bearer [a certain number of] yards of black cloth, and black cloth for two gentlewomen to wait upon you, and for two gentle-women and for eight yeomen; all which apparel you must cause in the meantime to be made up, as shall appertain. And concerning the habiliment of linen for your head and face, we shall before the day limited send the same to you accordingly. Given under our signet, at our manor of Greenwich, January.

P.S. For saving of time, if this order is shown to Sir William Poulett (living at the Friars-Augustine's, London), comptroller of our household, the cloth and linen for the head shall be delivered.

Henry VIII had been staying at Greenwich Palace when he received the news of Catherine's death. He showed distress, for although she had lost his love his first consort had never forfeited his esteem. He ordered his whole court to appear in mourning on the day of Catherine's funeral. Queen Anne, however, refused to obey the royal command. She and all the ladies of her household appeared dressed in yellow. Anne rejoiced openly at the news of the death of Catherine of Aragon, but was angered at the universal praise of Catherine's high qualities as a wife and queen. 'I am grieved', Anne confessed, 'not that she is dead, but for the vaunting of the good end she made'.

Although Anne herself was to make a 'bad' end four months after Catherine's death, she went to her execution calmly and, as an eyewitness vividly records, 'in fearful beauty'.

To Lady Jane Seymour, 1536

Certain of the biographers of Henry VIII's third queen describe Jane Seymour as 'the discreetest' of the king's wives: the slyest might more aptly be ascribed to her. It is true that she succumbed to the influence of her ambitious relatives in deliberately seeking to attract the king. Jane was of mature age, however, and could not be excused for the part she personally played in Anne Boleyn's tragedy.

Apart from the fact that she encouraged the courtship of Henry VIII at a time when Queen Anne was expecting a second child, and was indirectly responsible for the baby's being born dead, it is clear that arrangements for her marriage to the king were well advanced before Anne's head had rolled in the dust.

Jane Seymour's callousness was only excelled by that of the king himself, who was writing to her in the following strain at a time when Anne Boleyn was in the Tower awaiting sentence on a series of trumped-up charges, or so many historians believe.

My dear Friend and Mistress,

The bearer of these few lines from thy entirely devoted servant will deliver into thy fair hands a token of my true affection for thee, hoping you will keep it for ever in your sincere love for me. Advertising you that there is a ballad made lately of great derision against us, which if it go abroad and is seen by you, I pray you to pay no manner of regard to it. I am not at present informed who is the setter forth of this malignant writing: but if he is found out, he shall be straitly punished for it.[21]

For the things ye lacked, I have minded my lord to supply them to you as soon as he could buy them. Thus hoping shortly to receive you in these arms, I end for the present,

Your own loving servant and sovereign,

H.R.

To the queen consort, Catherine Parr, 1544

In 1544 Henry VIII invaded France with the intention of claiming the ancient possessions of the Plantagenets. During his absence he had appointed as regent his sixth and last consort, Catherine Parr. An able woman, she undertook her duties with great diligence, keeping the king – who had crossed the seas 'in a ship whose sails were of cloth of gold' – amply supplied with money and men.

The following fragment of a letter (the original was badly damaged by fire) that he wrote while on this campaign is an example of the amiable spirit in which Henry VIII conducted his personal correspondence at times. He details with soldier-like precision his attack on Boulogne, where he was to make triumphant entry ten days later. On the conclusion of a peace in 1546 Boulogne was restored to France on a payment of two million crowns.

... At the closing up of these our letters this day, the castle before named, with the dyke, is at our command, and not like to be recovered by the Frenchmen again (as we trust); not doubting, with God's grace, but that the castle and town shall shortly follow the same trade, for as this day, which is the eighth of September, we begin three batteries, and have three more going, beside one which hath done his execution in shaking and tearing off one of their greatest bulwarks.

No more to you at this time, sweetheart, but for lack of time and great occupation of business, saving, we pray you, to give in our name our hearty blessings to all our children, and recommendations to our cousin, Marget.[22] and the rest of the ladies and gentlewomen, and to our council also.

Written with the hand of your loving husband,

Henry R.

Less than three years later, on 28 January 1547, Henry VIII died at the age of fifty-six, at Whitehall Palace. Some time prior to his death this once elegant and gifted king had become fetid with ulcers and so corpulent and unwieldy that he had had to be propelled about in a chair. The nature of his illness made it hardly endurable to be in his presence.

As a monarch he was undoubtedly able, and succeeded in effecting a major revolution without losing his Crown or his hold on the country. All the same, however high his achievements as a ruler may be classed, thorough selfishness formed the basis of Henry VIII's character. His vices comprehended many of the worst qualities in human nature. It was said of him that 'he spared no man in his anger, no woman in his lust; everything must yield to his will'.

Henry VIII was buried in St George's Chapel, Windsor.

3

Edward VI (1537–1553)

Henry VIII's only son came to the throne when he was in his tenth year. Sickly, studious, and an ardent Protestant – undoubtedly more by training and persuasion than from personal conviction, in view of his age – during the six years that the youth reigned he was little more than a pawn in the hands of unprincipled statesmen – men of ability, but seeking their own individual ends.

His birth at Hampton Court Palace on 12 October 1537 had been heralded by Henry VIII and his court as an occasion for greatest rejoicings. The ceremony of his baptism lasted for many hours, during which time the child's mother had been borne from her sick-bed to take part in this State occasion and the celebrations that followed. These festivities, however, were quickly turned to mourning when, within a fortnight of the child's birth, Jane Seymour died.

The king, plunged into temporary gloom, departed for Windsor, leaving his son to the care of Lady Margaret Bryan, who had superintended the childhood of both the little prince's half-sisters – Mary and Elizabeth. Jane Seymour's child undoubtedly prospered under his foster-mother's care. She writes that 'he is in good health and merry', but complains that 'the princely baby's best coat is only tinsel, and that he hath never a good jewel to set on his cap'. This would have been regarded as a deep disgrace in those days. For centuries past the wearing of good jewellery and costly garments had been considered among good society as *de rigueur*.

On the whole, Edward's correspondence suggests that he was a precocious youth and more than inclined to pedantry. Certain of his letters, in fact, might have been written by a grey-beard of divinity. It is said that he received special instruction from his tutors on these compositions. From the nature of many of the letters this would appear to be only too true.

When Prince Edward to the king, 1543[1]

The following are brief excerpts from a lengthy epistle written by Edward to his father. The letter has been described as a 'wretched and miserable specimen' in its fulsome flattery and priggishness. It would certainly do little credit to the writer were one unaware that he was only six years of age at the time, but it does reflect discredit on his tutors. It is to be hoped that his royal parent regarded this screed from his 'little manikin', which was in Latin, as merely an exercise in that tongue, and a sample of his son's scholastic progress.

> In the same manner as, most bounteous king, at the dawn of day, we acknowledge the return of the sun to our world, although, by the intervention of obscure clouds, we cannot behold manifestly with our eyes that resplendent orb: in like manner your majesty's extraordinary and almost incredible goodness so shines and beams forth, that although at present I cannot behold it, though before me, with my outward eyes, yet never can it escape from my heart ... Therefore, as often as I recall my mind to that unbounded goodness of yours towards a little manikin like myself, and as often as I inwardly reflect upon my various duties and obligations, my mind shudders – yea, it shudders, so that while shuddering, it also

leaps with a marvellous delight: your majesty and the sweetest open-heartedness together carry me away ...

I see contained within the limits of your godlike mind all those eminent qualities which by constant reading I learn from the records of our forefathers were attributed to princes. For, from your earliest age even to the present time, that admirable goodness of yours, as if you had it from nature, has grown with you in proportion to your age, and that it may grow old with you is among my most ardent wishes ...

But now I will not detain your majesty by these trifles of mine from more grave matters. Wherefore of the great and good God I ask that He take into His protection your majesty.

Your majesty's very humble servant, Edward P.

At Cambridge, the 22nd of May, 1543.

To his half-sister, Princess Mary, *c.* 1546

The affection that existed between the heir apparent and his two half-sisters is somewhat remarkable in view of their family background. Chances of birth had destined each to be an enemy of the other two. Henry VIII had proclaimed Mary, his daughter by Catherine of Aragon, illegitimate in favour of Anne Boleyn's daughter, Elizabeth, and later declared both illegitimate in order to establish the superiority of Edward. Yet in spite of this obviously antagonistic relationship, between these three children of Henry VIII there existed a strong bond. Their unity lasted without any signs of dissension until the gentle-natured Edward on becoming king succumbed to the intrigues of his advisers, and was persuaded to disinherit both his half-sisters in their claims to the throne. This was in direct contradiction to his father's will, which was eventually to prevail.

Mary, at the time twenty-one years of age, had been present at the birth of Edward, and stood sponsor for him at his christening at Hampton court Palace. In the domestic upheaval that followed the sudden death of Jane Seymour, the king deputed his eldest daughter to bear all the principal responsibilities as to the funeral ceremony, at which she acted as chief mourner. From that time onwards, she watched over Edward's infancy with the care of a mother. For years they occupied a large portion of each other's thought and interest. The misunderstanding that was later to arise between them, after Edward had become king, was solely due to ministerial plottings and religious contentions. While it separated them, however, the cleavage failed – despite the indignities she had to suffer – to destroy Mary's love for her half-brother.

There is no hint in the following letter to Mary that it was dictated by any other agency than Edward's own heart.

Although I do not frequently write to you, my dearest sister, yet I would not have you suppose me to be ungrateful and forgetful of you. For I love you quite as well as if I had sent letters to you more frequently, and I like you even as a brother ought to like a very dear sister, who hath within herself all the embellishments of virtue and honourable station. For, in the same manner as I put on my best garments very seldom, yet these I like better than others; even so I write to you very rarely, yet I love you most. Moreover, I am glad that you have got well; for I have heard that you had been sick; and this I do from the brotherly love which I owe you, and from my good will towards you. I wish you uninterrupted health both of body and mind.

Farewell in Christ, dearest sister.

Edward the Prince

To his half-sister, Princess Elizabeth, 1546

Being close in age to each other a more intimate relationship existed between Elizabeth and Edward than in the case of

Mary, who was many years their senior. Edward never spoke of Elizabeth by any other title than his 'dearest sister', or his 'sweet sister Temperance'. The latter title was due to the fact that at this time Elizabeth affected extreme simplicity of dress, in conformity with the mode of women professing the doctrine of the Reformation. Such modest attire would, of course, have had the warm approval of her austere little brother.

One of Edward's principal tutors was Dr Richard Cox, afterwards to become Bishop of Ely in Elizabeth's reign. Although a Protestant, like many of his contemporary reformers Cox was imbued with asceticism. He unquestionably contributed much towards the shaping of the plastic mind of his pupil, which is easily traceable in the style in which the prince expresses himself in his correspondence.

Together Edward and Elizabeth had shared instruction at Hatfield House under Cox and the prince's other tutors, but in December, 1546, Elizabeth had been sent to the Earl of Rutland's home at Enfield. This separation so upset Edward that Elizabeth wrote him a comforting letter, and asked him to keep in correspondence with her. The following is Edward's reply to her request. It displays the sincerity of his affection for Elizabeth.

Change of place, in fact, did not vex me so much, dearest sister, as your going from me. Now, however, nothing can happen more agreeable to me than a letter from you; and especially as you were the first to send a letter to me, and have challenged me to write. Wherefore I thank you, both for your good will and despatch. I will then strive, to my utmost power, if not to surpass at least to equal you in good will and zeal. But this is some comfort to my grief, that I hope to visit you shortly (if no accident intervene with either me or you), as my chamberlain has reported to me. Farewell, dearest sister!

5th December, 1546 Edward the Prince

When king to Princess Mary, 1547

One of Edward VI's first acts on his accession was to write a letter of sympathy with Mary on their father's death. The original was in Latin, and concludes, as will be seen, in loving terms.

> Natural affection, not wisdom, instigates us to lament our dearest father's death. For affection thinks she has utterly lost one who is dead: but wisdom believes that one who lives with God is in happiness everlasting. Wherefore, God having given us such wisdom, we ought not to mourn our father's death, since it is His will, who worketh all things for good. However, so far as lies in me, I will be to you a dearest brother, and overflowing with kindness.
>
> May God endow you with his gifts. Farewell!
>
> From the Tower of London.[2] 8th February, 1547.

It is clear from the tone of the foregoing letter that Edward's counsellors had not yet had time to control his natural inclinations and kindliness of heart. The seed of consumption was already at work in him, and it is probable – who knows? – that he was subconsciously aware that his years were numbered. At this time he was much concerned about Mary's welfare and health, which was doubtless due, apart from affection, to his regarding her as his rightful successor.

There is no question but that Edward would never have disinherited Mary and Elizabeth had the boy on his death-bed not been terrorised into so doing by urgent representations from his advisers – among the first of whom was his godfather, Cranmer – that calamity would befall the nation if he did not appoint his cousin, the Protestant Lady Jane Grey, as heir to the Crown.

It may not, perhaps, be altogether irrelevant here to note the part that Edward's godfather played – after he had been made

Archbishop of Canterbury by Henry VIII – in the matrimonial problems of the king, whom Edward in his innocence likened to the sun for his 'boundless goodness'. Cranmer ruled the marriage of Catherine of Aragon and the king invalid. After giving judicial confirmation of the king's marriage to Anne Boleyn, he was later to declare her marriage null and void, as he was also to do in the case of Henry's fourth wife, Anne of Cleves. It was Cranmer, too, who gave information to the king as to the misconduct of his fifth consort, the unfortunate little Catherine Howard, who, like her cousin, Anne Boleyn, was to die on the block. All the same, Cranmer was one of the most useful men of the Reformation. Edward VI's reign, brief as it was, provided his godfather with a golden opportunity to promote the cause he had at heart, of which he took full advantage.

To his stepmother, the queen dowager, Catherine Parr, 1548

On the death of Henry VIII, Catherine Parr had been confident that as queen dowager she would be appointed regent until such time as the new king had reached his majority. She was considerably angered, therefore, on finding herself thrust aside by Edward's maternal uncle, Edward Seymour, Duke of Somerset, in his self-appointed role as guardian of the king, and as Lord Protector of the Realm.

Shortly after Edward's accession Catherine Parr wrote to the impressionable little monarch – over whom she retained a strong influence – on the subject of her great love for his late father. This was a somewhat curious topic for her to have dilated upon in view of the fact that with almost indecent haste she had secretly married the king's younger uncle, Thomas Seymour. By this alliance with the queen dowager, Thomas Seymour had hoped not only to acquire the wealth Catherine

Parr had accumulated while she was queen and to share in the dower to which she was entitled, but to attain, through her mediumship, easy access to Edward VI, and thereby oust his elder brother, Somerset, from the Protectorship.

When Catherine Parr's marriage became publicly known, by some wily method the artless Edward seems to have been persuaded into the belief that he personally had brought about the match between his stepmother and Thomas Seymour. From the following letter which the youth wrote in his own hand at this time to Catherine Parr it will be seen that he conveys his hearty thanks to her for acceding to his wish in this matter. The gallantry with which the boy king offers his protection to the intriguing newly-weds is not without its humorous aspect in view of the actual facts.

To the Queen's Grace.

We thank you heartily, not only for the gentle acceptation of our suit moved unto you, but also for the loving accomplishing of the same, wherein you have declared, not only a desire to gratify us, but to declare the good will, likewise, that we bear to you in all your requests. Wherefore ye shall not need to fear any grief to come, or to suspect lack of aid in need, seeing that he,[3] being mine uncle, is of so great a nature that he will not be troublesome by any means unto you, and I of such mind, that for divers just causes I must favour you. But even as without cause you merely require help against him whom you have put in trust with the carriage of these letters, so may I merely return the same request unto you, to provide that he [Seymour] may live with you also without grief, which hath given him wholly unto you. And I will so provide for you both, that if hereafter any grief befall, I shall be a sufficient succour in your godly or praisable enterprises.

Fare ye well, with much increase of honour and virtue in Christ. From St James's,[4] the five-and-twenty day of June.

Edward

Endorsed: 'The king's majesty's letter to the Queen after marriage, June 25th, 1548.'

To Barnaby Fitzpatrick, 1551

Edward VI wrote a series of letters to his friend, Barnaby Fitzpatrick, one of the gentlemen of his Privy Chamber, while the latter was engaged on the Continent. Apart from the prudish opening paragraph, the following letter throws a refreshing light on the otherwise solemn Edward's character. It is a pleasing example of the fact that despite his ardent pursuit of learning the young Edward was capable of interesting himself in sport and pastimes, and that he was not so entirely absorbed in the Greek and Latin authors, and matters of State, as to be disinterested in the inroads made by a remarkable tide that had occurred that year, and overflowed the coasts.

We have received your letters of the 28th of December, whereby we perceive your constancy both in avoiding all kind of vices, and also in following all things of activity, or otherwise, that be honest and meet for gentlemen, of the which we are not a little glad, nothing doubting your continuance therein ...

Here we have little news at this present, but only that the challenge that ye heard of before your going was very well accomplished. At tilt there came eighteen defendants; at tournay twenty; at barriers they fought eight to eight, on Twelfth Night. This last Christmas hath been well and merrily passed. Afterwards there was run a match at tilt, six to six, which was very well run ...

Of late there hath been such a tide here, as hath overflown all meadows and marshes, all the isle of Dogs, all Plumstead Marsh, all Sheppy, Foulness, in Essex; and the sea-coast was quite drowned. We hear that it hath done no less harm in

Flanders, Holland, Zealand, but much more, for towns and cities have there drowned[5] ...

The cause of our slowness in writing this letter hath been lack of messengers, as we had written before time.

Now, shortly, we will prove how ye have profited in the French tongue, for within a while we shall write to you in French. Thus we make an end, wishing you as much good as yourself.

At Westminster, the 25th of January, 1551.

Edward VI was the last of the Tudor kings. He died at Greenwich Palace on 6 July 1553, presumably from consumption, from which he had been ailing for some time. It was, all the same, openly hinted in some quarters that he had been poisoned, as his nails and his hair fell out during his last illness. John Dudley, Duke of Northumberland, came under suspicion in this connection. He had succeeded Somerset, who had been executed for high treason in 1552. The king was said to have taken a marked dislike to Northumberland towards the end of his life, and never to have forgiven him for being responsible for the beheading of both his uncles. If Northumberland was guilty of murdering Edward VI it was doubtless because he feared that the king might change his will and reinstate his half-sisters. Northumberland's action in hastily marrying his eldest son, Guildford Dudley, to the king's heir – Jane Grey – when it was known that the king was dying, suggests that he might not have been innocent of the crime of which he was suspected. Even more ambitious than Somerset, Northumberland was to lose his head on the block in Mary I's reign, six months before his son and daughter-in-law, 'Queen' Jane, suffered the same fate.

The one useful act of Edward VI's reign, and for which he was personally responsible, was the foundation of the system of grammar schools long associated with his name.

He was buried in Henry VII's Chapel in Westminster Abbey.

4

James I (1566–1625)

The reigns of the two succeeding sovereigns – Mary I (1533–58) and Elizabeth I (1558–1603) – having covered a period of exactly half a century, James VI of Scotland (as great-grandson of Henry VII's eldest daughter, Margaret) ascended the English throne. The strong and individual House of Tudor had vanished with the death of Elizabeth I, and by right of inheritance the Crown passed to the House of Stuart, whose origins and associations were not in England.

James, only child of Mary, Queen of Scots, by her second husband, Lord Henry Darnley, was born at Edinburgh Castle on 19 June 1566. Fourteen months after his birth, Mary Stuart, having reigned some eight years, was forced to renounce her Crown in favour of her son, following Darnley's mysterious death, and subsequent revolution in her kingdom. The tiny infant was duly crowned at Stirling as James VI, Mary fled to England for safety, and James Stuart, Earl of Moray (illegitimate son of the baby king's grandfather, James V) became regent.

When James VI of Scotland to Elizabeth I, 1586

James VI was later to be severely censured for taking no steps to prevent his mother's execution in 1587, or to revenge her death. This, however, was not just. He was barely twenty years old when her head was threatened, and owing to prevailing troubles in his realm, in his own words 'was, in reality, as complete a prisoner in Scotland as my mother was in England'. Despite this, he dispatched strong letters to his ambassadors in a desperate attempt to prevent his mother being put to death. He also wrote the following commendable letter to Elizabeth I. This letter, incidentally, is an example of one of James's best compositions.

Madam and dearest sister,

If you could have known what divers thoughts have agitated my mind since my directing of William Keith[1] unto you for the soliciting of this matter, whereto nature and honour so greatly and unfeignedly bind and oblige me; if, I say, you knew what divers thoughts I have been in, and what just grief I had, weighing deeply the thing itself, if so it should proceed, as God forbid! what events might follow thereupon, what number of straits I should be driven unto; and, amongst the rest, how it might imperil my reputation amongst my subjects; if these things (I yet again say) were known unto you – then, I doubt not but you would so far pity my case, as it would easily make you, at the first, to resolve your own best into it.

I doubt greatly in what fashion to write in this purpose, for you have already taken in so evil with my plainness, as I fear, if I should persist in that course, you will rather be exasperated to passions in reading the words, than by the plainest style, persuaded to consider rightly the simple truth. Yet, justly preferring the duty of an honest friend to the sudden passions of one, who, how soon they be past, can wiselier weigh the reasons that I can set them down, I am resolved, in few words and plain, to give you my friendly and best advice, appealing to your ripest judgment to discern thereupon.

What thing, madam, can greatlier touch me in honour, both as a king and a son, than that my nearest neighbour, being in strict friendship with me, shall rigorously put to death a free sovereign prince and my natural mother, alike in estate and sex to her that so uses her (albeit subject, I grant, to hard fortune), and touching her nearly in proximity of blood? What law of God can permit that justice shall strike upon them, whom He hath appointed supreme dispensators of the same under Him? Whom He hath called gods, and therefore subjected to the censure of none in earth. Whose anointing by God cannot be defiled by man nor unrevenged by the author thereof. Who, being supreme and immediate lieutenant of God in heaven, cannot therefore be judged by equals on earth. What monstrous thing is it, that sovereign princes themselves should be the example-givers of their own sacred diadem's profaning? Then, what should move you to this form of proceeding? (supposing the worst which, in good faith, I look not for at your hands) – honour? or profit? Honour were it to you to spare when it is least looked for. Honour were it to you (which is not only my friendly advice, but most earnest suit) to make me and all other princes in Europe eternally beholden unto you, in granting this my so reasonable request; and not (pardon, I pray you, my free speaking) to put princes to straits of honour; where through your general reputation and the universal (almost) misliking of you, may dangerously peril, both in honour and utility, your person and estate.

You know, madam, well enough how small difference Cicero concludes to be betwixt *Utile* and *Honestum*[2] in his discourse thereof, and which of them ought to be framed to the other. And now, madam, to conclude, – I pray you so to weigh these few arguments, that as I ever presumed of your nature, so the whole world may praise your subjects for their dutiful care of your preservation, and yourself for your princely pity – the doing whereof only belongs unto you, the performing whereof only appertains unto you, and the praise thereof only will ever be yours.

Respect then, good sister, this my first so long continued and so earnest request, despatching my ambassador with such a comfortable answer, as may become your person to give, and as my loving and honest heart unto you merits to receive. But in case any do vaunt themselves to know further of my mind in this matter than my ambassadors do – who indeed are fully acquainted therewith – I pray you not to take me to be a chameleon; but by the contrary them [such ill-advisers] to be malicious impostors, as surely they are.

And thus, praying you heartily to excuse my tedious and longsome letter, I commit you, madam and dearest sister, to the blessed protection of the Almighty, who might give you grace so to resolve on this matter, as may be most honourable for you and most acceptable to Him.

From my Palace of Holyrood, the 26th day of January, 1586.

Your most loving brother and cousin,

James R.

James's succession to the English throne in 1603 brought the two kingdoms under one sovereign. As far as his new subjects were concerned, however, the fact that their monarch came from north of the Border added little to his popularity. His native country was considered by the English to be populated by rapacious barbarians, whereas the court over which James I was to preside was accomplished, learned, and one of the most high-spirited in Europe.

In his journey from Edinburgh to London the thirty-seven-year-old king created no little adverse comment. The populace – used to the stately cavalcades and personal grandeur of the late sovereign – were astonished and disheartened at the unprepossessing appearance of their new ruler. They beheld 'a little fat personage, with large wandering eyes; a bonnet cast by chance upon his head, and sticking on as best it could; his legs too thin for his weight; his clothes so thickly padded out to resist a dagger-stroke,[3] of which he was in continual dread, that he looked more like a vast seal than a man; a flabby, foolish mouth, widened for the freer extrusion of remarkably broad Scotch – and all these surmounting a horse saddled after the manner of an armchair, with appliances for the rider's support, in spite of which his majesty not unfrequently managed to tumble most ungracefully to the ground.'

The appearance and demeanour of the king were discouraging enough in themselves, but in addition he earned contempt for the coarse manner in which he alluded to the late queen, and the ridiculous showering of knighthoods – either by way of propitiation or in return for monetary reward – on all and sundry in his progress south to the heart of 'The Promised Land'. This title of ancient chivalry was one that Elizabeth I had given sparingly to soldiers and statesmen alike. In his thirty-two-day journey from Edinburgh to London, however, James I knighted 237 gentlemen who were presented to him, for what specific reasons he alone could judge.

The king had, all the same, left Scotland with some inner trepidation. His new subjects had put his mother to death, and destroyed by faction or slain in battle her father and her grandfather, if they had not also by their intrigues induced the assassination of his own father, Lord Darnley. His fate might quite easily be similar, he considered. For this reason he left his consort, Anne of Denmark, behind at Edinburgh, and his son and heir, Prince Henry – a boy of ten – guarded by a strong garrison, in charge of the Earl of Mar, at Stirling Castle. The king had had no time to visit Prince Henry on departing for England, but sent him the following letter shortly before setting out on his journey.

When King of England to his son, Prince Henry, 1603

My Son,

That I see you not before my parting, impute to this great occasion, wherein time is so precious; but that shall, by God's grace, be recompensed by your coming to me shortly, and continual residence with me ever after. Let not this news[4] make you proud or insolent, for a king's son ye were, and no more are ye now; the augmentation that is hereby like to fall to ye, is but in cares and heavy burden. Be merry, but not insolent; keep a greatness, but *sine fastu*:[5] be resolute, but not wilful; be kind, but in honourable sort. Choose none to be your playfellows but of honourable birth; and, above all things, never give countenance to any, but as ye are informed they are in estimation with me.

Look upon all Englishmen that shall come to visit you as your loving subjects, not with ceremoniousness as towards strangers, but with that heartiness which at this time they deserve. This gentleman[6] whom the bearer accompanies, is worthy, and of good rank, and now my family servitor; use him, therefore, in a more homely, loving sort than others.

I send ye herewith my book lately printed.[7] Study and profit in it, as ye would deserve my blessing; and as there can nothing happen unto you whereof ye will not find the general ground therein, if not the particular point touched, so must ye level every man's opinions or advices with the rules there set down, allowing and following their advices that agree with the same, mistrusting and frowning upon them that advise ye to the contraire. Be diligent and earnest in your studies, that at your meeting with me I may praise ye for your progress in learning. Be obedient to your master for your own weal, and to procure my thanks; for in reverencing him, ye obey me and honour yourself. Farewell.

Your loving father,

James R.

To the queen consort, Anne of Denmark, 1603

The fact that her eldest son had been placed under the guardianship of the Earl of Mar – the usual custom in Scotland in the case of heirs-apparent – had for years been a source of bitter contention between the king and his consort. After James's departure for England, Anne of Denmark descended on Stirling Castle, with a supporting faction of nobles, and demanded that her son should be delivered into her own keeping. Her request being resolutely refused, however, the queen flew into such rages that she finally became seriously ill. To add to the general consternation she had created, she gave birth, prematurely, to a stillborn child.

When the news reached the king of his wife's dangerous illness, and the fate of his expected offspring, all his anger at her perverse behaviour was dissipated. He at once authorised that the queen should receive her son into her own custody at Holyrood.

In reply to a series of recriminations which he had received from his impetuous queen, James I wrote the following letter of remonstrance, which is at the same time in a reasonable and an affectionate vein.

My Heart,

Immediately before the receipt of your letter I purposed to have written to you, and that without any great occasion, excepting to free myself from the imputation of severeness; but now your letter has given more matter to write, though I take small delight to meddle in so unpleasant a process.

I wonder that neither your long knowledge of my nature, nor my late earnest exculpation to you, can cure you of that rooted error, that any one living dare speak to me anywise to your prejudice, or yet that ye can think those are your enemies who are true servants to me. I can say no more, but protest, on the peril of my salvation or condemnation, that neither the Earl of Mar nor any flesh living ever informed me that ye was upon any Papish or Spanish course, or that ye had any other thoughts than a wrong-conceived opinion that he had more interest in your son than you, and would not deliver him to you. Neither does he further charge the noblemen that are with you there, except that he was informed that some of them thought to have assisted you in taking my son by force out of his hands; but as for any Papist or foreign influence, he cloth not so much as allege it.

Therefore I say over again, leave these froward womanly apprehensions; for, I thank God, I carry that love and respect to you which by the law of God and nature I ought to do to my wife and the mother of my children – not for that ye are a king's daughter, for whether ye were a king's or a cook's daughter, ye must be alike to me, being once my wife. For the respect of your honourable birth and descent I married you; but the love and respect I now bear you is because ye are my married wife, and so partaker of my honour as of my other fortunes. I beseech you excuse my rude plainness in this; for casting up your birth is a needless impertinent argument to me.[8]

God is my witness that I ever preferred you to my bairns, [and] much more than to any subject; but if you will ever give ear to the reports of every flattering sycophant that will persuade you that, when I account well of an honest and wise servant for his true and faithful service to me, that it is to compare or to prefer him to you, then will neither ye nor I ever be at rest or peace.

I have according to my promise, copied so much of that plot [plan] whereof I wrote to you in my last as did concern my son and you, which is herein enclosed that ye may see I wrote it not without cause, but I desire it not to have any secretaries but yourself. As for the lamentations ye made concerning it, it is utterly impertinent at this time, for such reasons as the bearer will show to you, whom I have likewise commanded to impart divers other points to you; which, for fear of wearying your eyes with my rugged hand, I have herein omitted. Praying God, My Heart, to preserve you and all the bairns, and send me a blithe meeting with you, and a couple of them.

Your own,
James R.

The king and queen had more serious disagreements later, which terminated in Anne of Denmark deciding to live in a separate establishment. James I's favourites were never of the ladies of the court. By temperament he was insensible to their attraction. A leading favourite for some time was Robert Carr, a Scottish adventurer who had previously served as a page in James's Scottish court. Those with their own interests to exploit subsequently selected and trained Carr with a view to his attracting the king. He became James's confidential secretary, was weighted with costly gifts and honours, and swiftly created Viscount Rochester. The post of confidential adviser was primarily that of chief mediator between the king and his ministers. It demanded tact, diplomacy, and a wise concern for the monarch's best interests. In times long past, such position had been held by prelates, and not infrequently by the king's consort. It was soon evident to Anne of Denmark that Carr was totally unfitted for his appointment. Witnessing his increasing profligacy, and abuse of the king's favour, she abandoned hope of her influence being of aid, and withdrew from the situation.

As a result of an impassioned liaison with Carr, Frances, Countess of Essex, sought a separation from her husband in order to marry the king's favourite, her grounds for divorce being that Essex was impotent. The Earl of Essex's cryptic reply to this charge was that 'he was only impotent where his wife was concerned'. Nevertheless, a divorce was eventually secured, although not without difficulty, through the intervention of the king himself, in consideration of a fee of £25,000 for his advocacy. Being always generous hearted towards his favourites, James celebrated the marriage with royal pomp, and created the bridegroom Earl of Somerset.

Before very long, however, Somerset was to realise that a new arrival at court – George Villiers – was about to supplant himself in the king's favour. Angry scenes engendered by Somerset soon broke out publicly, not only with Villiers, whom Somerset considered was flagrantly encroaching on his preserves and offices at court, but with James I himself.

To Robert Carr, Earl of Somerset, *c.* 1615

There is no indication in the original script as to whom the king is addressing in the following letter. Although undated and without superscription, however, from certain unmistakable allusions it has been accepted as having been written to Somerset, and is considered one of the most important additions to the history of that critical time. It was evidently penned when the fallen favourite's jealousy of Villiers and his clique was at its height.

While much of James I's correspondence leaves an unfavourable impression, it is nevertheless extremely interesting, as in this case. In fact, in their intensity and emotional sincerity of expression certain passages in this letter to Somerset are remarkable.

First, I take God, the searcher of all hearts, to record that, in all the time past of idle talk, I never knew nor could, out of any observation of mine, find any appearance of any such court faction as you have apprehended; and so far was I ever from overseeing or indirectly feeling of it (if I had apprehended it), as I protest to God, I would have run upon it with my feet, as upon fire, to have extinguished it, if I could have seen any sparkle of it. As for your informations, you daily told me so many lies of myself that were reported unto you, as (I confess) I gave the less credit to your reports in other things, since you could not be an eyewitness of it yourself.

Next, I take the same God to record, that never man of any degree did directly or indirectly let fall unto me any thing that might be interpreted for the lessening of your credit with me; or 'that one man should not rule all,' and 'that no man's dependence should be but upon the King,' or any such like phrase; which, if I had ever found, then would I have behaved myself as became so great a king, and so infinitely loving a master.

Thirdly, as God shall save me, I meant not in the letter I wrote unto you to be sparing, in the least jot, of uttering my affection towards you, as far as yourself could require; my differing from your form in that point being only to follow my own style, which I thought the comeliest ...

I am far from thinking of any possibility of any man ever to come within many degrees of your trust with me, as I must ingenuously confess you have deserved more trust and confidence of me than ever man did, – in secrecy above all flesh, in feeling and impartial respect, as well as to my honour in every degree as to my profit. And all this, without respect either to kin or ally, or your nearest and dearest friend whatsoever; nay, unmovable in one hair that might concern me against the whole world. And in those points I confess I never saw any come towards your merit: I mean, in the points of an inwardly trusty friend and servant.

But, as a piece of ground cannot be so fertile, but if either by the own natural rankness or evil manuring thereof it become also fertile of strong and noisome weeds, it then proves useless and altogether unprofitable; even so, these before rehearsed rich and rare parts and merits of yours have been of long time – but especially of late, since the strange frenzy took you – so powdered and mixed with strange streams of unquietness, passion, fury, and insolent pride, and (which is worst of all) with a settled kind of induced obstinacy, as it chokes and obscures all these excellent and good parts that God hath bestowed upon you.

For although I confess the greatness of that trust and privacy betwixt us will very well allow unto you an infinitely great liberty and freedom of speech unto me – yea, even to rebuke me more sharply and bitterly than ever master durst do – yet, to invent a new act of railing at me – nay, to borrow the tongue of the devil, in comparison whereof all Peacham's[9] book is but a gentle admonition – that cannot come within the compass of any liberty of friendship.

And do not deceive yourself with that conceit, that I allowed you that sort of licentious freedom till of late. For, as upon the one part, it is true you never passed all limits therein till of late; so, upon the other, I bore, God Almighty knows! with those passions of yours, of old dissembling my grief thereat, only in hope that time and experience would reclaim and abate that heat, which I thought to wear you out of by a long suffering patience and many gentle admonitions ...

[Your ill-humour] being uttered at unseasonable hours, and so bereaving me of my rest, was so far from condemning your own indiscretion therein, as by the contrary it seemed you did it of purpose to grieve and vex me. Next, your fiery boutades were coupled with a continual dogged sullen behaviour, especially shortly after your fall and in all the times of your other diseases. Thirdly, in all your dealings with me, you have many times uttered a kind of distrust of the honesty of my friendship towards you. And, fourthly (which is worst of all) – and worse than any other thing that can be imagined – you have, in many of your mad fits, done what you can to persuade me that you mean not so much to hold me by love as by awe, and that you have me so far in your reverence, as that I dare not offend you, or resist your appetites. I leave out of this reckoning your long creeping back and withdrawing yourself from lying in my chamber – notwithstanding my many hundred times earnestly soliciting you to the contrary – accounting that but as a point of unkindness ...

To conclude, then, this discourse proceeding from the infinite grief of a deeply wounded heart – I protest, in the presence of the Almighty God, that I have borne this grief within me to the uttermost of my ability; and as never grief since my birth seated so heavily upon me, so have I borne it as long as I possibly can. Neither can I bear it longer without admitting an unpardonable sin against God in consuming myself wilfully; and not only myself, but in perilling thereby not only the good estate of mine own people, but even the state of religion through all Christendom, which almost wholly, under God, rests now upon my shoulders.

Be not the occasion of the hastening of his death through grief, who was not only your creator under God, but hath many a time prayed for you, which I never did for any subject alive but for you. But the lightening my heart of this burden is not now the only cause that makes me press you undelayedly to ease my grief. For your own furious assaults upon me at unseasonable hours hath now made it known to so many that you have been in some cross discourse with me, that there must be some exterior signs of the amendment of your behaviour towards me. These observations have been made, and collected [conclusions formed] upon your long being with me at un-seasonable hours, – loud speaking on both parts, – and the observation of my sadness after your parting, and my want of rest.

What shall be the best remedy for this I will tell you: be kind. But for the easing of my inward and consuming grief, all I crave is, that in all the words and actions of your life you may ever make it appear to me that you never think to hold grip of me save out of my mere love, and not one hair by force. Consider that I am a freeman, if I were not a king. Remember that all your being, except your breathing and soul, is from me. I told you twice or thrice, you might lead me by the heart and not by the nose. I cannot deal honestly, if I deal not plainly with you. If ever I find that you think to retain me by one sparkle of fear, all the violence of my love will in that instant be changed into as violent a hatred.

God is my judge, my love hath been infinite towards you; and only the strength of my affection towards you hath made me bear with these things in you, and bridle my passions to

67

the uttermost of my ability. Let me be met, then, with your entire heart, but softened by humility. Let me never apprehend that you disdain my person and undervalue my qualities; and let it not appear that any part of your former affection is cold towards me. A king may slack a part of his affection towards his servant upon the party's default, and yet love him; but a servant cannot do so to his master, but his master must hate him.

Hold me thus by the heart. You may build upon my favour as upon a rock that never shall fail you, that never shall weary to give new demonstrations of my affection towards you; nay, that shall never suffer any to rise in any degree of my favour, except they may acknowledge and thank you as a furtherer of it, and that I may be persuaded in my heart, that they love and honour you for my sake. Not that any living shall come to the twentieth degree of your favour.

For, although your good and heartily humble behaviour may wash quite out of my heart your by-past errors, yet shall I never pardon myself, but shall carry that cross to the grave with me for raising a man so high, as might make him presume to pierce my ears with such speeches ...

Thus have I now set down unto you what I would say if I were to make my testament. It lies in your hands to make of me what you please, – either the best master and truest friend, or, if you force me once to call you ingrate, which the God of heaven forbid, no so great earthly plague can light upon you! In a word, you may procure me to delight to give daily more and more demonstrations of my favours towards you, if the fault be not in yourself.

The mysterious death in the Tower of Somerset's intimate friend, Sir Thomas Overbury, in 1613, was to provide a court scandal of the first magnitude three years later.

From the outset of Somerset's arrival at court he had had to rely on the help and guidance of Overbury, being himself possessed of no intellectual abilities and incapable of coping with the onerous duties entailed as the king's confidential adviser. James I had recognised his favourite's shortcomings in this connection only too clearly. He had had no alternative, in the circumstances, therefore, but to submit to the arrangement, although he was personally jealous of Overbury.

Frances, Countess of Essex, was a grand-niece of Henry Howard, Earl of Northampton, who was himself plotting to replace Overbury – as Overbury well knew – as Somerset's indispensable aid. When, therefore, Overbury had heard of the impending divorce and proposed marriage between Somerset and Northampton's niece, he flew into a violent passion and threatened to expose Frances as a depraved character who covertly indulged in practices of witchcraft. Such a charge could, in fact, have been lawfully established against her. It was a capital offence. James I himself had taken so active an interest in the suppression of such practices that on his accession Parliament had passed a law imposing the death penalty for those proved guilty of exercising the 'black arts'.

In dread of exposure, Somerset and his mistress hastily concocted a plot, whereby Overbury was committed to the Tower on a charge of showing contempt for the king's authority. Shortly afterwards he died there, presumably from an internal complaint, and was quickly buried. No doubt was entertained by Somerset's enemies, all the same, but that Overbury had been poisoned. They withheld action, however, until such time as George Villiers had sufficiently won the king's affections to supplant the high favourite. Then they struck. Somerset and the countess were arrested – together with certain minor accomplices – for having occasioned the death of Overbury, and were both sent to the Tower to await trial. While this was pending, the five accomplices – including Elwes, lieutenant of the Tower at the time of Overbury's death and who had recently been appointed to that office by Northampton – were all summarily hanged at Tyburn.

To Sir George More, 1616

It is clear from the appended letter and other urgent missives that the king wrote to Sir George More – newly appointed lieutenant of the Tower by the king himself – that James I is labouring under some private anxiety regarding Somerset. It has been generally accepted, in view of the trickery employed by the king to wring a confession out of his late favourite, that the latter was in possession of a dangerous secret of which James I went in fear of exposure. What that secret was never came to light.

Good Sir George,

As only the confidence I hold in your honesty made me, without the knowledge of any, put you in that place of trust which ye now possess, so must I now use your trust and secrecy in a thing greatly concerning my honour and service. Ye know Somerset's day of trial is at hand, and ye know also what fair means I have used to move him, by confessing the truth, to honour God and me, and leave some place for my mercy to work upon. I have now, at last, sent the bearer hereof (an honest gentleman, and who once followed him), with such directions unto him, as if there be a spunk of grace left in him, I hope they shall work a good effect.

My only desire is, that ye would make his convoy unto him [Somerset] in such secrecy as none living may know of it, and that after his speaking with him in private, [the bearer] may be returned back again as secretly. So reposing myself upon your faithful and secret handling of this business, I bid you heartily farewell.

James R.

Endorsed by Sir George More: '9th of May, about one of the clock in the afternoon, 1616.'

To Sir George More, 1616

The tone of the king's letters to the lieutenant of the Tower suggests that James I was prepared to adopt any means possible, without placing himself in a hopelessly vulnerable position, to force Somerset to plead guilty. Somerset's obstinacy in this respect, combined with his dark hints regarding the king, was quite incomprehensible to More, especially in view of James I's indications that he would, in any event, pardon the prisoner. More communicated his perplexities to the king who, in the following reply, resorts to duplicity. He suggests that Somerset is accusing him of being an accessory to Overbury's murder.

Good Sir George,

I am extremely sorry that your unfortunate prisoner turns all the great care I have of him not only against himself, but against me also, as far as he can. I cannot blame you that ye cannot conjecture what this may be, for God knows it is only a trick of his idle brain, hoping thereby to shift his trial; but it is easy to be seen that he would threaten me with laying an aspersion upon me of being in some sort accessory to his crime.

I can do no more (since God so obstructs his grace from him) than repeat the substance of that letter the Lord Hay[10] sent you yesternight, which is this: If he would write or send me any message concerning this poisoning, it need not be private, if it be in some other connexion. That which I cannot now with honour receive privately, I may do it after his trial or confession proceed. I cannot hear a private message from him, without laying an aspersion upon myself of being an accessory to his crime; and I pray you to urge him to realise that I refuse him no favour which I can grant him without taking upon me the suspicion of being guilty of that crime whereof he is accused. And so farewell.

All attempts to persuade Somerset to plead guilty having failed, he was instructed to prepare himself forthwith for trial at Westminster Hall. This he refused to do, declaring that 'they should carry him in his bed first'. His threats against the king finally became so frightening to More that, although it was midnight, he hurried to Greenwich Palace, and was observed 'bouncing at the back stairs as if mad'. The king 'burst into a passion of tears' on hearing More's ill news, exclaiming 'On my soul, More, I wot not what to do! Help me in this great strait!'

A compromise was at length reached whereby the prisoner was to appear, sentence be pronounced, and the royal pardon bestowed. For abstaining from an attack on the king, Somerset was to be rewarded with a retiring pension of £4,000 a year. He still insisted upon pleading not guilty, but otherwise agreed the bargain.

Not many years after being released from imprisonment in the Tower, Frances, Countess of Somerset (who had pleaded guilty, but was pardoned), died of an incurable intestinal complaint. Somerset eked out his days in bitterness, an exile from court life that had been his world. He made several attempts to get back into the king's favour, but without success.

Somerset's rival, George Villiers – afterwards to be created first Duke of Buckingham – had the advantage of a more stabilised background than the displaced favourite. He was the son of a Leicestershire family of good standing, if in impecunious circumstances. In addition, Villiers was well-educated, skilled in all the high-born accomplishments of the day, and had broadened his knowledge by three years' travel on the Continent. His greatest appeal to the king, however, was his strikingly handsome appearance and charm of address, to which attractions alone his rapid and unmerited advancement – probably unparalleled in English history – was due.

In order to bring about Somerset's downfall his enemies
at court had devised the only plan that appeared practicable.
They had specially procured Villiers – who proved a willing
and an adept pupil in realising the behaviour that was
essential if he was to be a success with the king – as one who
would undoubtedly be a means of ousting Somerset. The king
lavished gifts, honours and estates on Villiers in the same way
that he had done with Somerset. He placed his new favourite
in a position of such power that from the time of their intimacy
to the end of James I's reign the history of the country is
related to little more than the personal aggrandisement and
career of Villiers. Sovereign in all but name, his injustices in
dispensing important posts and delegating responsibilities
created widespread and bitter discontent. Nevertheless, his
increasing influence was to remain unabated, and to continue
into the succeeding reign.

To George Villiers, Marquis of Buckingham, c. 1622

Villiers married Catherine, daughter and sole heiress of the
Earl of Rutland. The following letter was written by the king
to Buckingham when the latter's wife was expecting her first
child. It displays the king in the homely role of an adviser
on simple precautionary measures to ensure a successful
confinement. Incidentally, in a letter written by James I about
this time to Lord Cranfield, his High Treasurer, urgently
requesting Cranfield to liquidate his favourite's debts, the king
remarks that Buckingham's wife's 'lying-in and membling are
like to cost ten thousand pounds'.

My only sweet and dear child,
    The Lord of Heaven bless thee this morning and thy thing
my daughter! I pray thee, as thou lovest me, make her precisely

observe these rules: Let her never go in a coach upon the streets, nor never go fast in it. Let your mother keep all hasty news coming to her ears. Let her not eat too much fruit, and hasten her out of London after we are gone.

If thou be back by four in the afternoon, it will be good time. And prepare thee to be a guard to me, by keeping my back unbroken with business, before my going to the progress. And thus God send me a joyful and happy meeting with my sweet Steenie[11] this evening!

James R.

To George Villiers, Marquis of Buckingham

There is no date on the emotionally worded epistle that follows, and it is therefore difficult to place it in strict chronological arrangement. It was in all probability written about 1622. In any event, it shows the king's strong personal attachment to Villiers, whose picture, so James I himself confesses in one of his letters, he wore 'on a blue ribbon under my wash-coat next my heart'. What exactly the king meant by his 'wash coat' is an open question. He was strongly averse to ablutions, and in fact never even washed his hands, but only wiped the tips of his fingers on a damp napkin.

My only sweet and dear child,

I am now so miserable a coward, as I do nothing but weep and mourn; for I protest to God, I rode this afternoon a great way in the park without speaking to anybody, and the tears trickling down my cheeks, as now they do, that I can scarcely see to write. But, alas! what shall I do at our parting? The only small comfort that I can have will be to pry into thy defects with the eye of an enemy, and of every mote to make a mountain; and so harden my heart against thy absence. But this little malice is like jealousy, proceeding from a sweet root;

but in one point it overcometh it, for, as it proceeds from love, so it cannot but end in love.

Sweet heart! be earnest with Kate[12] to come and meet thee at New Hall[13] within eight or ten days after this. Cast thee to be here tomorrow, as near as about two in the afternoon as thou canst, and come galloping hither. Remember thy picture, and suffer none of the Council to come here – for God's sake! Write not a word again, and let no creature see this letter. The Lord of heaven and earth bless thee, and my sweet daughter, and my sweet little grandchild.[14] and all thy blessed family, and send thee a happier return – both now and thou knowest when – to thy dear dad and Christian gossip.

James R.

To his son, Charles, Prince of Wales, and George Villiers, Marquis of Buckingham, 1623

Despite the desire of his Parliament and his people that the Prince of Wales should marry one of his own religion, James I had for some time been negotiating with Spain for a matrimonial alliance between Charles and Maria, second sister of Philip IV.

In the early part of 1623 the capital was amazed by the news that the Prince of Wales and the Marquis of Buckingham – who was to receive ducal honours this same year – had set out for Madrid, travelling strictly incognito, under the assumed names of John and Thomas Smith. Arrangements for the marriage with the Spanish princess had practically been completed by the Earl of Bristol, ambassador to the court of the young Philip of Spain. Only a dispensation from the Pope was awaited. What was the object of this extraordinary escapade remains a mystery, but it created strong suspicion in England that James I was engaged in some deep plot of his own where Spain was concerned.

The following letter was written by the king a few weeks after the 'sweet boys and dear venturous knights, worthy to be put in a new romanso', as he termed them, had arrived in Madrid, in reply to a request for jewellery for presents and for their own adornment at court functions.

My sweet boys,

I write this now, my seventh letter, unto you upon the 17th of March, sent in my ship called the *Adventurer*, to my two boy-adventurers' whom God ever bless ... I send you your robes of the order, which ye must not forget to wear on St George's Day, and dine together in them – if they can come in time – which I pray God they may, for it will be a goodly sight for the Spaniards to see my boys dine in them.

I send you also the jewels as I promised, some of mine and such of yours – I mean both of you – as are worthy the sending, ay, or my Baby's presenting his mistress. I send him an old double cross of Lorrain, not so rich as ancient, and yet not contemptible for the value; a good looking-glass with my picture in it, to be hung at her girdle, which ye must tell her ye have caused it so to be enchanted by art-magic, that whensoever she shall be pleased to look in it, she shall see the fairest lady that either her brother or your father's dominions can afford.

Ye shall present her with two fair long diamonds, set like an anchor, and a fair pendent diamond hanging in them. Ye shall give her a goodly rope of pearls, ye shall give a carquanet or collar, thirteen great ballas rubies, and thirteen knots or conques of pearls; and ye shall give her a head-dressing of two and twenty great pear pearls; and ye shall give her three goodly pear pendent diamonds, whereof the biggest to be worn at a needle on the midst of her forehead, and one in each ear.

And for my Baby's own wearing, ye shall have two good jewels of your own, your round broach of diamonds, and your triangle diamond with the great round pearl. And I send you for your wearing The Three Brethren, that ye know full well, but newly set, and the Mirror of France, the fellow of the Portugal diamond, which I would wish you to wear alone in your hat, with a little black feather. Ye have also good diamond buttons of your own, to be set to a doublet or jerkin. As for your first, it may serve for a present to a Don.

As for thee, my sweet gossip, I send thee a fair table diamond – which I would once have given thee before, if thou would have taken it – for wearing in thy hat, or where thou pleases; and if my Baby will spare thee the two long diamonds in form of an anchor, with the pendent diamond, it were fit for an admiral to wear, and he hath enough better jewels for his mistress. Though he is of thine own, [I send] thy good old jewel, thy three pindars diamonds, the picture case I gave Kate, and the great diamond chain I gave her (who would have sent thee the least pin she had, if I had not stayed her).

If my Baby will not spare the anchor from his mistress, he may well lend thee his round broach to wear, and yet he shall have jewels to wear in his hat for three great days.

And now for the form of my Baby's presenting of his jewels to his mistress: I leave that to himself, with Steenie's advice, and my Lord of Bristol's.[15] Only I would not have them presented all at once, but at the more sundry times the better, and I would have the rarest and, richest kept hindmost. I have also sent four other crosses, of meaner value, with a great pointed diamond in a ring, which will save charges in presents to Dons, according to their quality. But I will send with the fleet divers other jewels for presents, for saving charges (whereof we have too much need); for till my Baby's coming away, there will be no need of giving presents to any but her.[16]

Thus you see how, as long as I want the sweet company of my boys' conversation, I am forced, yea, and delight to converse with them by long letters. God bless you both, my sweet boys, and send you, after a successful journey, a joyful happy return in the arms of your dear dad.

James R.

From Newmarket on St Patrick's Day, who, of old, was too well patronized in the country you are in.

To Charles, Prince of Wales, and the Marquis of Buckingham, 1623

The appended letter relates to a resolution taken on the advice of the ecclesiastical council at Madrid to delay the Infanta's voyage to England till the following spring. 'They are hankering upon a conversion', wrote Charles to his father, 'for they say there can be no friendship without union in religion'. This, Charles added, was quite out of the question, for he had neither the conscience nor taste for conversion.

Greenwich, June 14

My Sweet Boys,

Your letter, by Cottington, hath stricken me dead. I fear it shall very much shorten my days, and I am the more perplexed that I know not how to satisfy the people's expectation here, neither know I what to say to the Council, for the fleet that staid upon a wind this fortnight – Rutland and all aboard – must now be staid, and I know not what reason I shall pretend for the doing of it. But as for my advice and directions that ye crave, in case they [the Spaniards] will not alter their decree, it is, in a word, to come speedily away, and if ye can get leave, give over all treaty.

And this I speak without respect of any security they can offer you, except ye never look to see your old dad again, whom I fear ye shall never see, if you see him not before winter. Alas, I now repent me sore that ever I suffered you to go away! I care for match, nor nothing, so I may once have you in my arms again. God grant it, God grant it, God grant it! amen! amen! amen!

I protest ye shall be as heartily welcome as if ye had done

all the things ye went for, so that I may once have you in my arms again; and God bless you both, my only sweet son, and my only best, sweet servant, and let me hear from you quickly, and with all speed, as ye love my life. And so God send you a happy and joyful meeting in the arms of your dear dad.

James R.

In the end, the marriage treaty was to be broken off by reason of the unpopularity of the proposed union both in Spain and England. The Spanish had been distrustful of the English ever since the unfortunate marriage of Catherine of Aragon to Henry VIII. The English, for their part, had bitter memories of Philip of Spain's alliance with Mary I, and feared a renewed persecution of the Protestants.

To the honour of the Spaniards, all the costly presents made by Charles were returned entire after the betrothal was conclusively terminated.

The prince and Buckingham had been absent from England for seven months. They had squandered money lavishly, and returned without accomplishing anything, except that Buckingham had incensed the Spaniards by his arrogance and his depraved behaviour.

To George Villiers, Duke of Buckingham, 1625

The following letter was written by James I not so long before his death. Although it has been accepted by some historians as having been addressed to Charles it seems more likely that it was written to Buckingham. The favourite was at this time actively ingratiating himself with the Prince of Wales, who might any day become king, as James I's health was showing marked signs of decline.

The phrasing of the letter is curious, disclosing a loneliness of spirit and need of consolation.

My own sweet and dear child,

Notwithstanding of your desiring me to write yesterday, yet had I written in the evening, if at my coming in out of the park such a drowsiness had not come upon me, as I was forced to sit and sleep in my chair half an hour. And yet I cannot content myself without sending you this billet, praying God that I may have a joyful and comfortable meeting with you, and that we may make at this Christenmass a new marriage, ever to be kept hereafter; for, God so love me, as I desire only to live in this world for your sake, and that I had rather live banished in any part of the earth with you, than live a sorrowful widow-life without you.

And so God bless you, my sweet child and wife, and grant that ye may ever be a comfort to your dear dad and husband.

James R.

In March, 1625 James I was taken ill at his favourite residence, Theobald's Park, in Essex, and died there on the 27th of that month at the age of fifty-nine.

Referring to the state of the nation during his reign in England of twenty-two years, the French ambassador at one time wrote to his court, 'I discover so many seeds of disease in England, so much brooding in silence, and so many events inevitable, that I am inclined to affirm that for a century from this time the kingdom will hardly abuse its prosperity, except to its own ruin. The courage of the English is buried in the tomb of Elizabeth. His [James I's] vices debilitate his mind. The most important and urgent business cannot induce the king to devote a day, or even an hour to it, or to interrupt his pleasures. He does not care what people think of him, or what is to become of the kingdom after his death.'

This unquestionably prejudiced view of a foreigner is unfortunately supported by Burnet, the seventeenth-century bishop and historian. 'No king', he wrote, 'could be less respected, and less lamented at his death. England, which acted so great a part, and whose queen, Elizabeth, was the arbitress of Christendom and the wonder of her age, sank under his government into utter insignificance.'

On the other hand, perhaps the opinion of another historian[17] gives a more understanding and impartial estimate as to James's personal character.

'The truth is, he was an aggregate of confusions and incongruities. He was a spoiled child, in a deplorably literal sense, before he was born. Nature's intention with him seems to have been to produce the ablest Stuart that ever graced the line since it sprang from the daughter of Robert Bruce; but ... "black art" intervened to defeat nature's intention: and the child born three months after the shock received by Mary Stuart from the drawn swords of Rizzio's murderers was physiologically a wreck – damaged irretrievably in body and mind.'

He had had, in truth, an unfortunate start, and a tragic end if the charge later to be brought against Buckingham that he had poisoned the king were true. It was not without strong foundation.

James I was buried in Henry VII's Chapel in Westminster Abbey.

5

Charles I (1600–1649)

Although Charles I's birthplace had been in Scotland (he was born at Dunfermline on 19 November 1600), when he ascended the throne twenty-five years later he was regarded as one of their own countrymen by his English subjects. He had been a popular prince, and had created a favourable impression not only for his learning and marked taste in the arts, but for his dignity of behaviour and 'temperate, chaste and serious character'. This estimate is supported by Charles's private correspondence. His letters combine the fascination of romance with the truth of the history of his time and exhibit – particularly those written to his wife – the king's personal and domestic attributes. His possession of these high qualities is perhaps by no means so common knowledge as is the king's tragedy.

He had been born a sickly child, and so weak that his death had been hourly expected. If the wife of Sir Robert Carey (afterwards Earl of Monmouth) had not been specially selected by the queen herself as the baby's foster-mother he would probably not have survived early infancy. 'When the little duke was first delivered to my wife', wrote Carey in his *Memoirs*, 'he was not able to go, nor scarcely to stand alone, he was so weak in his joints, especially in his ankles, insomuch many feared they were out of joint. Many a battle my wife had with the king, but she still prevailed. The king was desirous that the string under his tongue should be cut, for he was so long beginning to speak that he thought he would never have spoken. Then he would have him put into iron boots, to strengthen his sinews and joints; but my wife protested so much against them both, that she got the victory, and the king was fain to yield.' Lady Carey's success with the prince caused no small amazement. He was to grow into a figure 'of manly beauty and kingly grace', as was said of him by Rosewell, a dissenting minister, who saw Charles I when, as a fugitive, he was sheltering under a broad oak, 'as beneath a golden canopy at Whitehall'.

When Duke of York to the king, *c.* 1610

When the prince reached his tenth year it was proposed to remove him from the care of his foster-parents, but the queen intervening, Carey remained in his position as master of the robes. This office placed him always in the company of Charles.

The following letter is probably one of the first that Charles wrote. His thanking his father for his 'best man' undoubtedly refers to his being allowed to retain Carey – for whom he had a strong attachment – in his service.

(Undated)

Sweet, sweet Father,

I learn to decline substantives and adjectives. Give me your blessing. I thank you for my best man.

Your loving son,
York

To Henry, Prince of Wales

This delightful letter from Charles to his brother, Henry – who had been created Prince of Wales in 1610 – is obviously one of his earliest communications, and displays his generous-hearted and impulsive nature as a small boy, offering everything he has because of his love. It is given here in its original orthography in order not to detract from its charm.

(Undated)

Sweet, Sweet Brother,

I thank yow for your Letter. I will keep it better than all my graith:[1] and I will send my pistolles by Maister Newton.[2] I will give anie thing that I have to yow; both my horses, and my books, and my pieces, and my cross bowes, or anie thing that yow would haive. Good Brother loove me, and I shall ever loove and serve yow.

Your looving brother to be commanded,

York

The death of the Prince of Wales in 1612 came as no surprise to the superstitious populace. In the autumn of that year James I had given instructions for his mother's coffin to be transferred from Peterborough Cathedral – where the Queen of Scots had been buried near Catherine of Aragon – to a costly tomb he had had prepared in Westminster Abbey. The old and popular belief that a grave was never disturbed without death claiming one or more of the deceased's relations was very active on this occasion. The reinterment was regarded as ominous for the royal family. Shortly after the removal of Mary Stuart's remains, the Prince of Wales was suddenly taken ill. The fears of the populace were all the more excited at this happening because a lunar rainbow occurred at the same time, and seemed to span the part of St James's Palace where the heir apparent's apartments were situated. This was considered a confirmatory sign of dire significance. Prince Henry died within a month of his royal grandmother's relics being placed in the tomb at Westminster Abbey.

To his mother, the queen consort, Anne of Denmark

It was freely rumoured at the Scottish court at the time of Charles's birth that the king was not Charles's father. There seems to have been foundation for such gossip, which linked Anne of Denmark's name with that of Alexander Ruthven – 'a learned, sweet, and hurtless young gentleman' – who had lost his life some months previously as a result of the Gowrie conspiracy. This plot was an alleged attempt on the life of James at Perth in 1600. It had caused as great consternation in Scotland at the time as, five years later, the 'Gunpowder Plot' was to do in England, although general opinion where the Gowrie conspiracy was concerned was that it had been a fabrication on the part of James himself with the object of eliminating certain of his personal enemies, in particular Alexander Ruthven. Whatever the truth of court rumour, Anne of Denmark was, in any event, in such a state of deep despondency at the time of the birth of her second son that she nearly lost her life as a consequence.

Charles's devotion to his gay-hearted mother is evidenced in the following letter. Although the communication is undated, from the school-boy reference to his being 'deprived of many good dinners' one can safely hazard a guess that he was still in his early teens.

Most worthy Mistress,

Seeing I cannot have the happiness to see your majesty, give me leave to declare by these lines the duty and love I owe you, which makes me long to see you.

I wish from my heart that I might help to find a remedy to your disease; the which I must bear the more patiently, because it is the sign of a long life. But I must for many causes be sorry; and specially because it is troublesome to you, and has deprived me of your most comfortable sight, and of many good dinners; the which I hope, by God's grace, shortly to enjoy. And when it shall please you to give me leave to see you, it may be I shall give you some good recipe, which either shall heal you or make you laugh; the which wishing I may obtain by your majesty's most gracious favour, kissing in all humility your most sacred hands, and praying for your health and long prosperity, I end, most worthy Mistress,

Your majesty's most humble and obedient Servant,
Charles

Anne of Denmark was afflicted with gout, the 'disease' to which Charles refers as being a sign of long life. She died, however, in her forty-sixth year. The distressed nineteen-year-old prince arrived shortly before her death, to place himself, as he said, 'at her service'. The dying queen smilingly replied, 'I am a pretty piece to wait upon, *Servant*!' This title, derived from the code of chivalry, was her favourite name for Charles, which she invariably used in their intercourse together. That same night, a few hours after his arrival, as the Hampton court clock struck one, the prince knelt by his mother's bedside to receive her last blessing. This she gave with great clearness. Charles was chief mourner at his mother's funeral. She left him all her personal property.

When Prince of Wales to the king, 1623

The unusual and romantic journey made to Spain by Prince Charles and Buckingham has already been mentioned. The letter that follows was written jointly by Charles and Buckingham (although penned by the latter) to James I on their arrival in Paris before eventually, 'to the wonder of the world', as Howell, a humorous letter-writer of the day described it, 'the prince and the Marquis of Buckingham arrived at this [the Spanish] court'.

The main interest in this letter to the king is the fact that it was when embarked on this escapade that Charles saw Henrietta Maria for the first time, when he went in disguise to a rehearsal of a ballet at the French court. 'There the prince saw those eyes', a contemporary biographer tells us, 'that after inflamed his heart so much that it was thought to be the cause of setting three kingdoms on fire'. It may have been so. All the same, Charles makes no special mention of Henrietta Maria in this or any other of his letters written during that escapade.

Paris, Saturday, February 22nd

Dear dad and gossip,

We are sure before this you have longed to have some news from your boys; but before this time we have not been able to send it you; and we do it with this confidence, that you will be as glad to read it as we to write, though it be now our best entertainment. And that we may give the perfect account, we will begin this where my last ended.

First about five or six o'clock on Wednesday morning, we wish to say, the first that fell sick was your son, and he that continued it longest was myself. In six hours we got over with as fair a passage as ever men had. We all got so perfectly well, when we but saw land, that we resolved to spend the rest of the day in riding post; and lay at Montreuil, three post off Boulogne. The next day we lay at Breteur, eleven post further; and the next to Paris, being Friday. This day, being Saturday, we rest at Paris, though no great need of it. Yet I had four falls by the way, without any harm. Your son's horses stumble as fast as any man's; but he is so much more stronger before than he was. He holds them up by main strength of mastery, and cries still on! on!! on!!!

This day we went, he and I alone, to a periwig-maker, where we disguised ourselves so artificially, that we adventured to see the King.[3] The means how we did compass it was this: We addressed ourselves to the King's governor, Monsieur du Proes, and he courteously carried us where we saw him our fill. Then we desired Monsieur du Proes to make us acquainted with his son, because we would trouble the old man no longer, which he did; and then we saw the Queen-mother[4] at dinner. This evening his son hath promised us to see the young queen, with her sister and little monsieur.[5]

I am sure now you fear we shall be discovered; but do not fright yourself; for I warrant you the contrary. And finding this might be done with safety, we had a great tickling to add it to the history of our adventures.

To-morrow, which will be Sunday, we will be (God willing) up so early, that we make no question but to reach Orleans; and so every day after we mean to be gaining something, till we reach Madrid. I have nothing more to say, but to recommend my poor little wife and daughter to your care; and that you will bestow your blessing upon

> Your humble and obedient son and servant, Charles
> Your humble slave and dog, Steenie

Since the closing of our last, we have been at court again (and that we might not hold you in pain, we assure you we have not been known), where we saw the young queen, little monsieur, and madame, at the practising of a masque that is intended by the Queen to be presented to the King. And in it there danced the Queen and madame, with as many as made up nineteen fair dancing ladies, amongst which the Queen is the handsomest, which hath wrought in me a greater desire to see her sister.[6] So, in haste, going to bed, we humbly take our leave.

The twenty-five-year-old Charles was proclaimed king on the day of his father's death. In view of his personal character the nation looked forward with reasonable expectation to being religiously and uprightly governed. As some indication of this, while retaining the same administration, Charles I set about reforming his court. All persons appointed were expected to display strictly moral conduct. Unfortunately, however, he chose to retain as his chief confidant and adviser the notorious and hated Buckingham, whose influence over him was almost as strong as that which Buckingham had held over the late king. This fact, combined with Charles's marriage to a Roman Catholic princess shortly after he came to the throne, caused dissension and dissatisfaction from the outset. The king was to have private problems to solve as well.

His marriage to Henrietta Maria of France had taken place at Canterbury on 22 June 1625, a marriage by proxy having been solemnised three weeks previously at Notre Dame according to the Roman Catholic rites, when Charles's cousin, the Duke of Chevreuse, had represented the king.

In the early days of their union the inevitable difficulties arising from their differing creeds created serious disagreements between Charles and his consort. In addition, his jealousy and dominating personality clashed violently with his girl-wife's haughty and wilful temperament, occasioning endless disputes between them. Finally Charles became obsessed with the conviction that Henrietta Maria's French attendants were not only influencing her opinions and actions, but were attempting to alienate his wife's affections. Their presence at his court proved daily more intolerable to him, until he determined that they must all be dismissed.

When king to George Villiers, Duke of Buckingham, 1625

Presumably, from the tone of the following letter, Charles had received advice from Buckingham, who was in Paris at the time, to treat Henrietta Maria with patience, and not to be too hasty in dismissing her French retinue. This counsel, all the same, would have been proffered by Marie de' Medici, and would not have been of Buckingham's own instigation.

He was a determined mischief-maker where Charles and his wife were concerned. The troubles that existed between the royal couple in these early days were greatly aggravated by Buckingham's studied insolence towards Henrietta Maria, who had good reason to resent the man who ruled the king, the court and the country.

Hampton court,[7]

10th November

Steenie,

You know what patience I have had with the unkind usages of my wife, grounded upon a belief that it was not in her nature but made by ill instruments, and aided by your persuasions to me that my kind usages would be able to rectify those misunderstandings. I hope your ground may be true, but I am sure you have erred in your opinion. For I find daily worse and worse effects of ill offices done between us – my kind usages having no power to mend anything.

Now necessity urges me to give vent to you in this particular, for grief is eased being told to a friend. And because I have many obligations to my mother-in-law (knowing that these courses of my wife are so much against her knowledge that they are contrary to her advice) I would do nothing concerning her daughter that may taste of any harshness without advertising her of the reasons and the necessity of the thing: therefore I have chosen you for this purpose, because you – having been one of the chief causes that hath withheld me from these courses hitherto – may well be one of my chief witnesses that I have been forced into these courses now.

You must therefore advertise my mother-in-law that I must remove all those instruments that are causes of unkindness between her daughter and me, few or none of the servants being free of this fault in one way or another. Therefore I would be glad that she might find a means of making them suitors to leave the country. If this be not done, I hope there can be no exceptions taken at my following the example of Spain and Savoy in this particular. So, requiring a speedy answer of thee in this business (for the longer it is delayed the worse it will grow) I rest

Your loving, faithful, constant friend,
Charles R.

Charles's attitude, as shown in the foregoing letter and other communications to 'Steenie' on the same subject, is more like that of a jealous young husband of strong possessive tendencies than of a ruling monarch of the dignity that he could rightly claim. In discussing his private relationship with his wife – an indiscretion which Henrietta Maria justly resented – the king could not have selected a worse counsellor, or one more determined to widen the breach between himself and the queen, than the latter's openly professed enemy.

In spite of the urgency the king expresses of getting rid of the French attendants, he was to have to endure the 'monsers', as he termed them, and the 'mesdames' too, for many months to come.

To George Villiers, Duke of Buckingham, 1626

By the summer of the following year Charles I's patience in his domestic problems had reached its tether-end. In this letter he is setting out his case in detail, and for the last time. While many of the complaints he makes seem trivial, Henrietta Maria's refusal to be crowned with him at Westminster Abbey, or even to be present on that occasion – solely on account of her bigotry – was an action without precedent in regal history. It placed the king at a serious disadvantage before all his subjects, and was an affront to the whole nation. This initial error of judgment was to have grave repercussions for Henrietta Maria, and to preclude her from ever becoming popular in England from that time onwards.

It is not unknown, both to the French king and his mother, what unkindnesses and distastes have fallen between my wife and me; which hitherto I have borne with great patience (as all the world knows), ever expecting and hoping an amendment – knowing her to be but young, and perceiving it to be the ill crafty counsels of her servants for advancing of their own ends, rather than her own inclination. For, at my first meeting of her at Dover, I could not expect more testimonies of respect and love than she showed; as, to give one instance.

Her first suit was, that she being young, and coming to a strange country, both by her years and her ignorance of the customs of the place, might commit many errors; therefore [she hoped] that I would not be angry with her for her faults of ignorance, before I had, by my instructions, learned her to eschew them; and [she] desired me, in these cases, to use no third person, but to tell her myself, when I found she did anything amiss.

I both granted her request and thanked her for it; but desired that she should use *me* as she had desired me to use her; which she willingly promised me – which promise she never kept. For, a little while after this, Madame St George,[8] taking a distaste because I would not let her ride with us in the coach – when there were women of better quality to fill her room – claiming it as her due (which in England we think a strange thing), set my wife in such a humour of distaste against me as, from that very hour to this, no man can say that ever she answered me, two days together, with so much respect as I deserved of her. But, on the contrary, has put so many disrespects on me, that it were too long to set down all.

Some I will relate, as I comprehend it was. On her first coming to Hampton court I sent some of my council to her with those orders that were kept in the Queen my mother's house, desiring she would command the Count of Tilliers[9] that the same might be kept in hers. Her answer was, that 'she hoped I would give her leave to order her house as she list herself.' Now, if she had said that she would speak with me, not doubting to give me satisfaction in it, I could have found no vault with her, whatsoever she would have said of this to myself, for I could only impute it to ignorance. But I could not imagine that she would have affronted me so as to refuse me in such a thing publicly.

After I heard this answer, I took a time, when I thought we had both best leisure to dispute it, to tell her calmly both her fault in the public denial and her mistaking the business itself. She, instead of acknowledging her fault and mistaking, gave me so ill an answer that I omit (not to be tedious) the relation of that discourse – having too much of that nature hereafter to relate.

Many little neglects I will not take the pains to set down. As, her eschewing to be in my company; when I have any thing to speak to her, I must means[10] her servant first, else I am sure to be denied; her neglect of the English tongue, and of the nation in general. I will also omit the affront she did me, before my going to this last unhappy assembly of Parliament; because there has been talk of that already ...

To be short, omitting all other passages, coming only to that which is most recent in memory: I having made a commission to make my wife's jointure, to assign her those lands she is to live on, and it being brought to such a ripeness that it wanted but my consent to the particulars they had chosen, she – taking notice that it was now time to name the officers for her revenue – one night, when I was in bed, put a paper into my hand, telling me it was a list of those that she desired to be of her revenue. I took it, and said I would read it next morning; but withal told her that, by agreement with France, I had the naming of them. She said, there were both English and French in the note. I replied, that those English I thought fit to serve her I would confirm; but for the French, it was impossible for them to serve her in that nature. Then she said, all those in the paper had breviates from her mother and herself, and that she could admit no other. Then I said, it was neither in her mother's power nor hers to admit any without my leave; and that, if she stood upon that, whomsoever she recommended should not come in.

Then she bade me plainly take my lands to myself! For, if she had no power to put in whom she would in those places, she would have neither lands nor houses of me! but bade me give her what I thought fit in pension. I bade her then remember to whom she spoke; and told her, she ought not to use me so. Then she fell into a passionate discourse, [saying] how miserable she was in having no power to place servants, and that business succeeded the worse for her recommendation; which, when I offered to answer, she would not so much as hear me. Then she went on, saying she was not of that base quality to be used so ill. Then I made her both hear me, and end that discourse.

Thus, having had so long patience with the disturbance of that which should be one of my greatest contentments, I can no longer suffer those, that I know to be the cause and fomenters of these humours, to be about my wife any longer. This I must du, if it were but for one action which they made my wife do, which is, to make her go to Tyburn in devotion to pray: which action can have no greater invective made against it than the relation.[11]

Therefore, you shall tell my brother [-in-law], the French king, as likewise his mother, that this being an action of so much necessity I doubt not but he will be satisfied with it; especially since he has done the like himself, not staying while he had so much reason. And being an action that some may interpret to be of harshness to his nation, I thought good to give him an account of it; because that, in all things, I would preserve the good relationship and brotherly affection that is between us.

July 12

In some justification of Henrietta Maria it should be mentioned that her attitude, in certain respects, was due to her mother's faulty and misleading instructions as to Henrietta Maria's religious observances in England. In a long letter to her daughter, Marie de' Medici implies that she is going into a country where, as the Host was not worshipped there, the deity of Christ was blasphemed: and by inference she urges the sixteen-year-old bride to enter the kingdom in the spirit of a missionary among heathens.

To George Villiers, Duke of Buckingham, 1626

This is the last letter from the king concerning the dismissal of the queen's foreign household. The style in which it is written discloses in a remarkable manner Charles's virulence towards his wife's attendants. Henrietta Maria blamed Buckingham for this happening. It will be seen, however, that he was acting by the king's express command, albeit he was doing so with relish.

Steenie,

I have received your letter by Dick Greame.[12] This is my answer. I command you to send all the French away to-morrow out of town. If you can, by fair means – but stick not long in disputing. Otherwise force them away – driving them away like so many wild beasts, until ye have shipped them. And so the devil go with them!

Let me hear no answer but the performance of my command. So I rest,

Your faithful, constant, loving friend,
Charles R.
7th of August

The French suite had first been evacuated from the court to Somerset House, the queen's private residence. Henrietta

Maria, watching the departure of her retinue from a window at Whitehall Palace, flew into such a fury that she smashed the panes in her determination to bid her friends a passionate farewell. The scene ended in a fierce struggle between the king and herself, Charles having to restrain his wife by main force.

Regarding Somerset House as their stronghold, the French attendants refused to leave the country, and Charles was compelled to send a strong body of yeomen to conduct them to the waiting barges on the Thames. Their departure was witnessed by a delighted crowd in the Strand, and ended in a street riot. During the uproar one of the mob was killed by an officer of the guard for stoning the elegant Madame de St George, against whom Charles had exhibited such marked animosity.

Although the conduct of the French train had been inexcusable, the king's high-handed action was undeniably a breach of the marriage contract, as was also his failure to relieve the English Roman Catholics from the operation of the penal laws – a strong bone of contention between himself and Henrietta Maria. Only by the wise counsel of Marie de' Medici's ambassador, the Duc de Bassompierre, was a serious situation with France averted.

Where their domestic happiness was concerned, the bold step that Charles I had taken in dismissing Henrietta Maria's French attendants would have been improved upon had he gone one step further and dispensed with Buckingham, whose interference in his private and public life had become a menace. As it was, the favourite's influence with the king, and antagonism towards Charles's high-spirited queen, was to continue to prove a source of bitter contention between the royal pair. It was not until after the fortuitous assassination of Buckingham – as being 'an enemy of the people' – in 1628 that all serious differences between Charles and his wife came to an end. Their unshaken love for each other thereafter, in its romance and tragedy, is unique in the history of the sovereigns covered by the reigns under review. The tenderness that existed between them is clearly evidenced by the letters that they wrote to each other during the Civil War which broke out in 1642.[13]

We are here in no way concerned with the political and religious issues that gave rise to this outbreak, or the rights and wrongs of the contending parties, except in so far as the correspondence that follows is of relative interest.

To the queen consort, Henrietta Maria, 1643

Early in 1642 Henrietta Maria had made a journey to Holland, ostensibly to conduct her eldest daughter, Mary – then aged ten – to the United Provinces as bride of William II of Orange, the marriage of the Princess Royal having taken place by proxy at Whitehall some months previously. The underlying objective of the queen's journey, however, had been to raise money and enlist aid for the king's cause, which commission she successfully performed.

The incident referred to by Charles I in the opening paragraph to the following letter occurred on the queen's return voyage to England in February, 1643, after an extended visit to Holland.

Henrietta Maria had sailed for England in *The Princess Royal*, but was driven back to The Hague by a storm of several days' duration. The queen had, however, great physical and moral courage at all times, and on her second attempt to reach England she managed to make a safe landing.

Dear Heart,

I never till now knew the good of ignorance. For I did not know of the danger that thou wert in by the storm, before I had certain assurance of thy happy escape – we having had a pleasing false report of thy safe landing at Newcastle, which thine of the 19th so confirmed us in that we at least were not undeceived of that hope till we knew certainly how great a danger thou hast passed – and of which I shall not be out of apprehension until I may have the happiness of thy company. For, indeed, I think it not the least of my misfortunes that for my sake thou hast run so much hazard, in which thou hest expressed so much love to me that, I confess, it is impossible to repay by anything I can do, much less by words.

But my heart being full of affection for thee, admiration for thee, and impatient passion of gratitude to thee, I could not but say some-thing, leaving the rest to be read by thee out of thine own noble heart.

The intercepting of mine to thee of the 23rd of February has bred great discourse in several persons and of several kinds … Some find fault as too much kindness to thee. Thou mayst easily vote from what constellation that comes. But I assure such that I want expression – not will – to do it ten times more to thee on all occasions. Others press me as being 'brought upon the stage'; but I answer that, having professed to have thy advice, it were wrong to thee to do anything before I had it … .

So daily expecting and praying for good news from thee,

Thine

The foregoing letter alone would serve to confirm the opinion of a contemporary Royalist, Sir Edward Hyde. 'The king's affection to the queen was a composition of conscience, love, generosity and gratitude, and all those noble affections which raise the passion to its greatest height; insomuch, that he saw with her eyes, and determined by her judgment. Not only did he pay her this adoration, but he desired that all men should know that he was swayed by her, and this was not good for either of them. The queen was a lady of great beauty, excellent wit and humour, and made him a just return of the noblest affections; so that they were the true ideal of conjugal attachment in the age in which they lived.'

Having been impeached by Parliament for 'levying war on England', Henrietta Maria's life became in danger very early in the Civil War. As a consequence, in view of the intensifying engagements between the Royalist forces and the Parliamentary army, Charles became fearful for his queen's safety, more especially as she was about to have another child. He insisted upon her seeking refuge in the loyal city of Exeter. Shortly after her confinement, however, the Earl of Essex (divorced husband of Frances, Countess of Somerset), who had joined the Parliamentary forces in their war against the king, advancing on Exeter sent a message that he intended to take the queen as a prisoner to London, to answer to Parliament for high treason. While in no way herself afraid of her enemies, Henrietta Maria realised that her personal danger might bring destruction on her husband's plans. With a price on her head and still seriously ill, she straightway fled the city and made her perilous way to France, where she was given accommodation at the Louvre. Her baby – Princess Henrietta Anne – was later smuggled over to France dressed as the child of a peasant woman (p. 132).

From the Louvre Henrietta Maria wrote to Charles expressing her longing for England. 'There I have what I have not here: *You*, without whom I cannot be happy; and I think I shall never have my health till I see you again.' She was never to see her husband again, and never again to enjoy full health.

The Civil War continued to drag on with no decisive results. Certain unexpected successes of the king's forces, however, were attributed to rivalry among the Parliamentary leaders, and the opposing views of Essex and Cromwell. Further, the religious differences of the Presbyterians and Independents soon extended to the Parliamentary army. With knowledge of this internal dissension among his opponents, the king decided to offer a treaty to the rebels to bring an end to the war.

Charles's 'mongrel parliament', as he himself termed it, sat at Oxford, and was composed of such peers as adhered – or professed to adhere – to the king's cause. The proceedings of this mixed assembly, however, caused the king grave misgivings at times. His parliament was small in numbers, and had a predominance of Roman Catholic peers who showed no anxiety to preserve the moderate course which it was Charles I's wish to maintain. As several of these nobles held office in Henrietta Maria's household, the king asked her to relieve him of some of them by commanding that they fulfil their duties in her court at the Louvre.

To the queen consort, Henrietta Maria, 1645

The Catholic Cavalier, Lord Algernon Percy, to whom the king refers in the following letter, more than justified the view of his character held by Charles I. He proved to be a Parliamentary spy, as was his sister, Lady Carlisle, one of the queen's trusted friends. (Lady Carlisle was to be put in charge of Princess Elizabeth, the king's second daughter, when she was held prisoner under the Commonwealth – p. 114.)

25th February

Dear Heart,

... As to our treaty, there is every day less hope than ever that it will produce a peace; but I will absolutely promise thee that if we have one it shall be such as will invite thy return. For I vow that without thy company I can neither have peace nor comfort within myself.

The limited days for treating with are now almost expired, without the least agreement upon any one article. Wherefore I have sent for enlargement of days, that the whole treaty may be laid open to the world. And I assure thee thou needst not doubt the issue of this treaty: for my commissioners are so well chosen (though I say it) that they will neither be threatened nor disputed from the grounds I have given them, which (upon my word) is according to the little note thou so well remembrest. And in this, not only their obedience but their judgments concur.

I confess, in some respects, thou hast reason to bid me beware of going too soon to London:[14] for, indeed, some amongst us had a greater mind that way than was fit – of which persuasion Percy is one of the chief, who is shortly like to see thee: of whom, having said this, will be enough to show thee how [little] he is to be trusted or believed by thee concerning our proceedings here.

In short, there is *little* or no appearance but that this summer will be the hottest for war of any that hath been yet. And be confident, that in making peace I shall ever show my constancy in adhering to bishops and all my friends, and not forget to put a short period to this perpetual Parliament.

But as thou lovest me, let none persuade thee to slacken thine assistance for him who is eternally

Thine

To the queen consort, Henrietta Maria, 1645

Charles I had faith in his wife's judgment and capacities – whether rightly or otherwise – before all others, as is clear from his correspondence. When, therefore, after the breaking off of the treaty it was suggested to him, as he mentions in this letter, that Henrietta Maria should act as an intermediary, he was only too willing to believe her to be the one best suited for 'so happy and glorious a work' as that of bringing about peace in his kingdom.

The queen had written to say that the Duke of Chevreuse was prepared to land in England with ten thousand men to aid the royal cause. The king's reference to this topic in more than one letter, combined with his giving the queen power to promise in his name that he would remove all the penal laws against the English Catholics if they would come to his assistance, reacted disastrously for Charles when his private cabinet fell into the hands of the enemy. From the time of the publication of these letters nothing was to prosper with the king's cause.

Oxford, Sunday 30th March

Dear Heart,

Since my last – which was but three days ago – there are no alterations happened of moment; preparations rather than actions being yet our chief business, in which we hope that we proceed faster than the rebels, whose levies both of men and money for certain goes on very slowly. And I believe they are much weaker than is thought even here at Oxford.

For instance, a very honest servant of mine, and no fool, showed me a proposition from one of the most considerable London rebels, who will not let his name be known until he have hope that this proposition will take effect. It is this: That since the treaty is broken off, neither the rebels nor I can resume it without at least a seeming total yielding to the other; [therefore] the treaty should be renewed upon thy motion, with a pre-assurance that the rebels will submit to reason.

The answer that I permitted my servant to give was that thou art much the fittest person to be the means of so happy and glorious a work as is the peace of this kingdom; but that upon no terms was thy name to be profaned. Therefore he was to be satisfied of the rebels' willingness to yield to reason before he could consent that any such intimation should be made to thee, and – particularly concerning religion and the militia – that nothing must be insisted upon but according to my former offers. This, I believe, will come to nothing. Yet I cannot but advertise thee of any thing that comes to my knowledge of this consequence.

I must again tell thee that most assuredly France will be the best way for transportation of the Duke of Lorraine's[15] army, there being divers fit and safe places of landing for them upon the western coasts, besides the ports under my obedience, as Shelsea[16], near Chichester, and others – of which I will advertise thee when the time comes.

By my next I think to tell thee when I shall march into the field, for which money is now his greatest want (I need say no more) who is eternally

Thine

To the queen consort, Henrietta Maria, 1645

Comment on this love letter from Charles I to his wife is unnecessary. The king's feelings on Henrietta Maria's enforced departure, left desolate as he then was to accomplish his destiny alone, are best described as given in the *Eikon Basilike*, or *Portrait of His Sacred Majesty in his Solitude and Sufferings,* excerpts from which will be found in Appendix A. The book, which was printed at the time of the king's execution, has not been accepted as his own work, chiefly because John Milton, deputed by Parliament to write an answer to the *Eikon*, questioned whether it was written by Charles I himself. All the same, Milton treated the work as written by the king 'as the best advocate and interpreter of his own actions'. On the Restoration, the authorship of the *Eikon Basilike* was claimed by Gauden, afterwards Bishop of Exeter. It remains a literary mystery, however.

Oxford, 9th of April

Dear Heart,

Though it be an uncomfortable thing to write by a slow messenger, yet all occasions of this which is now the only way of conversing with thee are so welcome to me as I shall be loth to lose any; but expect neither news nor public business from me by this way of conveyance. Yet, judging thee by myself, even these nothings will not be unwelcome to thee, though I should chide thee – which if I could I would – for thy too sudden taking alarms.

I pray thee consider, since I love thee above all earthly things, and that my contentment is inseparably conjoined with thine, must not all my actions tend to serve and please thee? If thou knew what a life I lead (I speak not in respect of the common distractions), even in point of conversation, which in my mind is the chief joy or vexation of one's life, I dare say thou wouldest pity me. For some are too wise, others too foolish, some too busy, others too reserved, many fantastic ...

I confess thy company bath perhaps made me, in this, hard to be pleased, but not less to be pitied by thee, who art the only cure for this disease. The end of all is this, to desire thee to comfort me as often as thou canst with thy letters. And dost not thou think that to know particulars of thy health, and how thou spendest thy time, are pleasing subjects unto me, though thou hast no other business to write of?

Believe me, sweet heart, thy kindness is as necessary to comfort my heart as thy assistance is for my affairs.

Thine

To the queen consort, Henrietta Maria, 1646

When the Parliamentary troops were closing in on Oxford – the Royalist's last stronghold – Charles I, realising that his difficulties were almost irretrievable, had no alternative but to plan immediate flight to avoid falling into the hands of the enemy. The French ambassador, Montreuil, had for some time been negotiating with the Scottish covenanters for the king to be received into their camp. It will be seen, however, from the following letter how desperate Charles considered his situation was in any event.

Oxford, April 15th

Dear Heart,

Since mine of the 13th to thee, not having heard anything from Montreuil, I find myself like to be drawn into very great straits. And being absolutely resolved, God willing, never to fall into the rebels' hands as long as I can by any industry or danger prevent it, I have also resolved to expose myself to all the difficulties and hazards that can occur to my deliverance; and, not to flatter myself in this purpose, whether I be obliged to go to the Scotch – or what other course soever I shall be forced to take – they [the difficulties] will be great enough to invite me to think of those things which will be of essential necessity, in case I do not save myself. One which, though not only necessary in that case, is the having my son with thee in France.

I do therefore charge thee, as soon as thou shalt receive this, if then he shall not be with thee (which I would not willingly doubt), that thou send mine and thine own positive commands to him to come unto thee. And this I write to thee now without any scruple; for that in every event that my present purpose can possibly produce, this counsel is not to be disputed. For, whether I save myself, or be taken prisoner, my son can be no where so well, for all the reasons I have to look upon in consideration of thee, myself, and him, as that he should be now with thee in France.

Therefore, again I recommend to thee that, if he be not with thee, thou send immediately for him; assuring thee that most certainly, if God let me live, I will either privately or by force attempt very suddenly to get from hence. I have not now time to tell thee the rest of the particulars I have in my thoughts, in case I hear from Montreuil that things are prepared for my reception in the Scotch [sic] or that I be forced to take any other course; but shall send thee an express to inform thee at large. So I conjure thee to pray for him who is entirely thine.

Charles R.

To his son, Charles, Prince of Wales, 1646

The firm attachment of Charles I to the established church is deserving of praise even by those who conscientiously differ from that denomination. The queen and her advisers later attempted to persuade the king to abandon his allegiance in the hope of securing peace, but he was adamant on this point. This will be clear from his letter to his eldest son, whom the king supposed to have arrived in France. The Prince of Wales, however, did not reach the Louvre until some months later.

Charles I is guardedly hinting in this communication that if the religious factions in England thought that they could persuade the Prince of Wales to their views, they would take his father's life and place himself on the throne.

Oxford, 22nd April

Charles,

Hoping that this will find you safe with your mother, I think fit to write this short but necessary letter to you. Then know, that your being where you are, safe froth the power of the rebels, is, under God, either my greatest security, or my certain ruin. For, your constancy to religion, obedience to me, and to the rules of honour, will make these insolent men begin to hearken reason, when they shall see their injustice not like to be crowned with quiet.

But if you depart from those grounds, for which I have all this time fought, then your leaving this kingdom will be (with too much probability) called sufficient proof for many of the slanders heretofore laid upon me.

Wherefore, once again I command you, upon my blessing, to be constant to your religion, neither hearkening to Roman superstitions, nor the seditious and schismatical doctrines of the Presbyterians and Independents. For I know that a persecuted Church is not thereby less pure, though less fortunate.

For all other things, I command you to be totally directed

by your mother; and, as subordinate to her, by the remainder of that council which I put to you at your parting from hence. And so, God bless you!

Charles R.

Both the Prince of Wales and his brother, James, Duke of York, had accompanied their father on his campaigns. Before the king's final preparations to depart secretly from Oxford, however, the Prince of Wales had been hurried off, and finally taken to Jersey for safety. James, who had been left behind at Oxford on its surrender to the Parliamentary forces, was sent by them as a prisoner to St James's Palace. He was his mother's favourite, and his escape was effected by her agents in England two years later.

It was with some private misgivings that the king – shorn of hair and beard, and riding behind his bedchamber man, John Ashburnham, as his servant – had set out from Oxford. For nine days he was to wander, uncertain whether to flee to France, Ireland, or his native country, Scotland. Eventually he decided on Scotland, with grievous results for himself.

The French ambassador's negotiations with the covenanters had held out hopes of sanctuary for Charles as their 'natural sovereign', but such promises, it seems, the representatives of the Scots had had little intention of fulfilling, although the actual facts are lost in obscurity. True, the Scots showed him every courtesy at first, but the king soon realised that he was a virtual prisoner in their hands, and that his fate was in the balance.

To his son, the Prince of Wales, 1646

The Scots conducted Charles I to Newcastle, and while in detention there and permitted to see no friends, he sent the following short letter – apparently deliberately non-committal – to his eldest son.

Newcastle, 2nd June

Charles,

This is rather to tell you where I am, and that I am well, than to direct you in anything, having written fully to your mother what I would have you do, whom I command you to obey in everything (except in religion, concerning which I am confident she will not trouble you). And see that you go no whither without her or my particular directions. Let me hear often from thee. So, God bless you.

Your loving father,
Charles R.

If Jack Ashburnham come where you are, command him to wait upon you, as he was wont, until I shall send for him, if your mother and you be together. If not, he must wait on her.

To the queen consort, Henrietta Maria, 1646

The king's suspicions as to the Scots' loyal intentions regarding himself increased with the passing months, and he finally planned an escape by sea. Whether it was his idea to get to France or seek safety in Ireland is not known. Evidently the queen's counsellors advised against this course, however, until Charles should be convinced beyond doubt of the Scots' treachery. 'And from these events', wrote a contemporary chronicler, 'it may be seen how badly the king was taught by his advisers not at once to flee from the bloody tyrants and usurpers, and to retire into France to his lady queen, or some foreign State where he would have been safe at least for a time.'

Newcastle, 5th December

Dear Heart,

… I will, according to thy conjuration, not think of an escape until the Scots shall declare that they will not protect me.[17] By which I perceive the opinion is – I say not it is thine – that it is less ill for my affairs that I should be a prisoner within my dominions than at liberty any where else: – for I cannot escape if I stay till the Scots declare against me. And indeed it may well be so. In which case [I trust] my friends will, upon my restraint, immediately and frankly declare for my release, of which I am sure thou wilt have a care, and therefore I will say no more ...

Thine

To the queen consort, Henrietta Maria, 1647

From the following letter it is clear that the Scots had become aware of the king's plot to escape from their custody. From this time onwards no one could obtain access to him without an order from the English Parliament.

Newcastle, January 2

Dear Heart,

I must tell thee that now I am declared what I have really been ever since I came into this army, which is a prisoner (for the governor told me some four days since that he was commanded to secure me, lest I should make an escape), the difference being only this: that heretofore my escape was easy enough, but now it is most difficult.

That which now is to be done is, that the Queen and the Prince of Wales declare publicly that my offers have been most reasonable, and that neither of you will persuade me to go further, but rather dissuade me, if I had a mind, to grant more. Because it is now clear that the demands concerning religion are destructive as well to my crown as conscience. I assure thee that somewhat fully to this sense (I say 'fully' for it must not be minced) is absolutely necessary for my preservation. For if there be the least imagination that the Prince of Wales will grant more than I, I shall not live long after. This is not my opinion alone, for the French ambassador fully concurs with me in it.

Having, as it is necessary, showed thee this sad truth (which to me is neither new nor strange), I need say no more; for I know thy love will omit nothing that is possible for my freedom. Yet I cannot but conjure thee never to despair of a good cause, and to remember that the Prince of Wales justly claims from thee a never-giving-over care of him, even as thou loves me, who am

Eternally Thine

The French ambassador goes from hence on Monday next, with my approbation, for he can have nothing more to do here; and I believe he will be useful to me in France, being no less confident of his affection to me than of his knowledge of these affairs, of which, on my word, there is no doubt. Wherefore I desire thee to give him all the countenance thou canst.

Finding the assistance of the Scots too costly, the English Parliament had been in negotiation with them for the withdrawal of their army from England. The sum the Scots finally agreed to accept for withdrawing was £400,000. Although the king's name was not mentioned in the preliminary negotiations, the fact that the Scots held him prisoner made it possible for them to demand this high figure, Parliament having originally only voted them £100,000. When, on the Scots' betrayal being known, it was suggested to the king that he should attempt to escape well into Scotland, and take refuge with the loyal Highlanders, he replied, 'I think it more respectable to go with those who have bought me, than stay with those who have sold me. I am ashamed that my price was so much higher than my Saviour's.'

Following final settlement of the negotiations, Charles I was carried off by the Roundheads on their marches south, and held at Hampton court, while the army and the Commons wrangled together as to which had the greater right to possession of the king's person.

To Colonel Whalley, 1647

The stealthy escape of the king from Hampton court was occasioned by a letter he had received from a friend in London signed 'E.R.' informing him that 'a secret meeting of the army agitators had taken place, in which murderous intentions were formed against him; and the fanatics ... had declared that His Majesty was no better than a dead dog.' Who was the writer of this warning letter is unknown. As the king mentions in his postscript to this communication to Colonel Whalley, his flight was not due to the letter that he had been shown that day – which was apparently from Cromwell.

Edward Whalley was to be among those who signed the warrant for the execution of Charles I, but it is said that the production of the following letter was instrumental in saving his life at the Restoration. He departed to New England, and died there in 1678.

Hampton court,
November 11th[18]

Colonel Whalley,

I have been so civilly used by you and Major Huntingdon that I cannot but by this parting farewell acknowledge it under my hand: as also to desire the continuance of your courtesy by your protecting my household stuff and moveables of all sorts, which I leave behind me in this house, that they may be neither spoiled nor embezzled.

Only there are three pictures here which are not mine, that I desire you to restore: to wit, my wife's picture in blue, sitting in a chair, you must send to Mistress Kirke; my eldest daughter's picture, copied by Belcam, to the Countess of Anglesey; and my

Lady Stanhope's[19] picture to Carry Rawley. There is a fourth which I had almost forgot – it is the original of my eldest daughter (it hangs in this chamber over the board next the chimney) which you must send to Lady Aubigny.

So, being confident that you wish my preservation and restitution, I rest

Your friend,
Charles R.

PS. I assure you it was not the letter you showed me to-day that made me take this resolution, nor any advertisement of that kind. But I confess that I am loth to be made a close prisoner, under pretence of securing my life.

I had almost forgot to desire you to send the black grewbitch ['Gypsey'] to the Duke of Richmond.[20]

The foregoing letter is interesting as exhibiting Charles I's fondness for works of art. During his reign he had introduced into the country some twelve hundred paintings of the finest merit and genius. Most of these were to be dispersed by public sale under the Commonwealth, and they produced to the republicans £38,000. Rubens, Vandyck, and other famous artists had all been familiar figures at Charles's court. The sculptor Bernini, however, could not be persuaded to come over from Italy, but agreed to make a bust of the king from portraits painted for this purpose by Vandyck. 'Something evil will befall this man!' exclaimed Bernini on seeing the portraits. 'He carries misfortune in his face'.

Charles I's letter to Whalley also indicates the facility with which the king could stoop to dealing with the disposal of trifles – or seeming trifles – amidst the dangers and embarrassments with which he was surrounded. Even when faced with execution, he was to have a thought for his dogs that had accompanied him on all his wanderings, and have them sent to Henrietta.

After his desperate dash for freedom, the king only succeeded in exchanging his imprisonment at Hampton court for detention at Carisbrooke Castle on the Isle of Wight by Colonel Hammond, a strong Parliamentarian and Governor of the Island.

To his daughter, Princess Elizabeth, 1648

The Princess Elizabeth had been named after Charles I's only surviving sister, Elizabeth, Queen of Bohemia. Her elder sister, being resident at The Hague as the wife of William II, was fortunately not destined to experience the intimate suffering in her father's tragedy that fell to Elizabeth's lot. She had been scarcely seven years old when the impending Civil War separated her from her parents, and had to pass the rest of her short life in the custody of comparative strangers.

The following little note was written by the king to Elizabeth while he was in detention on the Isle of Wight.

> Newport, 14th October

Dear daughter,

It is not want of affection that makes me write so seldom to you, but want of matter such as I could wish; and indeed I am loth to write to those I love when I am out of humour (as I have been these days by-past), lest my letters should trouble those I desire to please.

But having this opportunity, I would not lose it; though at this time I have nothing to say, but God bless you! So I rest

Your loving father,

> Charles R.

Elizabeth's last meeting with her father took place at St James's Palace on the eve of his execution. She was then in her fourteenth year, and has left her own account of this unhappy event (see Appendix B). She was treated with some harshness, it is said, when a prisoner with her little brother, Henry, Duke of Gloucester, at Carisbrooke Castle, and finally fell ill. Sir Theodore Mayerne, the royal physician, went to prescribe for the princess, but arrived too late. Among his papers was found the following record of her death, 'She died on the 8th of September, 1650, in her prison at the Isle of Wight, of a malignant fever, which constantly increased, despite medicine and remedies.'

Princess Elizabeth was buried obscurely at Newport.

To his son, the Prince of Wales, 1648

In the course of a long and last letter that the king wrote to his eldest son – excerpts from which follow – containing sincere and sound advice should the Prince of Wales be restored to the throne of England, Charles I remarks, 'A principal point of your honour will consist in your deferring all respect, love, and protection to your mother, my wife, who hath many ways deserved well of me; and chiefly in this, that having been a means to bless me with many helpful children[21] (all which, with their mother, I commend to your love and care), she hath been content with incomparable magnanimity and patience to suffer both for and with me and you.'

Newport, November 29

Son,

By what hath been said, you may see how long we have laboured in search of peace. Do not you be discouraged to tread those ways, to restore yourself to your right; but prefer the way of peace. Show the greatness of your mind, rather to conquer your enemies by pardoning than punishing. If you saw how unmanly and unchristianly this implacable disposition is in our evil-willers, you would avoid that spirit.

Censure us not for having parted with too much of our own right. The price was great. The commodity was security to us, peace to our people. And we are confident another Parliament would remember how useful a king's power is to a people's liberty.

Of how much we have divested ourself, that we and they might meet again in a due parliamentary way to agree the bounds for prince and people! And in this, give belief to our experience never to affect more greatness or prerogative than what is really and intrinsically for the good of our subjects (not satisfaction of favourites).[22] And, if you thus use it, you will never want means to be a father to all, and a bountiful prince to any you would be extraordinarily gracious to. You may perceive all men trust their treasure, where it returns them interest. And if princes, like the sea, receive and repay all the fresh streams and rivers trust them with, they will not grudge, but pride themselves, to make them up an ocean.

These considerations may make you a great prince, as your father is now a low one; and your state may be so much the more established, as mine hath been shaken. For subjects have learnt (we dare say) that victories over their princes are but triumphs over themselves; and so will be more unwilling to hearken to changes hereafter. The English nation are a sober people, however at present under some infatuation.

We know not but this may be the last time we may speak to you or the world publicly. We are sensible into what hands we are fallen; and yet we bless God we have those inward refreshments, that the malice of our enemies cannot disturb. We have learnt to own ourself by retiring into ourself, and therefore can the better digest what befalls us; not doubting but God can restrain our enemies' malice, and turn their fierceness unto His praise.

To conclude, if God give you success, use it humbly and far from revenge. If He restores you to your right upon hard conditions, whatever your promise, keep. Those men which have forced laws which they were bound to observe, will find their triumphs full of troubles. Do not think any thing in this world worth obtaining by foul and unjust means. You are the son of our love; and, as we direct you to what we have recommended to you, so we assure you, we do not more affectionately pray for you (to whom we are a natural parent) than we do pray that the ancient glory and renown of this nation be not buried in irreligion and fanatic humour: and that all our subjects (to whom we are a political parent) may have such sober thoughts as to seek their peace in the orthodox profession of the Christian religion, as it was established since the Reformation in this kingdom, and not in new revelations; and that the ancient laws, with the interpretation according to the known practices, may once again be a hedge about them; that you may in due time govern, as they be governed, as in the fear of the Lord.

C.R.

The commissioners are gone; the corn is now in the ground; we expect the harvest. If the fruit be peace, we hope the God of peace will, in time, reduce all to truth and order again: which that He may do is the prayer of

C.R.

To his last hour Charles I displayed nobility of character as a man and dignity as a sovereign. Still in the prime of life, he went to his execution with courage and serenity of spirit, fully justifying his own words, 'I fear not death: death is not terrible to me'. But perhaps the well-known lines of Andrew Marvell best serve to illustrate the king's behaviour on that occasion, 'He nothing common did, or mean, / Upon that memorable scene'.

Of the crowds that waited on that bitter winter day in Whitehall, shivering and stamping in the icy cold, few could have witnessed much of the final dramatic scene in the life of their king. The dense mass of troops surrounding the scaffold made any near approach impossible. One eyewitness, however – Philip Henry, later a Nonconformist preacher – was to record in his diary, 'The *Blow* I saw *Given*, and can truly say with a sad heart; at the instant thereof, I remember well, there was such a *Grone* by the *Thousands* there present as I heard never before and desire may lever hear again.'

One of the king's last acts on the scaffold was to remove the medallion of the Order of the Garter that he wore, and hand it to William Juxon, Archbishop of Canterbury, with the enigmatic remark, '*Remember*!' Below this medallion of St George was a secret spring which removed a plate ornamented with lilies, beneath which was a miniature of Henrietta Maria.

Historians have left varying and contrasting estimates of the character of Charles I. Nevertheless, in the light of the king's personal letters the view expressed by Clarendon is in no small degree substantiated. 'He was', says Clarendon, 'the worthiest gentleman, the best master, the best friend, the best husband, the best father, and the best Christian that the age in which he lived produced. And if he were not the best King, if he were without some parts and qualities which have made some kings great and happy, no other prince was ever unhappy who was possessed of half his virtues and endowments, and so much without any kind of vice.'

The king had expressed a wish that his remains might be buried in Westminster Abbey. By order of the Commons, however, the humble interment took place in St George's Chapel, Windsor, 'without either singing or saying'. This inscription alone was engraved on the coffin, 'Charles, *Rex*', and the year of his death.

6

Charles II (1630–1685)

The Commonwealth that came into being in 1649 was not to be of long duration, and after a series of experiments terminated within twelve years. It was evident that the parliamentary system of government could not work without a monarchy. As a consequence, Charles II, at the age of thirty, was restored to the throne in 1660, and what has been termed 'the long, lazy, lascivious reign' began.

In view of the calamities that had befallen the House of Stuart, and the early hardships that Charles personally had endured – knowing penury and danger, and experiencing all the miseries of a stateless wanderer – much might have been expected of him in development of character, in understanding, and in just government when finally he attained his kingdom.

Unfortunately, during his exile on the Continent, Charles had acquired tastes, ideas and habits unsuited to the country over which he was to reign. It was, in fact, a cynic and a libertine that ascended the throne of England, a monarch destined to become notorious mainly for his mistakenly termed 'merriness'. In his day, this word meant 'happy', but Charles was not happy. He was, in fact, subject to moods of deepest depression, and in his later years was to endure acute despondency over his wasted opportunities.

Unlike his father, Charles II was incapable of love in the

highest sense of the term. He was a slave to any woman who excited his desires and he had no liking for anyone who refused to be spoiled by him. By seventeen known mistresses – which even allowing for the times in which he lived seems a slightly excessive indulgence – he had thirteen children, foremost among them the hapless Monmouth. The males were to be created dukes and earls, and all his natural offspring provided in perpetuity with handsome revenues.

In his youth Charles was 'very well shaped', says Madame de Motteville, who had met him at Henrietta Maria's court at the Louvre. 'His brown complexion agreed well enough with his large bright black eyes; his mouth was exceedingly ugly, but his figure surpassing fine. He was very tall for his age, and carried himself with grace and dignity.'

When Prince of Wales to his sister, Mary, Princess Royal, 1642

The following letter was written by Prince Charles to his eldest sister, Mary (who, the reader will recall, had accompanied her mother to Holland in 1642), to whom the twelve-year-old Charles is sending news of home affairs, some of which he had obviously gleaned from his father's talks with him.

Most Royal Sister,

Methinks, although I cannot enjoy that former happiness which I was wont in the fruition of your society, being barred those joys by the parting waves, yet I cannot forget the kindness I owe unto so dear a sister as not to write – also expecting the like salutation from you, that thereby (although a while dissevered) we may reciprocally understand of each other's welfare. I could heartily, and with a fervent devotion, wish your return, were it not to lessen your delights in your loyal spouse, the Prince of Orange, who, as I conceived by his last letter, was as joyful for your presence as we sad and mourning for your absence.

My Father is very much disconsolate and troubled, partly for my royal Mother's and your absence, and partly for the disturbances of this Kingdom. I could wish and daily pray that there might be a conjunct and perfect uniting between my Father's Majesty and his Parliament, that there might be a perfect concordance with them in the subject, to the removal of the grievances of the Country, and the renewing of our decayed joys. For during the variance betwixt them, this Kingdom must of necessity lie under most palpable danger through fear of foreign or domestic enemies, they having now the lamps of the all discerning Parliament darkened, through the inconvenience of the many combustions now on foot.

As for the Militia of the Kingdom, it is not yet determined upon nor settled; which [Militia] of itself is one of the principal fortitudes wherewith this Kingdom is adorned.

Ireland was never in more danger than now of late, there being many Towns in the Province of Asper taken by the rebels; others endangered. But the last intelligence presented us with better news: wherein we understand of a fatal overthrow given the rebels' party, to their loss of ten thousand men; wherein O'Neal was supposed to be taken prisoner, Colonel Brunslow and divers other of their officers likewise following him in his sad misfortune.[1]

Dear Sister, we are, as much as we may, merry; and, more than we I would, sad, in respect we cannot alter the present distempers of these turbulent times.

My Father's resolution is now for York; where he intends to reside to see the event or sequel to these bad impropitious beginnings; whither you may direct your letter. Thus much desiring your comfortable answer to these my sad Lines, I rest

Your loving Brother,

Carol *Princeps*

Royston,[2] March 9th, 1642

Charles II's adventures during the years following his father's execution may be briefly summarised.

The fanatical hatred of the Scottish Presbyterians of popery and the English denominational creed determined them to acknowledge Charles II as king. After a compromise of sorts on the conditions the Scots laid down, Charles was crowned at Scone, and allowed to take command of the Scottish army. In the meantime he had had to submit to endless sermonising, strict supervision as to behaviour, the dismissal of his trusted servants as being 'ungodly persons', and perpetual lecturings on the sinfulness of his parents. The hypocrisy of the Presbyterian sect drove Charles to desperation, but, having his own aim in view, he endured with what grace he could summon.

In 1651 Charles marched his army into England. The failure of the English Royalists to support him in his war on Cromwell, however, terminated in his becoming a fugitive for six weeks in his own country, and with a price on his head. Eventually Charles escaped to France, and joined Henrietta Maria's court in Paris; but the ratification of the peace (1653–4) between France and Cromwell forced Charles to depart from the Louvre, and to become a wanderer in Europe.

In exile, to his aunt, Elizabeth, Queen of Bohemia, 1654

According to Clarendon, Charles remained for over two years at Cologne 'contending with the rigour of his fortune with great temper and magnanimity'. If the following letter is any criterion he was certainly pursuing his ways with the same 'merriness' that was to distinguish him when later he came to the Crown. An entry in Samuel Pepys's *Diary* affords sufficient comment on the king's inordinate passion for dancing and fiddlers. 'May 31st, 1664: I was told to-day that upon Sunday night last, being the king's birthday, the king was at my lady Castlemaine's lodgings (over the hither-gate at Lambert's lodgings) dancing with fiddlers all night almost; and all the world coming by taking no notice of it.'

Charles's aunt Elizabeth, to whom this letter is addressed, was James I's eldest daughter. In 1613 she had been married to Frederick V of Bohemia, when he was Elector Palatine. After Frederick's defeat at the Battle of Prague in 1620, she had taken refuge with her husband in Holland, where Frederick had died eleven years later.

The sister referred to by Charles was Mary, Princess of Orange, who was spending a holiday with her brother at the time.

Cologne, August 6th

Madame,

I am just now beginning this letter in my sister's chamber, where there is such a noise that I never hope to end it, and much less write sense. For what concerns my sister's journey and the accidents that happened on the way, I leave to her to give your Majesty an account of.

I shall only tell your Majesty that we are thinking how to pass our time in the first place, of dancing, in which we find two difficulties: the one for want of fiddlers, the other for somebody both to teach and assist at dancing the new dances. I have got my sister to send for Silvius[3] as one that is able to perform both. For the fideldedies [sic] my lord Taafe[4] does promise to be their convoy, and in the meantime we must content ourselves with those that make no difference between a hymn and a coranto.[5]

I have now received my sister's picture that my dear cousin, the Princess Louise,[6] was pleased to draw, and do desire your Majesty to thank her for me, for 'tis a most excellent picture, which is all I can say at present, but that I am, Madame,

Your Majesty's most humble and affectionate nephew and
servant,

Charles, R.

To the Queen of Bohemia, my dearest Aunt

To his brother, Henry, Duke of Gloucester, 1654

Henry, Duke of Gloucester, youngest son of Charles I, had
been permitted to be restored to his mother on the ratification
of peace between France and the Commonwealth. At the
same time Anne of Austria, queen regent of France, had felt
compelled to dismiss Charles II from her country. Before his
departure Charles had exacted a promise from his mother
that his youngest brother should not be brought up in the
Roman Catholic Faith. Nevertheless, Henrietta Maria was
privately determined that Henry should be converted, as she
was equally planning to bring about the conversion of all her
remaining family, if possible.

On the plea that Henry needed discipline, and owing to his
having been a prisoner in England lacked not only manners
but learning and languages, Henrietta Maria proposed to send
her young son to a Jesuit College for instruction. The boy
protested, but his mother remaining unmoved, he was forced
to appeal to Charles II.

The king's opinion of his mother's proceedings is forcibly
expressed in the following letter that he wrote to Henry on the
subject of the attempted conversion.

Cologne, November 10th

Dear Brother,

I have received yours without date, in which you tell me
that Mr Montague, the abbot of Pontoise.[7] has endeavoured
to pervert you from your religion. I do not doubt but you
remember very well the commands I left with you at my going

away concerning that point. I am confident you will observe them. Yet your letters that come from Paris say, that it is the Queen's purpose to do all she can to change your religion; in which, if you do hearken to her, or to anybody else in that matter, you must never think to see England or me again; and whatsoever mischief shall fall on me or my affairs, I must lay all upon you, as being the only cause of it. Therefore, consider well what it is to be, not only the cause of ruining a brother who loves you so well, but also of your king and country. Do not let them persuade you, either by force or fair promises; the first they never dare nor will use, and for the second, as soon as they have perverted you, they will have their end, and then they will care no more for you.

I am also informed, there is a purpose to put you into the Jesuits' college, which I command you, on the same grounds, never to consent unto; and whensoever anybody goes to dispute with you in religion, do not answer them at all. For, though you have reason on your side, yet they, being prepared, will have the advantage of anybody that is not upon the same familiarity with argument as they are. If you do not consider what I say unto you, remember the last words of your dead father, which were, to be constant to your religion, and never to be shaken in it; which, if you do not observe, this shall be the last time you will hear from,

Dear brother, your most affectionate,
Charles II

In consequence of the flouting of her authority, Henrietta Maria subjected the little duke to somewhat rigorous treatment. When this came to Charles's knowledge he claimed Henry as his subject, and took him from the Louvre. Henrietta Maria never saw her youngest son again after this parting. He accompanied the king and James, Duke of York, to England at the Restoration, but died of smallpox a few months after his arrival. Within three months of his death, Mary, Princess of Orange – who had joined her family in England to celebrate the Restoration – died of contagion, and was buried in the same Stuart vault with her brother in Westminster Abbey.

When king, to Catherine of Braganza, 1661

Efforts were made shortly after the Restoration to persuade Charles II to marry a Protestant princess, but his choice eventually fell on Catherine of Braganza, whose father, John, Duke of Braganza, had become king of Portugal in 1644. On his death in 1659 he had left the regency of the country in the hands of his widow, Donna Luiza of Medina-Sidonia, and it was she who skilfully negotiated for a treaty of marriage of her daughter with the king of England.

Catherine of Braganza's promised dowry undoubtedly provided the greatest attraction to Charles II. It incorporated an offer of £500,000 sterling, the assignment of Tangier, free trade for England with Brazil and the East Indies (hitherto denied to all nations save Portugal), and the gift of the island of Bombay – 'valued far above the portion in money', and which, incidentally, gave to England her first territorial possession in the East Indies. True, to the impecunious Charles's dismay part of the cash portion of the dowry was delivered by the queen regent's instructions in the form of sugar, spices, and other merchandise, but the king was not to know this at the time that he was writing the following letter to his bride-to-be.

On the signing of the marriage contract at Lisbon, Catherine of Braganza assumed the title of Queen of England, which, it will be noted, is the style in which Charles II addresses her.

My Lady and Wife,

Already, at my request, the good Count da Ponte has set off for Lisbon. For me, the signing of the marriage has been a great happiness, and there is about to be dispatched at this time after him one of my servants, charged with what would appear necessary; whereby may be declared, on my part, the inexpressible joy of this felicitous conclusion, which, when received, will hasten the coming of your majesty.

I am going to make a short progress into some of my provinces, in the meantime. Whilst I go for my most sovereign good yet I do not complain as to whither I go – seeking, in vain, tranquillity in my restlessness; and hoping to see the beloved person of your majesty in these kingdoms, already your own, and with the same anxiety with which – after my long banishment – I desired to see myself within them; my subjects (desiring also to behold me amongst them), having manifested their most ardent wishes for my return, well known to the world. The presence of your serenity is only wanting to unite us, under the protection of God, in the health and content I desire.

I have recommended to the Queen, our lady and mother[8] the business of the Count da Ponte[9], who, I must here avow, has served me in what I regard as the greatest good in this world, which cannot be mine less than it is that of your majesty; likewise not forgetting the good Richard Russell.[10] who laboured on his part to the same end.

The very faithful husband of your majesty, whose hand he kisses,

Charles, Rex
London, 2nd of July, 1661

To the Queen of Great Britain, my wife and lady, whom God preserve

To the Lord Chancellor, the Earl of Clarendon, 1662

Catherine of Braganza's journey to England from Portugal proved a long and stormy voyage, causing acute seasickness among the passengers. The bride-to-be was met at Portsmouth by James, Duke of York, the king being detained on 'imperative business' in London. On Charles II's arrival at Portsmouth some days later, the marriage ceremony took place at the king's house there, and was duly recorded in the register of the parish church of St Thomas-à-Becket, 'on vellum and in letters of gold'.

As his consort had not recovered from her sea voyage, the king 'took his supper with the queen on her bed, showing, in every way, how much pleased he was with her', and, on the advice of her physicians, she was left to sleep off the effects of her journey. Charles's own views on this marriage-night arrangement will be seen from the letter he wrote the next morning to his Lord Chancellor.

Portsmouth, May 21, 8 in the morning

I arrived here yesterday about two in the afternoon, and as soon as I had shifted myself, I went to my wife's chamber, who I found in bed, by reason of a little cough, and some inclination to a fever, which was caused, *as we physicians say*, by having certain things stopped at sea which ought to have carried away those humours. But now all is in due course, and I believe she will find herself very well in the morning as soon as she wakes.

It was happy for the honour of the nation that I was not put to the consummation of the marriage last night; for I was so sleepy by having slept but two hours in my journey as I was afraid that matters would have gone very sleepily. I can now only give you an account of what I have seen a-bed; which, in short, is, her face is not so exact as to be called a beauty, though her eyes are excellent good, and not anything in her face that in the least degree can shock one. On the contrary, she has as much agreeableness in her looks altogether, as ever I saw; and if I have any skill in physiognomy, which I think I have, she must be as good a woman as ever was born. Her conversation, as much as I can perceive, is very good; for she has wit enough and a most agreeable voice. You would much wonder to see how well we are acquainted already. In a word, I think myself very happy; but am confident our two humours will agree very well together. I have not time to say any more. My Lord Lieutenant[11] will give you an account of the rest.

To the Lord Chancellor, the Earl of Clarendon, 1662

Four days after his marriage the royal bridegroom wrote the following brief letter to his chancellor. His cheerful comments give every promise of a happy union. Unfortunately Charles was easily pleased with new toys, and was quickly bored once his initial delight of possession had cooled.

Portsmouth, 25th of May.

My brother[12] will tell you all that passes here, which I hope will be to your satisfaction. I am sure 'tis so much to mine, that I cannot easily tell you how happy I think myself, and I must be the worst man living (which I hope I am not) if I be not a good husband. I am confident never two humours were better fitted together than are ours. We cannot stir from hence till Tuesday, by reason that there are not carts to be had to-morrow to transport all our *guarde-infantas,* without which there is no stirring. So you are not to expect me till Thursday night at Hampton court.

The *guarde-infantas* to which the king alludes were farthingales, or large hooped petticoats, pertaining to the bride's wardrobe and those of her lady attendants, and not, as one might at first conclude, a grim escort of females appointed by the queen regent to watch over the young bride. The ladies in her retinue, all the same, were of sufficiently rigid demeanour. Catherine of Braganza's chamberlain, Lord Chesterfield, whimsically complained of the difficulty in pleasing the 'Portingall ladies', as he styled them. They were so 'over-delicate' about their accommodation that they refused to sleep in any beds that had been occupied by men.

One of the reasons that Catherine of Braganza enjoyed uninterrupted harmony in her relationship with her husband in the first few weeks of their marriage was due to the fact that his presiding mistress – expecting a child by him – had been forced to absent herself from court festivities. She gave birth to a son at Hampton court a few days after the royal marriage had taken place.

In view of the irate letter that follows, an outline of this particular lady's career is of interest. At the age of eighteen Barbara Villiers, daughter of Viscount Grandison – who had died in the Royalist cause – had married Roger Palmer, heir to a great fortune. Both she and her husband had joined the exiled court of Charles II, and intimacy between Mrs Palmer and the king had taken place before he returned to England. Their association, in fact, was notorious all over Europe, and had, of course, reached the ears of the queen regent of Portugal. Donna Luiza had told her daughter before her marriage of the king's liaison, and had advised her in no circumstances to receive his mistress at court.

To the Lord Chancellor, the Earl of Clarendon, 1662

In order to give Mrs Palmer the necessary rank, so that she could be appointed first lady of the bedchamber to his consort, Charles had created her husband Earl of Castlemaine. He probably had no alternative. His mistress's rages could bring the king to his knees, and her tyranny over him was a by-word.

His Lord Chancellor, Clarendon, protested that the king's proposal that the queen should accept Lady Castlemaine was 'one with which flesh and blood could not comply', with which opinion the Duke of Ormonde had humbly but firmly agreed.

Hampton court, Thursday evening

I forgot, when you were here last, to desire you to give Brodericke[13] good counsel not to meddle any more with what concerns my lady Castlemaine, and to let him have a care how he is the author of any scandalous reports; for if I find him guilty, I will make him repent of it to the last moment of his life.

And now I am entered on this matter, I think it very necessary to give you a little good counsel in it, lest you may think, by making a further stir in the business, you may divert me from my resolution, which all the world shall never do; and I wish I may be unhappy in this world and in the world to come if I fail in the least degree of what I have resolved, which is of making my lady Castlemaine of my wife's bedchamber; and whosoever I find use any endeavours to hinder this resolution of mine (except it be only to myself), I will be his enemy to the last moment of his life.

You know how true a friend I have been to you. If you will oblige me eternally, make this business as easy to me as you can, of what opinion soever you are of, for I am resolved to go through with this matter, let what will come of it, which again I solemnly swear before Almighty God.

Therefore, if you desire to have the continuance of my friendship, meddle no more with this business, except it be' to bear down all false and scandalous reports, and to facilitate what I am sure my honour is so much concerned in. And whosoever I find to be my lady Castlemaine's enemy in this matter, I do promise, upon my word, to be his enemy as long as I live. You may show this letter to my lord lieutenant,[14] and if you both have a mind to oblige me, carry yourselves as friends to me in this matter.

Charles R.

This intimidating letter succeeded in bringing both Clarendon and Ormonde to heel, although very much against their better feelings. Charles was not so successful with the queen at first. She stoutly refused to agree to the proposal. He ignored her protests, however, and introduced Lady Castlemaine to Catherine of Braganza before the court. The shock was so great to the queen that 'blood gushed from her nostrils', and she was carried from the apartment in a fit. Clarendon then tried to reason with her, but she would not listen to him, so to break her spirit, the king sent away all her Portuguese attendants. The queen was thus left alone to bear the studied insults to which she was subjected as best she was able, and finally was forced to accept Lady Castlemaine as one of her household.

To his sister, Henrietta Anne, Duchess of Orleans, 1663

Henrietta Anne, who had been smuggled over to France after her mother's flight from Exeter, was married in 1660 to Philip, Duke of Orleans, brother of Louis XIV. Possibly the nearest approach that Charles II ever came to loving was the deep affection he held for his youngest sister. After he had been restored to the throne the greater part of his correspondence was addressed to his 'chere Minette' to whom he avowed, 'You have my heart, and I cannot give you more'.

The marriage to which the king refers in this letter was that of his eldest illegitimate son, James Fitzroy Crofts, by Lucy Walters. He had been brought over from France, where he had been educated at Henrietta Maria's court, and a State marriage had been arranged between the youth and the little Lady Anna Scott, the heiress of Buccleugh. The bride was twelve years of age, and the Duke of Monmouth, as he had been created, 'a most pretty spark', according to Pepys, 'of about fifteen years old; who I perceive', adds Pepys, 'do hang much on my lady Castlemaine, and is always with her'. No happiness came of this marriage.

Whitehall, April 20

To Madame

You must not by this post expect a long letter from me, this being James's marriage day. And I am going to sup with them, where we intend to dance and see them a-bed together; but the ceremony shall stop there, for they are both too young to lie all night together.

The letters from France are not yet come, which keeps me in pain to know how Queen-mother does.[15] I hope James Hamilton will be on his way home before this comes to your hands.

I send you here the title of a little book of devotion in Spanish, which my wife desires to have. By the directions you will see where 'tis to be had, and pray send two of them by the first conveniency. My dearest sister, I am entirely yours,

C.

When later on in his reign suggestions were made that the Duke of Monmouth was the lawful heir to the throne, Charles II was forced to issue a public denial that he had been legally married to Lucy Walters. He asserted that he was 'never married nor gave any contract to any woman whatsoever but to my wife, Queen Catherine, to whom I am now married'.

To Henrietta Anne, Duchess of Orleans, 1664

In December 1664 Charles II – who had a decided taste for scientific pursuits and was the founder of the Observatory at Greenwich – watched with great interest for several nights for a sight of a new comet that had appeared, as he mentions to his sister in this letter. 'Mighty talk there is of this Comet', notes Pepys in his *Diary*, 'that is seen a'nights; and the King and Queene did sit up last night to see it, and did, it seems'.

Whitehall, December 26

To Madame

... We have seen here the Comet, but the weather has been so cloudy I never saw it but once. It was very low, and had a tail that stood upwards. It is now above twelve days since I saw it. But upon Christmas Eve and the night before, there was another seen very much higher than the former. I saw it both nights, and it looks much lesser than the first, but none of the astronomers can tell whether it be a new one or the old one grown less and got up higher; but all conclude it to be no ordinary star. Pray inquire of the skilful men, and let me know whether it has been seen at Paris. This new one was seen here, the 23rd and 24th of this month, and had a little tail which stood north-east.

I have no more to trouble you with, but that I am yours,

C.

As in the case of the lunar rainbow of 1612, the comet caused alarm and foreboding among the superstitious-minded, by whom its advent was regarded with scarcely less terror than that with which the Anglo-Saxons had beheld a comet in 1066, on the eve of the Norman invasion. As though to confirm the worst fears of those who anticipated the comet's evil portent, shortly after its appearance was to occur the Great Plague, which carried off some hundred thousand people. This calamity was followed by the Great Fire of London in 1666.

As Sir Edward Hyde, Clarendon had followed the fortunes of Charles I, and had subsequently shared in the long exile of Charles II. At the Restoration he had been created Earl of Clarendon, and became chief minister and virtual ruler of the nation. Of arrogant temper and impatient of opposition, Clarendon nevertheless had a strong sense of moral and religious obligations, and reverence for the country's laws. His habits of thought and procedure were diametrically opposed to the levities of the king and the younger courtiers, but for some years his great abilities were indispensable to Charles II.

Of the enemies Clarendon created Lady Castlemaine proved to be one of the most implacable. She never forgave Clarendon's championship of Catherine of Braganza. Aided by her faction, in 1667 she was instrumental in framing against the Lord Chancellor a series of serious charges to effect his downfall. The national temper, irritated to extremes by the evils which the country was labouring under at this time, demanded a scapegoat, and this Clarendon was made. He was impeached for high treason. Contention between the two houses became so alarming that Clarendon was advised to quit England. He at first refused, as he had refused to resign office. When, however, Charles II commanded him to retire to the Continent, Clarendon had no alternative but to hand in the seals of office.

In the following letter to the Duke of Ormonde – Clarendon's great friend, who was at the time over in Ireland attending to affairs as Lord Lieutenant – the king is excusing his own action on the grounds that his chancellor's temper had grown 'unsupportable'.

Whitehall, 15th September

I should have thanked you sooner for your melancholy letter of the 26th of August, and the good counsel you gave me in it, as my purpose was also to say something to you concerning my taking the Seals from the Chancellor; of which you must need have heard all the passages, since he would not suffer it to be done so privately, as I intended it. The truth is, his behaviour and humour was grown so unsupportable to myself and to all the world else, that I could no longer endure it; and it was impossible for me to live with it, and do those things with the Parliament that must be done or the Government will be lost.

When I have a better opportunity for it you shall know many particulars that have inclined me to this resolution, which already seems to be well liked in the world, and to have given a real and visible amendment to my affairs.

This is an argument too big for a letter. So I will add but this word to it: to assure you that your former friendship to the Chancellor shall not do you any prejudice with me, and that I have not in the least degree diminished that value and kindness I ever had for you. This I thought fit to say to you on this occasion because it is very possible malicious people may suggest the contrary to you.

To My Lord-Lieutenant

The explanation given to Ormonde as to the reason for Clarendon's dismissal was not the true one. Charles II had discarded his minister, who had laboured for over a quarter of a century in his father's and Charles's own service, because Clarendon's integrity had become hateful to Charles II and to his frivolous court. The courtiers' delight – in particular that of Lady Castlemaine – as well as that of the monarch himself knew no bounds once they had been freed from Clarendon's restraining supervision.

An exile thereafter at Montpelier, Clarendon dedicated his remaining years to his literary work, by which perhaps his name is best remembered in history, although as a statesman he was of no mean stature, and as a man he was immeasurably superior to those who had brought about his fall from power.

To Henrietta Anne, Duchess of Orleans, 1668

Renowned for her beauty as 'La Belle Stuart', Frances Stuart, a relative of the king's, had for long attracted his open admiration, to the anxiety of the queen and the fury of the Duchess of Cleveland, as Lady Castlemaine had now become. Although there were justifiable fears at one time that Charles II might divorce Catherine of Braganza in order to marry Frances, 'La Belle Stuart' was not to be won even on those terms. The king's attentions became so troublesome, however, that she finally 'had no way', according to Pepys, 'but to marry and leave the court ... that the world might see she sought not any thing but her honour'. Her marriage to her cousin, Charles, third Duke of Richmond, caused them both to bring down the king's wrath on their heads. Two years after her marriage 'La Belle Stuart' fell a victim of smallpox, which was to disfigure her permanently. In his anxiety for her welfare during her illness Charles II, risking chances of infection, paid several calls on her.

At the same time, as will be gathered from the following letter, the king was perturbed over his wife's condition, who, as our invaluable diarist of the period confirms, 'hath miscarryed of a perfect child, being gone about ten weeks; which do show that she can conceive, though it be unfortunate that she cannot bring forth'. Charles was also concerned about the health of his 'Chère Minette'. But, on the other hand, to dispel his anxieties he was enjoying the company of 'two comic actresses' – Moll Davies and Nell Gwynne. The latter was to be made one of the queen's maids-of-honour.

Whitehall, May 7th

To Madame

I have so often asked your pardon for omitting to write to you, as I am almost ashamed to do it now. The truth is, the last week I absolutely forgot it till it was too late, for I was at the Duchess of Richmond's, who, you know, I have not seen this twelve months, and she put it out of my head that it was post day. She is not much marked with the smallpox, and I must confess this last affliction made me pardon all that is past, and cannot hinder myself from wishing her very well. And I hope she will not be much changed, as soon as her eye is well, for she has a very great defluction in it, and even some danger of having a blemish in it, but now I believe the worst is past.

I did receive your letter by Fitzgerald the same day that the physicians were doing the very prescriptions you advise in your letter. But now that matter is over, for my wife miscarried this morning. And though I am troubled at it, yet I am glad 'tis evident she was with child, which I will not deny to you till now I did fear she was not capable of. The physicians do intend to put her into a course of physic which they are confident will make her hold faster next time ...

I will not go about to decide the dispute between Mam's[16] masses of Mr de Mayerne's pills,[17] but I am sure the suddenness of your recovery is as near a miracle as anything can be. And though you find yourself very well now, for God's sake have a care of your diet, and believe the plainer your diet is the better health you will have. Above all, have a care of strong broths and gravy in the morning.

I ask pardon for forgetting to deliver your message to James,[18] but I have done it now. He shall answer for himself, and I am sure he has no excuse, for I have often put him in mind to acknowledge, upon all occasions, the great obligations he has to you for your goodness to him, which I assure you he expresses every day here. If he does fail in writing, I fear he takes a little after his father. And so I will end this long trouble with the assuring you that I cannot express the kindness and tenderness I have for you.

To Charles's grief, Henrietta Anne died suddenly two years after the foregoing letter was written. She was only twenty-six, and the general belief was that she had been poisoned. Her effeminate husband and his favourite, the Chevalier de Lorraine, both came under strong suspicion. In the end, however, Charles had to be satisfied with the assurance of

Louis XIV that, according to his physicians' report, Henrietta Anne's death had been from natural causes.

The saddened king quickly sought consolation in the companionship of Renée de la Kerouaille, who had attracted his interest when she had attended Henrietta Anne on her last visit to England. Within a few weeks of his sister's death, Charles II sent a secret envoy and specially chartered yacht over to France, and Renée de la Kerouaille came to England. Charles compelled Catherine of Braganza to accept his new mistress as one of her household 'for the sake of his sister's memory'. The cultured and clever Renée, who was created Duchess of Portsmouth after she had borne the king a son, remained mistress-in-chief thereafter. Notorious for her huge gambling debts and her political intrigues, the lovely Kerouaille lived to the ripe age of ninety.

To Charlotte Fitzroy, Countess of Lichfield, 1682

Charles II appears to have written very few private letters during the last ten years or so of his reign. Among those that he did write were several short epistles to his eldest daughter by the Duchess of Cleveland, the young Countess of Lichfield. The one that follows is a fair example of his fatherly indulgence.

Whitehall, October 2, 1682

I have had so much business since I came hither that I hope you will not think that I have neglected writing to you out of want of kindness to my dear Charlotte. I am going to Newmarket[19] tomorrow, and have a great deal of business to dispatch tonight. Therefore I will I only tell you now that I have five hundred guineas for you which shall be either delivered to yourself, or any whom you shall appoint to receive it, and so, my dear Charlotte, be assured that I love you with all my heart, being your kind father

C.R.

Twenty-five years after he had been restored to the throne Charles II died at the age of fifty-five. No more enlivening pen than that of Macaulay's could be employed to describe the scene that had taken place at Whitehall Palace five days prior to the king's unexpected death.

'The Palace had seldom presented a gayer or a more scandalous appearance than on the evening of Sunday, the 1st of February, 1685. The great gallery of Whitehall, an admirable relic of the magnificence of the Tudors, was crowded with revellers and gamblers. The king sat there chatting and toying with three women, whose charms were the boast, and whose vices were the disgrace, of three nations. Barbara Palmer, Duchess of Cleveland, was there, no longer young, but still retaining some traces of that superb and voluptuous loveliness which twenty years before overcame the hearts of all men. There, too, was the Duchess of Portsmouth, whose soft and infantine features were lighted up with the vivacity of France. Hortensia Mancini, Duchess of Mazarin, and niece of the great cardinal, completed the group. Charles himself, during his exile, had sought her hand in vain. No gift of nature or of fortune seemed to be wanting to her. But her diseased mind required stronger stimulants, and sought them in gallantry, in basset, and in usquebaugh. While Charles flirted with his three sultanas, Hortensia's French page, a handsome boy, whose vocal performances were the delight of Whitehall, and were rewarded by numerous presents of rich clothes, ponies, and guineas, warbled some amorous verses. A party of twenty courtiers was seated at cards round a large table on which gold was heaped in mountains. Even then the king had complained that he did not feel quite well. He had no appetite for his supper; his rest that night was broken ...'

The following morning the king had an apoplectic fit. Consternation reigned throughout the palace. All leading medical experts were summoned to his bedside. It was soon evident, however, that the king could not recover. In his last messages he consigned his numerous natural offspring to the care of his brother, the Duke of York and asked pardon of the queen, 'And do not', he added, 'let poor Nelly starve'. On this last score he need not have worried. 'Sweet Nell of Old Drury' was to die within a year or so at the age of thirty-seven. (It was said that Catherine of Braganza – who was generous-natured and extremely wealthy – allowed Nell's son, the Duke of St Albans, £2,000 a year after his mother's death.)

The historian Hallam, in commenting on the contribution rendered to civilisation by the vices of Charles II's court, remarks, 'We are, however, much indebted to the memory of Barbara, Duchess of Cleveland, Louise, Duchess of Portsmouth, and Mrs Eleanor Gwynne ... They played a serviceable part in ridding the kingdom of its besotted loyalty ... They pressed forward the great ultimate security of English freedom – the expulsion of the House of Stuart.' Although this opinion suggests discredit on Charles II's abilities as a king, it must be conceded that he maintained the throne to which he had been restored for a quarter of a century – no easy task in those unrestful times – and replanted the institution of monarchy so firmly that it remains with us to the present day.

Charles II was buried in Henry VII's Chapel in Westminster Abbey.

7

James II (1633–1701)

James II, who at the age of fifty-two succeeded his brother in 1685, was to lose his throne after a brief and troubled reign of less than four years. As Duke of York he had in early days been exceedingly popular with the nation on account of his physical courage and resourcefulness both by land and sea. When in exile during the Commonwealth he had served in the Continental wars with distinction, and became Lord High Admiral at the Restoration. Later, however, he was to fall from favour, mainly owing to the fact that, when nearing his forties, he had embraced the Roman Catholic faith. As a consequence, efforts were made to get him excluded from the succession, but despite this, and his being virtually sent into exile, James clung to his religious convictions. On his accession he made no secret of his Papist leanings, but at the same time vowed before his privy council to uphold the rights of the established church. These rights he nevertheless soon tried to undermine, to his own swift undoing and the loss of his crown.

In certain respects James II was similar in character to his father, in that he was proud of his kingship, scrupulously conscientious in given points of conduct, and unswervingly obstinate in his views and procedure. But there the likeness ended. While imitating his brother in his perpetual amours, he had not Charles II's selectivity for lovely women. In fact, his mistresses were usually so physically unattractive that Charles II declared that he believed they were given to his brother by his priests as a penance.

Shortly before the Restoration James had secretly married – because she was about to have a child by him – the ugly but 'gay' Anne Hyde (whose father was to become Earl of Clarendon), at the time when she was a maid-of-honour to his eldest sister, Mary, Princess of Orange. When the truth leaked out, Henrietta Maria and Mary were highly incensed at the heir presumptive's choice of wife. Clarendon himself also professed rage at the unsuitable alliance, even to the extent of suggesting his daughter should be sent to the Tower. Charles II, however, decided to forgive his sister-in-law. It is said that she carried her rank as Duchess of York with great dignity. Of the many children that she bore James before her death in 1671, only Mary and Anne survived; in due course they were to take part in waging war against their father, and to help to oust him from the throne.

When Duke of York to the Earl of Clarendon, 1662

James's personal correspondence is clear-cut, businesslike and terse in expression. In fact, the few of his letters that are available read, in many instances, very like governmental minutes, as instanced by the following note to his father-in-law, the Lord Chancellor. The 'minute' relates to Charles II's intention to bring his illegitimate son, James Crofts, as he was known at the time, to court.

> My brother hath spoken with the Queen yesterday concerning the owning of his son, and in much passion she told him 'that, from the time he did any such thing, she would never see his face more'.[1]

The queen's threat, as we know, was of no avail. The king not only brought his son to court and created him Duke of Monmouth, as already mentioned, with precedence over every other duke in the land with the exception of the Duke of York, but he also lavished favours and titles on the youth to such a degree that it was concluded that Charles II had actually been married to Lucy Walters and that he intended to make Monmouth his successor. In such circumstances, it is not surprising that in course of time the Duke of Monmouth should be persuaded that he was legitimate and the rightful heir to the Crown. His attempt to seize the throne shortly after James II's accession ended in his being executed on Tower Hill, and brought about the slaughter or sale into slavery of thousands of those who had rallied to his standard.

To the Earl of Peterborough, 1673

After the death of Anne Hyde, Charles II and his cabinet decided to take an active part in the selection of a second wife for the heir-presumptive, whose idle fancies were once more straying in unsuitable quarters. Their choice was eventually to fall on Mary Beatrice of Modena. Although only in her mid-teens the princess spiritedly declared that she had 'an invincible aversion to marriage', and further argued that either of her aunts – Eleanora and Mary d'Este, who were somewhere in their thirties – would prove more suitable in age than herself, the Duke of York being old enough to be her father.

For some long time the Earl of Peterborough – to whom James wrote the following letter – had been touring abroad in search of a likely bride eligible for the royal duke and it was not without difficulty that he had finally persuaded Mary Beatrice's mother, the Duchess of Modena, to give her consent to the matrimonial alliance.

When you shall have contracted the Princess in my name, you are to present her, as a token of my esteem, with such part of my jewels in your custody as you shall judge convenient; and the morning of the day of performing the solemnity of the marriage, you shall present her with the remainder of my said jewels, as a further pledge of my affection, and of my satisfaction of what you have done for me.

When the marriage shall be over,[2] and you have adjusted all the manner of your coming into France – which journey will, I think, be most conveniently performed by sea to Marseilles, whither the galleys of the most Christian king[3] will be ordered to bring her, and whither you must attend her – it will be fit that then, or before, you must dismiss most of your retinue, lest their attendance may not consist with the figure the Princess may probably desire to take of travelling incognita, or embarrass you in the conveniences of your journey, retaining only as many as will fill one coach. And thus follow her all the way until she arrive at Paris or Calais, at one of which places my servants shall be appointed to attend on her.

The manner in which the Duke of York received news of the confirmation of his State marriage is related in a gossiping letter written by Lady Rachel Vaughan to a relative, 'The news came on Sunday night to the duke of York that he was married. He was talking in the drawing-room when the French ambassador brought the letter, and told the news; the duke turned about to the circle, and said, "Then I am a married man." His bride proved to be the princess of Modena, but she was rather expected to be Canaples' niece [a descendant of the royal blood of France]. She is to have 100,000 francs and more. They say she has more wit than any woman had before, as much beauty, and more youth than is necessary. The duke of York sent his daughter Lady Mary word the same night, "that he had provided a playfellow for her".'

Peterborough safely delivered the reluctant bride at Dover in November, 1673, when a second marriage took place. While his Italian bride was approved for her beauty, her husband's unpopularity was increased by the fact that he had married a Roman Catholic.

There is no information as to whether the young princess was delighted or otherwise with the jewels which James instructed the Earl of Peterborough judiciously to dole out in acknowledgment of the bargain of marriage. The story goes, however, that Mary Beatrice was compelled to sell these, together with the rest of the jewellery she possessed, during her subsequent exile following 'The Glorious Revolution' of 1688.

To his son-in-law, William, Prince of Orange, 1678

The arranged marriage between James's eldest daughter by Anne Hyde with her cousin, William, Prince of Orange – the 'stunted, sour, determined man with the sharp eyes' – had taken place in 1677. During the early time in Holland Mary suffered much from ill-health, partly on account of climatic conditions and partly owing to her personal unhappiness.

In the autumn of 1678 she contracted typhoid fever, and was dangerously ill for a time. Sir Henry Sidney, an official at The Hague, made the following note in his diary relative to this occurrence: 'Sir Gabriel Sylvius and Dr Ken [Mary's almoner at The Hague] were both here, and both complain of the prince, especially in his usage of his wife; they think she is sensible of it, and that it doth greatly contribute to her illness. They are mightily for her going to England, but they think he will never consent.' On Mary's convalescence her sister Anne and Mary Beatrice of Modena decided to pay her a visit, probably to ascertain the truth of reports that were being received as to the behaviour of William of Orange. The

Duke of York, who was extremely fond of both his daughters, is announcing the proposed visit in the following letter to his son-in-law.

London, September 27

... The duchess and my daughter Anne intend to make your wife a *very incognito*, and have yet said nothing of it to anybody here but his majesty, whose leave they asked, and will not mention it till the post be gone. They carry little company with them, and sent this bearer, Robert White, before, to try to get a house for them as near your court as he can. They intend to stay only whilst we shall be at Newmarket.

I was very glad to see by the last letters that my daughter continued so well, and hope now she will go out her full time. I have written to her to be very careful of herself, and that she would do well not to stand too long, for that is very ill for a woman in her state.[4]

The *incognite* ladies intend to set out from hence on Tuesday next, if the wind be fair. They have bid me tell you they desire to be very *incognito*, and they have lord Ossory for their governor.[5] I have not time to say more, but only to assure you that I shall always be very kind to you.

For my son[-in-law], the Prince of Orange

To William, Prince of Orange, 1682

The first three children of Mary Beatrice of Modena had died in infancy. When, therefore, after a lapse of nearly five years it was announced abroad that she was expecting another child, the prospect was received with no little interest by both the Duke of York's friends and enemies alike. The appearance of a comet on the day of the child's birth in August, 1682, was regarded in this instance, for some unknown reason, as a good omen. It was supposed to prognosticate 'a great and glorious destiny' for the little princess – Charlotte Maria, as she was christened – and there was widespread rejoicing throughout the country. Unfortunately the child died of a fit within two months of its birth, thus once more proving a comet to be a bad omen.

William of Orange wrote a letter of sympathy to James on the death of his fourth child by Mary Beatrice. The Duke of York, however, would appear by this time to have regarded his son-in-law with some suspicion, if one may judge from the following crisp reply he made on the subject.

October 24th

I had yours of the 23rd at Newmarket, before I came thence, but could not answer It sooner than now. I see by it you were sensibly touched with the loss I had of my little daughter, which is what I had reason to expect of you, that are so concerned at all that happens to me.

When king to William, Prince of Orange, 1685

James II's younger daughter, Anne, by his first Duchess, had been married in 1683 to the brother of King Christian V of Denmark, grand-nephew of Anne of Denmark. Luckily for Princess Anne, the large, lazy, heavy-drinking Prince George of Denmark – who in earlier days had proved a fine soldier – was quite content to reside in England and share his wife's fortunes. From a material angle these were by no means to be despised. On James's accession Anne received an allowance of £32,000 a year, together with settlement of her enormous debts, mostly incurred at the card tables.

Five weeks after James's coronation Anne gave birth to a daughter. A few days later the king became anxious over Anne's health, as will be seen from the following hasty note to his son-in-law.

My daughter was taken ill this morning, having vapours which sometimes trouble women in her condition. This frightened us at first, but now, God be thanked, our fears are over.

She took some remedies, and has slept after them most of this afternoon and evening, and is in a very good way, which is all I can say to you now, but to assure you of my kindness.

The king became so troubled about his daughter, in fact, that he spent hours by her bedside, which indicates that Anne held a special place in her father's affections. His consistent kindness to Anne is worth noting in view of the ingratitude she displayed at a later stage.

To William, Prince of Orange, 1688

The year 1688 was an eventful and a memorable one in the lives of the king and the royal family generally, as it was to be in the history of the whole country.

Over five years had elapsed since the death of Mary Beatrice of Modena's last child, and in view of the fact that the king was without lawful issue, the next in the line of succession was, presumably, his eldest daughter, the Princess of Orange. In June of that year, however, the queen gave birth to a son, to the consternation of the Protestant faction in England, and more particularly to that of Mary and Anne. The advent of a Prince of Wales threatened the end of the sisters' hopes of succeeding to the Crown.

It was an equally unpleasant shock, too, for William of Orange, who, in view of his wife's prospects, had been long 'concerned', as James II himself cryptically remarks in a previous letter, with all that happened to his father-in-law. It must have been with some sense of satisfaction, therefore, that the king wrote the following letters to William announcing this important event, for by this time James II was not unaware of his son-in-law's treacherous intentions towards the existing monarchy.

June 12, 1688

The queen was, God be thanked, safely delivered of a son on Sunday morning, a little before ten. She has been very well ever since, but the child was somewhat ill, this last night, of the wind; but is now, blessed be God, very well again, and like to have no returns of it, and is a very strong boy.[6]

Last night I received yours of the 18th. I expect every day to hear what the French fleet has done at Algiers. 'tis late, and I have not time to say more, but that you shall find me to be as kind to you as you can expect.

For my son [-in-law], the Prince of Orange
St James's, June 18, 1688

The queen was somewhat feverish this afternoon. My son is, God be thanked, very well, and feeds heartily and thrives very well.

Although there was a general outbreak of rejoicings at the news, the king's triumph, all the same, was to be short-lived. His son's birth was only to cause their Catholic king's deposition to be pressed forward with greater urgency by the Protestant ministers, whose plots in this connection had been secretly operating for some time.

To William, Prince of Orange, 1688

Instigated by the Protestant party – the leaders of which had already issued a secret invitation to William of Orange to come over to England, redress the country's wrongs, and enquire into the legitimacy of the Prince of Wales – the slanders and libels which were speedily broadcast far and wide caused tremendous national concern and excitement.

'Those', declared Protestant prejudice, 'whose interest it was to have a Prince of Wales would be at no loss to procure one'. The fantastic report that the baby of a bricklayer's wife had been smuggled into the queen's bed was to gather strength and become a conviction among those whose interests it might be expected to serve, and the credulous-minded masses.

In the meantime, his son-in-law's deceitful message of congratulations on the birth of an heir apparent drew from the king – fully alive at last to William's schemes – the following cold and distrustful 'minute'.

> July 22nd, 1688
>
> I have had yours by M. Zulestein, who has, as well as your letter, assured me of the part you take on the birth of my son. I would not have him return without writing to you by him, to assure you I shall always be as kind to you as you can with reason expect.

Count Zulestein, referred to by the king in this letter, was the Prince of Orange's 'silvery-tongued' envoy. He was an illegitimate brother of William's father, and proved one of the most active instruments in the long-projected revolution. Elegant, bawdy-minded, skilled in diplomacy, Zulestein's sagacity at intrigue was exceptional. He plunged with delight into the plots to depose James II. It was reputedly Zulestein who only three months after this visit was insolently to command the king to 'quit Whitehall without delay, as his master' – William, who had landed at Tor Bay – 'required to occupy the Palace himself'.

To his daughter, Mary, Princess of Orange, 1688

The king's eldest daughter was unquestionably an intelligent woman and had strategic abilities, as was proved when she came to the throne. All the same, from a filial angle, her deception of her father as to William's intentions of invading England discloses an unfavourable aspect of her character, if one is to judge from the correspondence between herself and James II. Is it likely that she knew nothing of her husband's plan to wrest the Crown from her father, and honestly assumed that William's preparations were intended to repel an expected attack by the French? Yet James himself seems to have believed this, or so the appended letter that he wrote to Mary suggests.

From the date of this communication and his final letter it will be seen that the king was in constant correspondence with his daughter up to within a short time of William's landing at Tor Bay.

Whitehall, September 28th, 1688

This evening I had yours of the 4th, from Dieren,[7] by which I find you were then to go to the Hague, being sent for by the Prince. I suppose it is to inform you of his design of coming to England, which he has been so long a-contriving. I hope it will have been as great a surprise to you[8] as it was to me, when I first heard it, being sure it was not in your nature to approve of so unjust an undertaking.

I have been all this day so busy, to endeavour to be in some condition to defend myself from so unjust and unexpected an attempt, that I am almost tired, and so I shall say no more but that I shall always have as much kindness for you as you will give me leave to have.

To Mary, Princess of Orange, 1688

The gentle, restrained tone of this last letter that the king wrote to Mary must surely have troubled her conscience if she retained any love at all for her father. James II is obviously searching for excuses for her conduct, and hoping against hope that her deception of him was not of her own volition, but that she was torn between two opposing loyalties.

> Whitehall, October 9th, 1688
>
> I had no letter from you by the last post, which you see does not hinder me from writing to you now, not knowing, certainly, what may have hindered you from doing it. I easily believe you may be embarrassed how to write to me, now that the unjust design of the Prince of Orange invading me is so public. And though I know you are a good wife, and ought to be so, yet for the same reason I must believe you will be still as good a daughter to a father that has always loved you so tenderly, and that has never done the least thing to make you doubt it.
>
> I shall say no more, and believe you are very uneasy all this time, for the concern you must have for a husband and a father.
>
> You shall still find me kind to you, if you desire it.

In fairness to Mary, it should be mentioned that she had not seen her father for nine years, when he had last visited her at The Hague in 1679. This long separation, added to the fact that she was not in a position to obtain first-hand and impartial information as to the crisis in her father's affairs, had undoubtedly influenced her attitude. Furthermore, in later years Mary confessed that in her behaviour at this time she had 'acted under orders'.

Perhaps the most vulnerable blow that the king sustained in the early days of the revolution was the discovery of the treachery of his two daughters.[9] Almost to the last he had refused to countenance any suggestion that Princess Mary was seriously in league against him. The affection and loyalty of Princess Anne he had never doubted. When, therefore – following the swift and startling desertion of his generals, including Prince George of Denmark, to join the invading forces – he was to learn of Anne's flight from Whitehall to throw in her lot with William of Orange, disillusionment and grief caused the king to break down completely.

An interesting account of the sensation created in London on the news of Anne's disappearance is given by Daniel Defoe, 'I cannot but remember the consternation among the people, when it was first noised abroad that the princess was missing: it being at first warm among the people that they had murdered or made away with her. I want words to express the compassion that appeared in the countenances of the people: and so much was she then beloved that the very soldiers talked of setting Whitehall on fire, and cutting the throats of all the papists about the court. The people ran raving up and down, and the confused crowds thronged into the apartments of Whitehall, inquiring of everyone they met if they had seen the princess. Had it not presently been made public that she was withdrawn; nay, had not the letters she left behind been made public, some fatal disturbance had been seen in the very palace, and that within a very few hours.'

The recurrence of such scenes as these so alarmed the king that he straightway made arrangements for his family to be smuggled out of the country. The queen, disguised as an Italian washerwoman and carrying her six-month-old baby under her arm as a bundle of linen, left Gravesend on a small sailing barque. Her escort, Count de Lauzun, had strict instructions from the king that should her disguise be discovered and there be any hint of handing the queen over to the Dutch, Lauzun was to shoot the captain dead.

To Lord Dartmouth, 1688

Lady Oglethorpe, who held an office in the royal household, left it on record 'that the king was so deeply affected when the Princess Anne went away, that it disordered his understanding.' After James II had sent the queen and his son over to France this morbid state of mind was greatly increased, some suggestion of which is shown in the following letter that he wrote to Lord Dartmouth.

Dartmouth was the English admiral in charge of the king's fleet in the Channel, and had been a favourite naval pupil of James when he himself had been Lord High Admiral.

> Whitehall, December, 1688
>
> Things having so bad an aspect, I could no longer defer securing the Queen and my son, which I hope I have done, and that to-morrow by noon they will be out of the reach of my enemies. I am at ease now I have sent them away.
>
> I have not heard this day, as I expected, from my commissioners with the Prince of Orange,[10] who, I believe will hardly be prevailed on to stop his march; so that I am in no good way – nay, in as bad a one as possible.
>
> I am sending the Duke of Berwick[11] down to Portsmouth, by whom you will know my resolution concerning the fleet under your command, and what resolution I have taken; till when, I would not let you stir from the place where you are, for several reasons.

Dartmouth had disapproved of the king's decision to send the Prince of Wales out of the country. He seems to have been a man of sound common sense, to judge by a letter of advice that he had sent to James II on hearing of the latter's plans, in the course of which Dartmouth says, 'I most humbly hope you will not exact it from me, nor longer entertain so much as a thought of doing that which will give your enemies an advantage, though never so falsely grounded, to distrust your son's just right, which you have asserted and manifested to the world in the matter of his being your real son, and born of the queen, by the testimonies of so many apparent witnesses. Pardon, therefore, sir, if on my bended knees I beg of you to apply yourself to other counsels, for the doing of this [sending his son out of the country] looks like nothing less than despair, to the degree of not only giving your enemies encouragement, but distrust of your friends and people, who I do not despair will yet stand by you in the defence and right of your lawful successor.'

To Louis XIV, 1688

Having determined that the only course open to him was to place his family and himself under the protection of his cousin, the king wrote the following letter to Louis XIV after his own attempt at flight had been frustrated.

> Sir, and My Brother,
>
> As I hope that the Queen, my wife, and my son have last week landed in one of your ports, I hope you will do me the favour of protecting them. Unless I had been unfortunately stopped by the way, I should have been with you to ask the same for myself, as well as for them. Your ambassador will give you an account of the bad state of my affairs, and assure you, also, that I have done nothing contrary to the friendship that subsists between us. I am, very sincerely, sir, my brother,
>
> Your good brother,
James, R.
At Whitehall, December 1688

Shortly after having written the foregoing letter, the king made a second attempt to flee the country. 'I saw the king take barge to Gravesend, a sad sight!' notes Evelyn in his *Diary* under the date of 18 December 1688. 'The prince [William] comes to St James's and fills Whitehall with Dutch guards'.

James II landed safely in Picardy on Christmas Day, and was given accommodation with the queen at St Germains.

To Louis XIV, 1692

The king's friends in general had strongly advised James II not to quit England, as it was the very course that his enemies seemed to desire. Although he himself had obviously conceived no such prospect, he was thereafter to be an exile from his own country to the day of his death twelve years later. Plots for his restoration were to continue for years. Any hope, however, of James II reclaiming his throne can be said to have terminated in 1692, when – aided by Louis XIV – his attempted counter-invasion of England was defeated at the Battle of La Hogue, with the loss of sixteen French men-of-war.

An impression that he was born to fulfil a tragic destiny, in which any who tried to come to his assistance were doomed also to suffer ruin, is conveyed by the king in the following letter to Louis XIV.

> My evil star has had an influence on the arms of Your Majesty, always victorious but when fighting for me. I entreat you, therefore, to interest yourself no more for a prince so unfortunate; but permit me to withdraw, with my family, to some corner of the world, where I may cease to be an interruption to Your Majesty's wonted course of prosperity and glory.

James II was overwhelmed by the disaster at La Hogue, which it was considered had, once again, temporarily unhinged his mind. This was doubtless true, for in earlier times James had been notably valiant in contending with the fortunes of war.

The following character of the exiled king, and a reasonably temperate one, was given by Burnet, 'He [James II] was a prince that seemed made for greater things than will be found in the course of his life, more particularly in his reign. He was esteemed in the former parts of his life a man of great courage, as he was, quite through it, a man of great application to business. He had no vivacity of thought, invention or expression, but he had a good judgment where his religion or his education gave him not a bias, which it did very often. He was bred with strange notions of the obedience due to princes, and came to take up as strange ones of the obedience due to priests. He was naturally a man of truth, fidelity and justice, but his religion was so infused in him and he was so managed in it by his priests, that the principles which nature had laid in him had little power over him when the concerns of his church stood in the way. He was a gentle master, and was very easy to all who came near him, yet he was not so apt to pardon as one ought to be that is the vice-regent of that God who is slow to anger and ready to forgive. He had no personal vices but of one sort: he was still wandering from one amour to another, yet he had a real sense of sin, and was ashamed of it. In a word, if it had not been for his popery, he would have been, if not a great, yet a good prince.'

James II died in 1701. His coffin remained uninterred in the church of the Benedictines at St Germains. When this church was destroyed during the French Revolution, the king's relics were taken to Paris, and since the corpse was found to be in an extraordinary state of preservation, it was exposed to public view for a fee of a few sous. It was to be over a hundred years before James II's bones were given burial. On the instructions of George IV the remains of the last of the Stuart kings of England were taken back to St Germains and buried in the church, where a monument was raised to his memory.

8

William III (1650–1702)

William, Prince of Orange, was born prematurely at The Hague three days after the death of his father, William II of Orange, at the early age of twenty-four. On his young mother dying of smallpox ten years later, the orphaned William was consigned to the protection of his grandmother, the old princess dowager, Wilhelmina. At the request of his mother, however, both his uncles – Charles II and James of York – served in the nature of William's guardians. It was, in part, due to Charles II's demand that the title of Stadholder, denied to William on his father's death, was some years later restored to him.

By the time he was twenty-three years of age William became renowned throughout Europe as a soldier and a politician, and in due course was to disclose qualities as a ruler. Yet he had been born a weak, diminutive child, and all his life suffered from acute asthma. Added to early ill-health, the political contentions with which he had had to cope in his own country from the age of fifteen years might have broken a stronger spirit. They developed strength of character in William, however, to a marked degree, and an iron nerve. Unfortunately they left him with a difficult and an unprepossessing personality.

'Long before he reached manhood', says Macaulay, 'he knew how to keep secrets, how to baffle curiosity by dry and guarded answers, how to conceal all passions under the same show of grave tranquillity. Meanwhile he made little proficiency in fashionable or literary accomplishments. The manners of the Dutch nobility at that age wanted grace which was found in the highest perfection among the gentlemen of France, and which, in an inferior degree, embellished the court of England; and his manners were altogether Dutch. Even his own countrymen thought him blunt.'

In addition, William fell far short of being an ideal husband. His neglectful treatment of his young wife combined with the public preference he displayed for certain ladies of her household – in particular Elizabeth Villiers – caused Mary no little sorrow from the outset.

When Prince of Orange to James II, 1685

In view of the strong efforts that had been made to exclude his father-in-law from the succession, apparently William of Orange had never supposed that the Duke of York would inherit the throne. In this mistaken confidence, he had been entertaining the Duke of Monmouth on a grand and friendly scale at The Hague shortly before Charles II's unexpected death. 'The Prince of Orange', wrote D'Avaux, French ambassador at The Hague, 'knows not how to caress Monmouth sufficiently. Balls and parties are unceasingly given for him'. Of this fact William's father-in-law was not ignorant. On the latter's accession, therefore, William of Orange realised that he would be in an embarrassingly awkward position should the new sovereign choose to regard him in the light of an antagonist. He accordingly attempted, as the following note shows, to make good his error of judgment.

Nothing can happen which will make me change the fixed attachment I have for your interests. I should be the most unhappy man in the world if you were not persuaded of it, and should not have the goodness to continue me a little in your good graces, since I shall be, to the last breath of my life, yours, with zeal and fidelity,[1]

William

William of Orange's personal letters are usually worded, as in this case, in a style strangely at variance with his general behaviour. Few of his available epistles consist of more than two or three well-turned phrases, and contain little matter, especially of a narrative character. His complex nature must have proved an enigma to most people. Probably the only person who learnt to understand him, in the course of the years, was his wife, the realisation of whose unselfish devotion was to be brought home to him on her early death at the age of thirty-two.

To Lawrence Hyde, Earl of Rochester, 1685

Doctor Ken, Mary's almoner at The Hague, had made himself unpopular with William of Orange because of his open disapproval of the prince's treatment of his wife. 'He [Ken] is horribly unsatisfied with the Prince of Orange', wrote Sir Henry Sidney in his journal on 21 March 1680. 'He thinks he is not kind to his wife, and he is determined to speak to him about it, even if he kicks him out of doors.'

In consequence, Ken had been replaced by Doctor Covell, who, however, formed the same opinion as his predecessor. Covell expressed his views on the unsatisfactory state of affairs prevailing in Mary's household with some asperity in a letter to Bevil Skelton, the English ambassador at The Hague, in the course of which he says, 'Your honour may be astonished at the news, but it is true, that the princess's heart is like to break; and yet she every day, with Mistress Jesson and Madame Zulestein,[2] counterfeits the greatest joy, and looks upon us as dogged as may be. We dare no more speak to her. The prince hath infallibly made her his absolute slave, and there is an end of it ... None but infamous people must expect any tolerable usage here.'

This letter William intercepted. He sent a copy of it to Mary's maternal uncle, Lawrence Hyde, accompanied by the following epistle from himself, which, in its wrath, is perhaps the most expressive letter ever written by William. Since he confesses to using Covell's cipher, the prince must have picked the lock of the old doctor's desk, but why he chose to send on to Mary's relative the very information that Covell hoped would be conveyed to England is somewhat incomprehensible.

As was the case with Ken, Covell was also dismissed from Mary's household, together with all those whom William suspected of being antagonistic to himself.

I had for some time suspected that Dr Covell was not a faithful servant to the Princess. The last time I was at the Hague, a letter fell into my hands which he had written to Skelton,[3] the ambassador. I opened it, and at my return to Dieren, where the doctor was with the Princess, I took the doctor's cipher and deciphered it, as you will see by the copy annexed; the original (which I have), written and signed by his own hand, he acknowledged when I showed it to him. You will, no doubt, be surprised that a man of his profession could be so great a knave.

With the flight of James II from England, prolonged and confused discussions had taken place in Parliament as to who should fill the vacant throne. It could not be decided whether the king had 'deserted', 'abdicated', or 'forfeited' the Crown. Any suggestion of the little Prince of Wales succeeding, under a regency, was dismissed without consideration, for apart from the slur cast on his birth the prince would be a Roman Catholic. The simplest course seemed to be to make Princess Mary queen. Here, however, the Prince of Orange himself interposed. He would not, he declared, accept any share in the English government merely by courtesy as the queen's husband. Sovereignty must be invested in himself personally, or he would return to Holland and 'meddle no more with English affairs'. This being his ultimatum, Parliament finally resolved, by the Declaration of Right of 1689, that William and Mary should be proclaimed joint sovereigns, administration being left in the hands of William.

On the more powerful Irish Catholics refusing submission to William III, James II – having obtained money, arms and ammunition from Louis XIV – set sail for Ireland to make war on his son-in-law. The Battle of the Boyne at the beginning of July 1690 terminated in the defeat of the deposed king's recruited and ill-equipped army, and his own ignominious retreat on a French vessel.

Mary II, probably from policy, celebrated the Boyne victory over her father with a magnificent ball at Whitehall, to the exasperation of the Earl of Devonshire, Lord Steward of the Household, who was being worn out by the continuous balls that the queen regnant deemed it necessary to give throughout William's absence in Ireland.

When king to the Earl of Deponshire, 1690

In the meantime, William III's interests had not been well served in home waters, where the Earl of Torrington, in charge of the English fleet, had been instructed by Mary II and her council to attack the French fleet approaching the coast. Instead, Torrington had not only hesitated, but had finally let the brunt of the conflict fall on the Dutch squadron under Eversten, and suffered defeat by the French off Beachy

Head. Invasion of England appeared imminent, but after satisfying themselves by burning the Devonshire fishing village of Teignmouth the enemy ships retired.

The following letter from William III to Devonshire was written from the seat of war.

> At the Camp of Welles, this July 17
>
> I am very much obliged by the part you take in what concerns my person, and the advantage that I have gained over my enemies.[4] The misfortune that has befallen my fleet has sensibly touched me, but I hope that it will soon be in a state to put to sea. It will be necessary to chastise severely those who have not done their duty.
>
> If it had been possible, without abandoning all here, I should have set out as soon as yesterday morning, when I received your dispatches; but, without losing all the advantages I have gained, I cannot leave the army for five or six days. Of this I have written to the Queen and to the lords of the committee, to whom I refer you, and hope very soon to have the satisfaction of seeing you, and assuring you of my constant friendship and esteem, on which you may entirely rely.
>
> William, R.

Torrington was deprived of his command and sent to the Tower. Although acquitted by a court martial he was never employed again.

To Sir James Dalrymple, 1692

In 1691 an order had been issued for the politically unruly Highlanders to take an oath of allegiance before the Crown Commissioners on or before the last day of December of that year. The chiefs all obeyed with the exception of MacDonald of Glencoe, who, owing to the snows and adverse conditions, was unable to put in an appearance before the appointed day had expired. Due solely to clannish hatreds MacDonald's absence was deliberately interpreted as a refusal to take the oath. As a consequence, William III, unaware of the true facts, hastily issued the following instructions, which were in the nature of a warrant.

William R[5]

As for the M'Donalds of Glencoe, if they can well be distinguished from the rest of the Highlanders, it will be proper, for the vindication of public justice, to extirpate that sect of thieves.

W.R.

This communication resulted in the massacre of Glencoe. The houses of the clan were burnt to the ground, their cattle driven off or destroyed, and men, women and children either slaughtered outright or left to die of hunger and cold in bogs and caverns.

Initiated by James II and his adherents, the news of the massacre created a great outcry throughout Europe, the even worse slaughter that had followed the Monmouth Rebellion in 1685 being conveniently forgotten by the Jacobites and their partisans.

In 1693 William III felt compelled to order an investigation into the matter, but nothing more came of it than the dismissal from office of Dalrymple of Stair, president of the commission, who had directed the massacre. A bitter enemy of the MacDonalds, Dalrymple had assured William III that Glencoe was the great obstacle to the pacification of the Highlands. 'In return for many victims immolated', says Macaulay, 'only one victim was demanded by justice, and it must ever be considered a blemish on the fame of William that the demand [of the Scottish Parliament, in 1695, for a further investigation] was refused.'

To the Earl of Marlborough, 1700

The personal dislike that William III had always shown towards his sister-in-law, which Princess Anne equally reciprocated, was aggravated by the fact that on his joint accession to the throne with Mary II serious dissension arose between the two sisters themselves. Sarah, Duchess of Marlborough, in her *Conduct* says that the trouble arose 'from the conviction of William III that the princess and her husband, George of Denmark, had been of more use [in assisting in the revolution] than they were ever like to be again.' This statement, all the same, was intentionally misleading, and obscured the true cause of the split between Mary II and Princess Anne, which was due to Anne's infatuation for the intriguing and subversive-minded Sarah, her first lady.

As an indication of the extreme pettiness to which their mutual dislike had descended, the duchess tells an unconsciously amusing story of William and his sister-in-law, on an occasion when they were dining together. 'There happened to be right before her [Anne] a plate of green peas, the first that had been seen that year. The king without offering the princess the least share of them, drew the plate before him and devoured them all ... The princess confessed, when she came home, that she had so much mind for the peas that she was afraid to look at them, and yet could hardly keep her eyes off them.' Both William and Anne were inclined to gluttony – particularly Anne. The king doubtless puckishly considered it an opportunity of annoying Anne that should not be missed.

On the death of the childless Mary II in 1694, the relationship between William and Anne became even more strained. William was not only in great distress through being bereft of his wife and, as he had come to discover, his only devoted friend, but he was aware of the loss of an able ruler. In addition, it was evident to the king that he had also lost his sole link of hereditary right to the Crown by the death of the queen regnant, and that he himself remained an elective monarch, 'whom a breath had made, and a breath could unmake'.

Despite the king's dislike of Princess Anne, he had shown some indication of affection for her only remaining child, the Duke of Gloucester. In July 1700, while William was absent at The Hague, the Earl of Marlborough, as the little duke's official governor, informed the king of the death of Anne's son. It was some months before William III replied to Marlborough's news, and then only in the following brief manner.

Loo,[6] October, 1700

I do not think it necessary to employ many words in expressing my surprise and grief at the death of the duke of Gloucester. It is so great a loss to me, as well as to all England, that it pierces my heart with affliction.

In January 1702, while out riding in Bushey Park, the king's horse stumbled in a molehill and flung him to the ground. He sustained a broken collarbone, but seemed in no danger, although his physical health had not been good for some while. A few days later he contracted a fever, and died at eight o'clock on the morning of 7 February. He was in his fifty-second year.

As a statesman William III probably had no equal among his contemporaries. He was far better suited to save a nation than adorn a Crown, but to the last he was a foreigner to the English in speech, tastes and habits. 'He never became an Englishman', says Macaulay. 'He saved England, it is true; but he never loved her, and he never obtained her love. To him she was always a land of exile, visited with reluctance and quitted with delight. Even when he rendered to her those services of which, at this day, we feel the happy effects, her welfare was not his chief object. Whatever patriotic feeling he had was for Holland.'

The king had purchased Kensington Palace in 1689. He had had it considerably altered, and it was his principal residence while in England. It was there he died. He was buried in Henry VII's Chapel in Westminster Abbey.

9

George I (1660–1727)

Anne reigned for twelve years as queen regnant, and on her death in 1714, George Louis of Hanover came to the throne as the next in the line of Protestant succession, the Act of Settlement passed on the death of Anne's son having excluded all Roman Catholics from succeeding to the Crown.

Eldest son of Ernest Augustus, Elector of Hanover, and Sophia, youngest daughter of Elizabeth Stuart, Queen of Bohemia and sister of Charles I, George Louis had been born at Osnbrück in 1660. While he had inherited her claim to the English throne, the stolid George Louis had inherited none of the physical attraction, charm or wisdom of his accomplished mother. He had no particular merits. Nevertheless, when he became Elector of Hanover on his father's death in 1698, although in private life he continued as profligate as ever, he showed signs of solidity and consistency in his public conduct.

It is to their credit that neither the Dowager Electress nor her son had stooped to intrigue for the Crown of England. On the contrary, they would never have challenged the right of the Chevalier de St George had he chosen to change his religion at the time that the Act of Settlement was under discussion. As a Protestant Stuart, Sophia of Hanover had been agreeable, in the circumstances, to step into the breach, and as a great lover of England had looked forward to becoming Queen Sophia of

Great Britain. George Louis, on the other hand, having paid one visit to this country in his youth, showed no desire at all to return.

When Prince of Hanover, to his mother, the Electress Sophia, 1680

As hereditary Prince of Hanover, George Louis had come to the court of Charles II in 1680 as a suitor for the hand of Princess Anne. The following letter to his mother was written on the occasion of this visit.

London, December 30, 1680

After wishing your Serene Highness a very happy New Year, I will not delay letting you know that I arrived here on the 6th of December, having remained one day at anchor at Greenwich till Mr Beck[1] went on shore to take a house for me. He did not fail to find out Prince Robert,[2] to let him know of my arrival at Greenwich, who did not delay telling King Charles II. His majesty immediately appointed me apartment at Whitehall. M. Beck requested Prince Robert to excuse me; but King Charles, when he spoke thus, insisted that it should absolutely be so, for he would treat me '*en cousin*,' and after that no more could be said.

Therefore M. Cotterel[3] came on the morrow, to find me [on the ship at Greenwich] with a barque of the King, and brought me therein to Whitehall. I had not been there more than two hours, when *milor* Hamilton[4] came to take me to the King, who received me most obligingly. Prince Robert had preceded me, and was at court when I saluted King Charles.

In making my obeisance to the King, I did not omit to give him the letter of your Serene Highness, after which he spoke of your Highness, and said 'that he remembered you very well.' When he had talked with me some time, he went to the

Queen.[5] and as soon as I arrived he made me kiss the hem of her Majesty's petticoat.

The next day I saw the Princess of York,[6] and I saluted her by kissing her, with the consent of the King. The day after I went to visit Prince Robert, who received me in bed, for he has a malady in his leg: which makes him very often keep his bed; it appears that it is so without any pretext, and that he has to take care of himself ...

They cut off the head of Lord Stafford yesterday, and made no more ado about it than if they had chopped off the head of a pullet.[7]

I have no more to tell your Serene Highness, wherefore I conclude, and remain your very humble son and servant,

George Louis

The prospect of this matrimonial alliance, however, had not been regarded by William of Orange with favour. If George of Hanover married Anne, and Mary, Princess of Orange, died first without offspring – as was to prove the case – William would, he foresaw, have to give way before their prior claim to the succession. To prevent this happening, the Prince of Orange had indulged in secret intrigues. As a consequence, George Louis was recalled to Hanover to contract a marriage with Sophia Dorothea of Zell.

Her Hanoverian suitor's inexplicable behaviour was an insult that Princess Anne, not in possession of the facts, never overlooked in after-years. After she had become queen regnant, the thought of George Louis as a prospective successor to her Crown became abhorrent to her. As a consequence, in the earlier days of her reign Anne showed marked indications of favouring the cause of her half-brother, the Chevalier de St George, whom in her remorseful moods she genuinely pitied.

When Elector of Hanover to Robert Harley, Secretary of State, 1710

There are more than a few letters extant which show the manner in which the British statesmen, even at the outset of Queen Anne's reign, approached the heirs expectant with a view to establishing their own individual fortunes should the tide of events suddenly change.

Where the House of Hanover was concerned, the Dowager Electress Sophia being advanced in years, the ministers' chief homage was to George Louis. Among the foremost intrigants in this connection was Robert Harley, later created Earl of Oxford. Like other of his contemporaries, preferring to keep a foot in both camps Harley was to correspond with the Jacobite faction – soon to become once more markedly active in the country – while at the same time giving George Louis every assurance of his loyalty to the Hanoverian succession.

Towards the close of the year 1710 Harley had written to George Louis offering 'testimony of his devotion'. He could not, he averred, be 'a faithful or acceptable servant to her Majesty without studying to serve your Highness's interest … I have taken the liberty to write this in English, because I know your Electoral Highness has an English heart, that you may be assured it comes from a heart entirely devoted to your service.' This message Harley took care to have delivered by hand direct. The following is George Louis's formal reply.

Hanover, December 15, 1710

Sir,

Madame Cresset has delivered to me the letter that you have taken the trouble to write to me.

I have received with much pleasure the assurances that it contains of your devotion to the interests of my House, and it is with much pleasure that I learn that the Queen honours with her confidence a Minister who realises so completely the true interests of Great Britain, and who has always shown so much zeal for his native land.

As nothing is more valuable to me than the goodwill of which her Majesty has given me indication, you could not oblige me more ably than acting as a contributor to the maintenance of it. I cherish it with all the care imaginable, and will always be very glad to make you see the consideration I have for you personally, and the sincerity with which I am, Sir,

Yours very kindly,

George Louis, Elector

To Mr Robert Harley

Queen Anne's hatred of her Hanoverian successors became increasingly acute with the passing of time. She was in a state of perpetual dread that either George Louis or his son – afterwards George II – would come over to her court and claim right as heir. This fear was not without some justification, but the possibility was mainly due to the intrigues of her scheming minsters. In the same way Anne was smitten with terror that her half-brother might at any moment land on her shores. The queen was, in fact, a very sick woman, at the mercy of her advisers, and tossed and turned with every fresh current of opinion like a foundering barque.

In the grip of these growing alarms, Anne finally issued a proclamation setting a price of £5,000 'for the apprehension of the Pretender, dead or alive, if he were found within Great Britain or Ireland'. At the same time she wrote angry and challenging letters, not only to George Louis and his son but to the Dowager Electress Sophia. In the course of her communication to her aunt – as Sophia was known – Anne insinuates the existence of a plot 'to fix a prince of your blood in my dominions, even whilst I am yet living'. These letters from the queen, it was said, proved the aged Sophia's death-blow. The day following their receipt, while walking in the gardens at Herrenhausen with her grandson's wife – Caroline of Anspach – she fell dead in the princess's arms. Nevertheless, it seems unlikely that Anne's letters were the cause of Sophia of Hanover's sudden end. She was eighty-four years of age, and had surely, during the long years, learnt enough of human nature and the caprices of fortune not to be slain by a few unjust words uttered by a woman whose 'gout had gone to her head'.

To Queen Anne, 1714

Sophia of Hanover was not only an exceptionally high-minded and talented princess, but all her life she had upheld the character of her royal English ancestry with honour and distinction. It fell to her son, George Louis, to break the news of his mother's death to the queen.

Herrenhausen, June 11, 1714

Madame,

I received the letter of the 30th of May, with which it has pleased your Majesty to honour me. But having had the misfortune two days after receiving it of losing Madame the Electress, my mother, by a sudden death, which has filled me with distress – and of which I do not neglect to notify your Majesty in a manner suitable to the respect I owe – I find myself compelled by such an acute grief to put off for the time being answering the contents of your Majesty's letter.

I pray you to be persuaded of the care and of the earnestness that I shall always employ to cultivate the honour of your good opinion, and of the respect with which I am, Madame,

Your Majesty's very humble and obedient servant,
George Louis, Elector

To Her Majesty the Queen of Great Britain

On receipt of this letter Anne's terrors were greatly increased, and she herself was to die of an apoplectic fit only two months later, when in her fiftieth year.

To Robert Harley, Earl of Oxford, 1714

It is evident from the tone of this letter written by George Louis to the Earl of Oxford not long before Anne's death, that some such plot as the queen avowed was definitely afoot where the House of Hanover was concerned, and that the Elector of Hanover himself, in any event, was agreeable to the proposal to send a prince of his house into England.

Hanover, June 15, 1714

My Lord,

I have seen with much pleasure, in your letter of the 30th of May, the fresh assurances that you give me of your zeal for the Protestant succession, and of your attachment to my interests. These kind sentiments were never more necessary than at the present time, seeing that I myself am concerned to dispel the shadows that suggest a stain on me and my House, imputing to us designs prejudicial to the authority of the Queen. As to this, I flatter myself that the letter that I have had the honour to write to her Majesty will serve to make known to her the sincerity of my intentions, to which you will infinitely oblige me, My Lord, if you will join your good offices.

You will see from the Memorandum that I herewith deliver to you by your relative that I desire to conjoin with the Queen in all that is deemed necessary for the strengthening of the Protestant succession; and you will not ignore sundry distinguished persons of one Party or the other who have this succession at heart and who are faithful subjects and zealous servants of the Queen; and who judge that the presence of one of the Princes of my House will be the most efficacious means of contributing to the safety of the person and the realms of her Majesty against the designs of a Pretender; and one who will always uphold the wishes of the Queen and on whom she can rely against an alien force.

In point of fact, My Lord, if the nation of itself seeks security against the Pretender during the life of her Majesty, it will of itself in such case be even more affected when God shall inflict on Great Britain the retirement of a Queen who has governed it with so much glory; and in this last resort, the presence of a Prince of the Protestant line will be of no little utility in preventing the disorders from within or the invasions from without.

If you know of any other means of procuring to the succession a security equivalent you will greatly oblige me to make it known ...

I pray you to continue your labours [for the strengthening of the Protestant succession], and to be persuaded that you will receive from me all the recognition that you have the right to expect, and that it will be a great comfort to me to see you given such distinction, being very sincerely

My Lord, yours very affectionately,
George Louis, Elector

George Louis's friendly and courteous acceptance of the Earl of Oxford's loyalty and aid in the Protestant cause must have been most reassuring to the latter's hopes when George should become king. Oxford was to receive a bad shock, however. On the arrival of the new king some four months later, Oxford found it almost impossible to obtain an audience. When he finally did so George I's chilly demeanour was such that the earl sensed his fortunes were on the wane. He was not wrong. He soon found himself impeached for high treason and committed to the Tower. On being later acquitted by his peers, Oxford wisely retired into private life, and spent his few remaining years accumulating literary treasures, on which the valuable Harleian Library was founded.

On the death of Queen Anne the new sovereign showed no particular haste to come to England. Seven weeks, in fact, were to elapse before George Louis was to arrive from Hanover, which he had left in tears and in the spirit of one going into exile. He brought no consort with him. His political marriage to Sophia Dorothea of Zell had swiftly come to an end, and tragically for Sophia Dorothea with the murder of her lover, Philip Konigsmark, one of the family of that name that had a notorious history. George Louis never lived down his ruthless treatment of his wife, whom he had had confined in the Castle of Ahlden on the Aller; her repeated attempts to escape from her imprisonment were to succeed only by her own death, shortly before George I departed.

To ease his acute homesickness, however, the fifty-four-year-old monarch brought with him to England his two elderly German favourites, Mlle Schulemberg and Mme Kielmansegge, later to become Duchess of Kendal and Countess of Darlington. These intriguing ladies proved extremely unpopular with ministers and populace alike on account of their avaricious tendencies. The universal dislike they created was in no way lessened by their personal appearances. The Schulemberg was described as being 'conspicuous for the awkwardness of her long, gaunt, fleshless figure'. She was known by wags as 'The Maypole'. Mme Kielmansegge, by way of contrast, had 'two acres of cheeks spread with crimson, an ocean of neck that overflowed and was not distinguishable from the lower part of her body, no portion of which was restrained by stays'. Madame was nicknamed 'the Elephant'. Whenever they set out by coach to take the air they were invariably greeted by the London mob with ribald remarks. On one such occasion when the crowd had become particularly offensive, Mlle Schulemberg – said to have been George I's half-sister by one of his father's mistresses – having picked up a smattering of English, thrust her face out of the coach window and cried, 'Goot pipple! What for you abuse us? We come for all your goots'. 'Yuss, damn you!' shouted a voice from the mob, 'an' fer our chattels, too!'

Their new king's genuine attachment to his native land, while being an admirable trait, was not to endear him to his English subjects. In addition, he did not understand one sentence of the English tongue, and was ignorant of the country's history, customs and traditions. Fortunately he was fairly fluent in French, in which language he conversed and corresponded with his ministers, leaving those among the latter who were no linguists somewhat at a disadvantage.

Long before coming to England strong mutual antagonism had existed between George I and his heir, George Augustus. (George I's only other child by Sophia Dorothea of Zell became the queen of Frederick William I of Prussia, and mother of Frederick the Great.) George Augustus, for one thing, could never forget the ill-treatment of his mother, with whom the king had forbidden him any intercourse whatsoever.

On arrival in England their loathing for each other increased to such an extent that their violent quarrels soon became a public scandal. Apart from the fact that George I had insisted upon taking his son's children under his own personal direction, forbidding the parents to visit their offspring except with his consent, the king was intensely jealous of the Prince of Wales assuming any semblance of power. For this reason he adamantly refused to appoint George Augustus regent on his own periodical trips to his much-loved Herrenhausen. He compromised by endowing the Prince of Wales with the obsolete title of 'Guardian of the Realm and Lieutenant', with as many restrictions on his son's authority as the king could find to impose. Such office had never been known in England since the days of Edward, the Black Prince, over three centuries earlier. Maybe it was only as a 'black' prince that George I saw his son.

His daughter-in-law, Caroline of Anspach, the king invariably referred to as '*cette diablesse madame la princesse*'. The Princess of Wales, all the same – 'she-devil' or not – was not unattractive to her father-in-law's pale blue, bulbous eye. In addition to being an outstandingly clever woman, with a witty if coarse sense of humour, Caroline was physically pleasing, and of the colouring and build that appealed to the king in his later years. It was suggested that Caroline of Anspach's feminine charms were another cause of George I's jealousy of his son.[8]

With the guidance of his more than able wife, George Augustus finally responded to his father's treatment by setting up his own court party in opposition to that of the king's court at St James's. He removed his household to Leicester House, Leicester Square, and waited with what patience he could muster for his sire's death to bring George Augustus to the Crown. This came suddenly, after a reign of twelve years, on 10 June 1727. The king, on a visit to Hanover in the company of the Duchess of Kendal, suffered a stroke while journeying in his coach. With a loud cry of 'Osnabrück! Osnabrück!' he compelled the drivers to speed up their horses. It was at Osnabrück that he had been born, and at Osnabrück that his brother, the prince-bishop, had his palace. '*C'est fait de moi!*' the king murmured a short while later. All was over with him, indeed. At midnight the coach, dashing over the cobbles of the palace courtyard, brought only the corpse of the Elector of Hanover and England's first Hanoverian monarch.

His English subjects received the news of their sovereign's death with composure. The vast majority did not bother their heads about it. Yet he had been a moderate ruler. He had kept his compact with the people, and his reign, on the whole, had been one of prosperity for the country. George I's aim had been to leave England to itself, and be out of it himself as much as possible. True, he had never been liked by his subjects as a person. But far less liked had been his German mistresses, his German secretaries, his German attendants, cooks and bottle-washers, all of whom had plundered the country of whatever booty on which they could lay their hands.

George I was buried in his native Hanover.

10

George II (1683–1760)

George II was the last foreigner by birth to come to the English throne. Born at Hanover in 1683, George Augustus, who was to wear the Crown for thirty-three years, was certainly no improvement on his father, whom he all too closely resembled in character. Possessing no kingly qualities, he was a plain-faced, dull little man of low tastes. He hated the sight of a book – unless an account-ledger – and was blind to the charms of what he termed, in his German accent, 'bainting' and 'boetry'.

On the other hand, George II was far from being blind to the charms of the female sex. Their alluring attractions, together with his love for hard cash, occupied much of his time and interest. His mechanical habits and aggravating tricks of behaviour – such as the persistent jingling of the coins in his purse – drove those about him to exasperation. One court beauty, having no desire to bestow her favours in return for some of George II's tinkling lucre, was so irritated that she struck the purse from the king's hand and walked from the room.

While lacking the finer sensibilities, George Augustus had great physical courage – he saw active service at Oudenarde (1708), and many years later at Dettingen (1743), said to be the last battle in which a King of England personally took part – but was prone to bore his listeners with tales of his prowess in the field of war.

'I am sick to death', exclaimed Princess Caroline, the most likeable of his five daughters, 'of hearing of his personal courage *every* day of my life!' Subject to sudden, uncontrollable fits of temper, the king would shake his fist in the faces of the courtiers, fling his coat or wig on the floor, stamp on it and scream. The only person who could exercise restraint over him or command him was his wife. Why did the handsome, cultured Caroline of Anspach marry that 'ridiculous, red-faced, staring princeling?' her admirers often asked themselves. The explanation was probably a simple one. Caroline had been deeply devoted to George Augustus's grandmother, Sophia of Hanover, who had taken the orphaned princess under her wing in youth. Doubtless Sophia's influence effected this marriage. Very early on she had recognised the abilities and ambitious tendencies of Caroline, and she would have visualised her protégée as eminently suited to be a prospective Queen of England.

When Prince Elector of Hanover to Queen Anne, 1714

A few days after his grandmother's death, George Augustus wrote, on black-edged notepaper, and in his own hand, the following letter to Queen Anne, in the desire to be restored to the latter's favour. The letter was in all probability dictated by Caroline, whose eyes had been focussed on England, and England's unrestful political state, for some time.

Hanover, June 15, 1714

Madame,

It is with much regret that I have noted from the letter of the 30th of May with which your Majesty has honoured me that persons have striven to render me suspect, and have represented me as capable of exciting trouble and of encouraging factions in your Realms.

As to any such designs may I be pardoned if I had even so much as a thought, and I ardently desire to be permitted to add that your Majesty would have been undeceived of this to the fullest extent had I personally been known to you more nearly.

I am persuaded that my conduct will induce you ere long to render me justice, and to accord me the honour of your good graces, for which I shall always strive with the utmost zeal, being, with much respect, your Majesty's

Very humble and very obedient servant,

George Augustus, Prince Elector

When king to the queen consort, Caroline of Anspach, 1735

Caroline of Anspach is reputed to have been sorely wounded by her absurd little husband's constant infidelities. It is difficult, all the same, wholly to credit this, or to see the masterful Queen Caroline in the light of a wronged wife. George Augustus frankly discussed his *affaires* with his consort, the merits or demerits of his mistresses, and even confided to her most intimate details of his relationships with other women. Caroline knew, in any event, that she was first and foremost in her husband's esteem. While she lived no other woman had any possibility of usurping her prerogatives or authority. There must, in fact, have been more than one occasion on which Caroline, with her statesmanlike abilities, was only too relieved that the circumstances of the king's liaisons precluded him for the time being from meddling in court or national policy. The queen and her Prime Minister, Robert Walpole, were two of a kind, and more than capable of ruling without George II's fussy interference.

Mrs Howard – afterwards Lady Suffolk – had become George Augustus's mistress in early days, when he was Prince of Wales. She was an intellectual woman, the friend of men of such mental stature as Dean Swift, Dr John Arbuthnot, and Alexander Pope. Further, she was much liked by her own sex, in particular by Mary Bellenden, the lady who had struck the king's purse from his hand. (A pleasing letter from Mary Bellenden to her 'dear Howard' will be found in Appendix C.)

Possibly Mrs Howard considered the allowance of £1,200 a year which George Augustus made her sufficient compensation for enduring the companionship of her royal, empty-headed 'Jingling Geordie'. When he became king, George II increased this sum to £3,200 annually, and gave Mrs Howard – according to Queen Caroline – £12,000 towards building her villa at Twickenham. She retained her position as bedchamber woman to Caroline when Caroline became queen. The latter, however, exacted such strict observance of customs where this office was concerned that Mrs Howard felt at last forced to resign. This she did in 1734, and the following year, at the age of forty-nine, she married George Berkeley, fourth son of the second Earl of Berkeley and a member of the opposition.

The king was in Hanover at the time, and deeply involved in a fresh liaison that was to cause anxiety to both the queen and Robert Walpole. The following is George II's brief comment on the news which the queen had sent him regarding the woman who had been his close associate for nearly twenty years.

> ... I am greatly surprised at the resolution, of which you have sent me word, that my old mistress has made to commit her body in marriage to that gouty old George Berkeley, and I am myself extremely glad. I would not make such gifts to my friends, and when my enemies rob me, God grant it will be always in this fashion.

George II had no love for the Berkeley family. Shortly after his accession, Queen Caroline had found in the late king's cabinet a proposal from the Earl of Berkeley, First Lord of the

Admiralty, to seize the Prince of Wales, as her husband then was, and transport him to America, 'where he should be heard of no more'. It appears that George I had given very serious consideration to this suggested abduction.

George Augustus returned from his extended visit to Hanover in a bad mood. He snubbed all those with whom he came into contact, and publicly insulted his queen, his family, and his Prime Minister. The king's announcement that he hated everything English – the people, their customs, and the very sight of the country itself – caused justifiable resentment. The reason for his ill-humour, however, was not far to seek. He had procured a new object of adoration in the person of Amelia Sophia, Madame von Walmoden, the young and fashionable wife of a German baron. The latter had been willing to renounce his marital claims for the not extortionate cash sum of 'one thousand dollars'. Whereupon the elderly, goggle-eyed king and his young mistress had proceeded to emulate their conception of the romance of Antony and Cleopatra in a Hanoverian setting. They indulged in revels and orgies of every description, in the company of a host of hangers-on as refined as themselves. The king brought home with him – not having dared to bring his mistress – a collection of paintings made of these bacchanalian entertainments, with portrait likenesses of those who had taken part, which he delighted in exhibiting to the queen and anyone who happened to be around.

Shortly after his return the love-sick George Augustus – writing to his adored by every post – announced his intention of hastening back to Hanover with all speed. Walpole's efforts to prevent him bore no fruit. He appointed the queen, as was usual on his trips abroad, as regent, and hastily packed himself off. Walpole, aware of public tension created by the king's prolonged absences, advised the queen to suggest that George Augustus bring his mistress over to England.

To the queen consort, Caroline of Anspach, 1736

The following excerpt from a letter that George II wrote to Queen Caroline when she had invited Madame von Walmoden to accompany the king to England indicates the regard he had for his wife's exceptional qualities.

> Herrenhausen
>
> ... You are sensible of my passions, my dear Caroline! You know my weaknesses. My heart can hide no secrets from you; and God grant that you will not fail to correct me with the same facility that you explore me!
>
> God grant that I may emulate you in all that I know you to admire, and that I may learn of you all the virtues that you make me see, savour, and love.

The queen complacently set about making preparations for the new sultana's reception, but her unconventional proposal that Madame von Walmoden should become one of her household shocked the broad-minded Walpole to the core. While it was one thing for the king to take one of her bedchamber women as his mistress, Walpole protested that public opinion would be scandalised by the queen's voluntarily receiving a mistress into her establishment. He and Caroline might have saved themselves this headache. Madame von Walmoden wisely declined to come to England on any terms. She had no fancy for close quarters with the queen.

The disgruntled king once more set out alone for his English kingdom. On account of heavy storms that were sweeping the coasts, however, his non-arrival at the expected time caused anxiety at court. As far as the general public were concerned, their hope was freely expressed that George II was at the bottom of the deep blue sea. The nature of the king's visits to Hanover was well known, and his reckless squandering of the country's money in so worthless a cause met with strong and open disapproval. As an indication of his unpopularity in this respect, while the king was missing, and tossing about in the North Sea, the following notice was posted up on St James's Palace gates.

> Lost or Strayed out of this house a man who has left a wife and six children on the Parish. Whoever will give any tidings of him to the church wardens of St James's Parish, so that he may be got again, shall receive four shillings and sixpence. N.B. This reward will not be increased, nobody judging him to deserve a crown.

While Walpole was striving to stem the flood of public censure, news was suddenly received that the king was stranded at Helvoetsluys in Holland. The Prime Minister and the queen heaved sighs of relief, and the public groaned.

To his son, Frederick Louis, Prince of Wales, 1737

Family history was to repeat itself in the antagonistic relationship between George II and his eldest son, Frederick Louis. All members of the royal family, in fact, united with the king in their detestation of the Prince of Wales. This suggests that he must have been a far from attractive character. 'Popularity always makes me sick', ejaculated the queen, referring to her son's studied attempts to steal the limelight, 'but, my God! Fritz's popularity makes me vomit!' Princess Caroline's emphatic support of her mother's views resolved itself into a single phrase where her brother was concerned, 'That nauseous beast!' This abusive epithet must have become somewhat monotonous to her hearers since Princess Caroline repeated it several times a day.

Frederick Louis had remained in the background for some years after his arrival in England from Hanover on the death of George I. Once, however, he had learnt the English tongue, and become aware of his own importance as Prince of Wales, he entered with avidity into opposition against his parents. He was a weak character, fond of adulation, and easily led by flatterers. He had cast himself in the royal family drama, of which he was the author, as a man of intrigue, but he so overacted his part that he finally found himself expelled from his father's court, and an enemy of the king and queen for life.

The reason for George II's decision to be rid of his son is explained in the following letter that he wrote to the Prince of Wales following the latter's treatment of his wife – Augusta of Saxe-Gotha – during her pregnancy. Frederick Louis had no comprehensible explanation for his actions, and left his parents to suspect that Augusta's first-born had been brought in to the lying-in chamber in a warming-pan, as was suggested of Mary Beatrice of Modena's son. 'That nauseous beast', exclaimed Princess Caroline, 'is capable of anything – even *that!'*

September 10, 1737

The professions you have lately made in your letters of your particular regard to me are so contradictory to all your actions that I cannot suffer myself to be imposed upon by them.

You know very well you did not give the least intimation to me, or the Queen, that the Princess was with child or breeding, until within less than a month of the birth of the young Princess. You removed the Princess [Augusta] twice in the week immediately preceding the day of delivery from the place of my residence, in expectation, as you have voluntarily declared, of her labour; and both times upon your return, you industriously concealed from the knowledge of me, and the Queen, every circumstances relating to this important affair. And you at last, without giving any notice to me, or the Queen, precipitately hurried the Princess from Hampton court in a condition not to be named. After having thus, in execution of your own determined measures, exposed both the Princess and her child to the greatest perils, you now plead surprise and tenderness for the Princess, as the only motives that occasioned these repeated indignities offered to me and the Queen, your mother.

This extravagant and undutiful behaviour, in so essential a point as the birth of an heir to my Crown, is such an evidence of your premeditated defiance of me, and such a contempt of my authority, and of the natural right belonging to your parents as cannot be excused by the pretended innocence of your intentions, nor palliated or disguised by specious words only.

But the whole tenor of your conduct for a considerable time has been so entirely void of all real duty to me that I have long had reason to be highly offended with you.

And until you withdraw your regard and confidence from those by whose instigation and advice you are directed and encouraged in your unwarrantable behaviour to me and to the Queen, and until you return to your duty, you shall not reside in my Palace; which I will not suffer to be made the resort of them who, under the appearance of an attachment to you, foment the division which you have made in my family, and thereby weaken the common interest of the whole.

In this situation I will receive no reply; but when your actions manifest a just sense of your duty and submission, that may induce me to pardon what at present I most justly resent.

In the meantime, it is my pleasure that you leave St James's with all your family,[1] when it can be done without prejudice or inconvenience to the Princess. I shall for the present leave to the Princess the care of my granddaughter until a proper time calls upon me to consider of her education.

G.R.

Upon the Prince of Wales's receipt of the foregoing letter from his father, Augusta found herself unceremoniously bundled off to Kew with her newly born infant. She had survived her confinement only by a miracle. Groaning and in fear,

Augusta had been hoisted into a carriage at night, and driven full gallop from Hampton court to St James's Palace, where naturally there were no preparations for a lying-in. No suitable requirements were available, not even sheets, apparently. Frederick Louis and his mistress – Lady Archibald Hamilton, who had accompanied this nightmare expedition – were compelled to put the Princess of Wales to bed between two tablecloths, and only just in time for the birth of a baby girl, 'about the bigness of a good large toothpick', to take place. This 'toothpick', all the same, despite her chaotic entry into the world, grew up to be a handsome woman. As Princess Augusta of England, she married Charles William Ferdinand, Duke of Brunswick-Wolfenbüttel, and became mother of Caroline of Brunswick.

To Augusta, Princess of Wales, 1737

Since her husband himself had been forbidden to write to the king, once arrived at Kew Augusta did so, asking for the king's forgiveness of Frederick Louis, and begging for an interview. The following is George II's curt reply.

> Hampton court, September 18, 1737
>
> I am sorry, Madam, that anything should happen to give you the least uneasiness. It is a misfortune to you, but not owing to me, that you are involved in the consequences of your husband's inexcusable conduct. I pity you – to see you first exposed to the utmost danger, in the execution of his designs, and then made the plea for a series of repeated indignities offered to me.
>
> I wish some insinuations in your letter had been omitted, which, however, I do not impute to you, as I am convinced it is not from you they proceed.
>
> G.R.

The king's reference to insinuations that had better 'been omitted' was made because of an ill-conceived remark in Augusta's own letter. 'How much am I to be pitied, Sir', she wrote, 'that an *incident* so grateful to me, and at the same time *so agreeable to the Public*, should unfortunately become the unhappy cause of a *division* in the Family!'

The queen wrote more kindly to Augusta on this occasion. A dying woman during the time of this domestic and public upheaval, Caroline of Anspach nevertheless refused to have anything more to do with her eldest son.

Accounts of eyewitnesses of the scenes that took place in Queen Caroline's death-chamber two months later have their humorous as well as their tragic aspect. The self-dramatising little king stole the act, and unwittingly turned the solemn drama into a serio-comic event. When he was not burying his face in the bedclothes in blubbering remorse, he was shouting and storming about the chamber, enjoining his wife 'Not to stare so! You look like a dying calf!' or, alternately, in an excess of self-pity, beseeching her not to die, as he could not live without her. The queen, in her physical agonies concerned only with being freed of 'this fever called living', advised her husband to marry again as soon as possible. 'No, no!' he wept, repelled at such a disrespectful suggestion, 'I will have mistresses!' All the weariness of past experience was contained in the queen's contemptuous retort, 'My God! Nothing can prevent that'. Between the intervals of such recurring scenes the Archbishop of Canterbury was prayerfully visiting and revisiting the death-chamber, the broken-hearted princesses moving softly to and fro, and Frederick, Prince of Wales, knocking in vain at the palace doors.

The king's despondency after the death of his consort in November, 1737, posed a problem for Robert Walpole. George II resolutely declined to consider a new queen. In the end, Madame von Walmoden – afterwards Lady Yarmouth – arrived from Hanover to console the royal widower. She

193

was to remain his chief stay during the many ensuing years that George Augustus occupied the throne. His end came as suddenly as had his father's. At Kensington Palace, five days before his seventy-seventh birthday, the king rose early, as was his habit, drank his morning chocolate, uttered a groan, and fell dead.

As a monarch George II showed great moderation in exercising his prerogatives, and once his confidence had been obtained, no minister had just cause – despite the king's violent language at times – to complain of him. George II probably realised how well served he was. Apart from the wisdom and governing qualities of his queen, seldom had any sovereign such ministers of pre-eminent ability as the sturdy Walpole and the stately Pitt to make his kingdom strong and his reign great.

George II was the last monarch to be buried in Henry VII's Chapel in Westminster Abbey.

11

George III (1738–1820)

George III – eldest son of Frederick, Prince of Wales, and Augusta of Saxe-Gotha – was born on 4 June 1738, at Norfolk House, St James's Square, where his father had temporarily set up his town residence after being dismissed from the king's palaces. A delicate, seven-month-old baby, he was handed over to the care of a healthy young peasant – the wife of a gardener – and it was solely due to his wet-nurse's tending that George William Frederick survived infancy. He grew to be a tall, sturdily built youth, albeit highly strung, and, according to his mother, 'a dull, good boy'.

For forty-six years the country had been ruled by German princes, more interested in their native land than in being kings of England. George III was different. He was London-born, spoke the English tongue, and sincerely loved all that was English. In return he was to become genuinely loved by his people, particularly cottage folk and those of humble stock. It was perhaps from his wholesome nurse that George III acquired his fondness for the good earth, and those that followed the plough. It was to earn him the affectionate nickname of 'Farmer George'.

Two years before his death from pleurisy in 1751, Frederick, Prince of Wales had formed a close friendship with an obscure Scot – Lord Bute. Bute possessed little material wealth, and no greater advantages, apparently, than a quick intelligence and an engaging, if autocratic, manner. The influence he had exercised over Frederick, Bute continued to wield, after the former's death, over Frederick's widow and eldest son. Gossip insisted that the Dowager Princess of Wales was Bute's mistress. It was probably true, but there is no definite evidence to support the rumour. She was all the same, hypnotically swayed by Bute, and in her turn she kept the shy, awkward George under her thumb until the day of her death – twelve years after he came to the throne. The firm grip that Bute and his own mother retained on him, combined with George II's intense dislike of his daughter-in-law, resulted in the youth of George III being passed under agitated conditions.

Having appointed himself 'governor' of the heir apparent, Bute set out determinedly to mould the lad's character and way of life along the lines he considered they should go. He had very quickly visualised himself as prospective unofficial regent, for the old king could not last much longer.

When Prince of Wales to Lord Bute, 1756

The following letter, written when the prince was eighteen years old, shows how completely Bute's spell was uppermost at this time. In fact, it is so catechetical in its style that it bears indication of having been written under instruction. George's letters were always earnest and plain-spoken, but there is here definite lack of spontaneity in the studied phrasing and pointedly expressed sentiments.

Kew,[1] June 30th, 1756

My dear Lord,

I have had the pleasure of your friendship during the space of a year, by which I have reaped great advantage, but not the improvement I should if I had followed your advice; but you shall find me make such progress in this summer, that shall give you hopes, that with the continuation of your advice, I may turn out as you wish.

It is very true that the Ministers have done everything they can to provoke me; that they have called me a harmless boy, and have not even deigned to give me an answer when I so earnestly wish to see my Friend about me. They have also treated my Mother in a cruel manner (which I shall neither forget nor forgive to the day of my death), because she is so good as to come forward and to preserve her son from the many snares that surround him. My Friend is also attacked in the most cruel and horrid manner, not for anything he has done against them, but because he is my Friend, and wants to see me come to the Throne with honour and not with disgrace and because he is a friend to the blessed liberties of his country and not to arbitrary notions. I look upon myself as engaged in honour and justice to defend these my two Friends as long as I draw breath.

I do therefore here in the presence of Our Almighty Lord promise, that I will ever remember the insults done to my Mother, and never will forgive anyone who shall offer to speak disrespectfully of her.

I do in the same solemn manner declare, that I will defend my Friend and will never use evasive answers, but will always tell him whatever is said against him, and will more and more show to the world the great friendship I have for him, and all the malice that can be invented against him shall only bind me the stronger to him.

I do further promise, that all the allurements my enemies can think of, or the threats that they may make pour out upon me, shall never make me in the least change from what I do solemnly promise in this paper.

I will take upon me the man in every thing, and will not show that indifference which I have as yet too often done.

As I have chosen the vigorous part, I will throw off that indolence which if I don't soon get the better of will be my ruin, and will never grow weary of this, though — [George II] should live many years.

I hope my dear Lord will conduct me through this difficult road and will bring me to the goal. I will exactly follow your advice, without which I shall inevitably sink.

I am young and inexperienced and want advice. I trust in your friendship which will assist me in all difficulties.

I know few things I ought to be more thankful for to the Great Power above, than for its having pleased Him to send you to help and advise me in these difficult times.

I do hope you will from this instant banish all thoughts of leaving me, and will resolve, if not for my sake for the good of your country to remain with me. I have often heard you say, that you don't think I shall have the same friendship for you when I am married as I now have. I shall never change in that, nor will I bear to be in the least deprived of your company. And I shall expect that all my relations shall show you that regard which is due to the Friend of the whole Family.

I sign my name with the greatest pleasure to what I have here written, which is my firm and unalterable resolution.

George P.

To the king, 1756

In his desire to withdraw the young Prince of Wales from the influence of his mother and 'that puppy Bute', George II proposed that when his grandson became nineteen years of age he should receive a settlement of £40,000 a year, and take up his residence at St James's Palace, a most attractive proposition, one would have thought, for a young man in his circumstances and under such subjection at the hands of his mother and Bute.

However, the prospect did not – or was not permitted to – appeal to the enslaved George. He was in any event terrified of his grandfather. He pleaded that he did not wish to be in a separate establishment from the Dowager Princess of Wales, or to be deprived of the companionship of Bute. The exasperated king was finally persuaded by his advisers to concede to his grandson's wishes, and also to make Bute groom-of-the-stole. Evidently George II's ministers, realising that the king was nearing his end, thought it as well, in their own interests, to get into the good graces of his successor by humouring the Prince of Wales in this way.

In the following letter George is expressing his gratitude to the king.

Kew, October 5

Sir,

I humbly beg, with a heart full of duty and gratitude, to lay myself at your Majesty's feet; and to return my most humble thanks for the great tenderness your Majesty has been pleased to show me, in so graciously permitting me to remain with the Princess my mother; and for condescending to inform me of your Majesty's favourable dispositions to my humble request concerning the Earl of Bute.

It has been and always will continue the desire of my life to merit your Majesty's gracious favour and protection. I dare affirm to your Majesty that I shall never be wanting in the sincerest returns of duty and gratitude that l owe your Majesty both as a son and a subject; I shall think myself bound to promote as far as lies in my power the most perfect union and harmony in the Royal Family, and by every action convince the world of my sincere love and unalterable attachment to your Royal Person. It is with these sentiments I presume to subscribe myself, [etc.].

To Lord Bute, 1759

Whatever methods Bute had used to gain his strong hold over the Prince of Wales remain a mystery, but he certainly used his power to keep his royal charge in subservience to an abject degree. From the following letter one is left with the impression that his 'governor' was unsympathetic to George's emotions where the opposite sex were concerned, and even deprecated any hint of his sowing the mildest of wild oats. Such harsh restraints on the youth's natural feelings suggest determination in the phlegmatic Scot to exclude all influence save his own.

(Undated)

You have often accused me of growing grave and thoughtful. It is entirely owing to a daily increasing admiration of the fair sex, which I am attempting with all the philosophy and resolution I am capable of to keep under. I should be ashamed after having so long resisted the charms of those divine creatures now to become their prey. Princes when once in their hands make miserable figures: the annals of France and the present situation of Government in the Kingdom I most love, are convincing proofs of it.[2]

When I have said this you will plainly feel how strong a struggle there is between boiling youth of twenty-one years and prudence. The last I hope will ever keep the upper hand. Indeed if I can weather it but a few years, marriage will put a stop to this combat in my breast.

I believe you will agree that application is the only aid I can give to reason, that by keeping the mind constantly employed is a likely means of preserving those passions in due subordination to it. Believe me I will with the greatest assiduity attempt to make all that progress which your good counsels, if properly attended to, have reason to expect.

The letter also gives indications of having been written under extreme nervous tension. It may, perhaps, have been indirectly concerned with an infatuation that the Prince of Wales had conceived for a Wapping tradesman's daughter whose uncle was in business as a linen-draper near the court. The Prince's chance meeting with the attractive Quakeress – Hannah Lightfoot – had resulted in love at first sight. Gossip of the day affirmed that he had married her. The rumour, however, is hardly worth consideration. Had he done so the honest and straightforward George would have honoured the marriage bond, and the Wapping tradesman's daughter would have become a Queen of England, no Royal Marriage Act being in force at that time.

A more serious romance was to stir the court and split it into two camps shortly after George III had ascended the throne. On this occasion the object of his adoration – acclaimed one of the most beautiful women of her time – was the Lady Sarah Lennox, youngest daughter of the Duke of Richmond, and sister-in-law of Henry Fox, one-time Secretary of State and afterwards Lord Holland. Fox and the Lennox family were naturally more than anxious to promote the marriage. On the other hand, the Dowager Princess of Wales and Bute strenuously opposed it. They had everything to lose by such an alliance.

The young king was desperately in love, and Lady Sarah seems to have been more than agreeable to his advances. She would, it is said, 'play at hay-making, in rustic attire', in the meadows of Holland House – the Kensington residence of her brother-in-law – when she expected her lover-king to come riding by. This Arcadian scene must have enchanted the eyes of the latent 'Farmer George'.

However, 'The Petticoat and the Boot' – as the current caricaturists lampooned the Dowager Princess of Wales and Bute – won the day. George's attentions were directed to a foreign princess as a consort. The lovely Sarah, having contracted three marriages in the course of her long life, died at the age of eighty-two in 1826. As daughter of the second Duke of Richmond, she was believed to be the last surviving great-granddaughter of Charles II.

When king to Lord Bute, 1762

George III came to the throne in 1760 at the age of twenty-two. His reign of sixty years was to witness many upheavals both at home and abroad. England was to undergo the revolt of the American colonies, and submit to defeat and separation, it was to withstand the impact of the French Revolution, and to grapple and struggle for existence with the Napoleonic menace.

Within a year of his ascending the throne his marriage to Princess Charlotte, of the ancient Protestant House of Mecklenburg-Strelitz, provided the populace with a coronation that was of such gorgeous pageantry that it lived long in public memory.

From the outset of his reign George III had had an idealistic aim to promote the welfare of his people and the interests and honour of England. With this objective in view he was to find his administration encompassed with difficulties, and in his pathetic belief in the innate goodness of human nature, with the passing years the king was to suffer bitter disillusionment. It was, in fact, all too quickly brought home to him that politicians, as he himself declared, were guided solely by the incitements that too frequently directed their conduct – 'the shadow of popularity (for the reality must consist alone in what is of real advantage to the country), and a desire of giving trouble'. On another occasion he trenchantly remarked, 'The business of politics is a most villainous business. It is the business of a coxcomb. It is not the profession of a gentleman.'

On the resignation of the Duke of Newcastle, who had been premier when George III came to the throne, Bute became Prime Minister in his stead. His unpopularity, however, as the king's intimate friend, and his extreme favouritism of his own countrymen – the Scots – combined with his total inability for the onerous post to which he had so long aspired, terminated in his retiring within twelve months. Bute's resignation took the king by surprise. Although it was Bute's hope that he would be recalled at a later date, this never transpired. He had to content himself thereafter by acting as a 'minister of the back stairs', busying himself with State matters in a private capacity only.

The following letter was written by the king to Bute at this time of government crisis, when ministers were either resigning or being dismissed from office weekly, and while the youthful and inexperienced George III strove desperately to establish his authority.

December, 1762

... Now I come to the part of my dear Friend's letter that gives me the greatest concern, as it overturns all the thoughts that have alone kept up my spirits in these bad times. I own I had flattered myself when Peace was once established[3] that my dear Friend would have assisted me in purging out corruption, and in those measures that no man but he that has the Prince's real affection can go through. Then when we were both dead our memories would have been respected and esteemed to the end of time. Now what shall we be able to say: that Peace is concluded, and my dear Friend becoming a courtier – for I fear mankind will say so – the Ministry remains composed of the most abandoned men that ever held those offices. Thus instead of reformation, the Ministers being vicious, this country will grow if possible worse. Let me attack the irreligious, the covetous, etc., as much as I please, that will be no effect, for the Ministers being of that stamp, men will with reason think they may advance to the highest pitch of their ambition, through every infamous way that their own black hearts or the rascality of their superiors can point out ...

To Lord North, 1770

The king's youngest brother, Henry Frederick, Duke of Cumberland, had made himself sensationally conspicuous in 1770 by figuring in a court trial. The principal party implicated was the wife of the Earl of Grosvenor, whom Henry Frederick had attempted to seduce. The earl won his action, and was awarded heavy damages against the Duke of Cumberland.

The following letter from George III to his First Lord of the Treasury is self-explanatory in this connection.

Richmond Lodge,[4] November 5

Lord North,

A subject of a most private and delicate kind obliges me to lose no time in acquainting you that my two brothers have this day applied to me on the difficulty that the folly of the youngest has drawn him into. The affair is too public for you to doubt but that it regards the lawsuit; the time will expire this day sennight, when he must pay the damages and the other expenses attending it. He has taken no one step to raise the money, and now has applied to me as the only means by which he can obtain it, promising to repay it in a year and a half.

I therefore promised to write to you, though I saw great difficulty in your finding so large a sum as thirteen thousand pounds in so short a time; but they pointed out to me that the prosecutor would certainly force the House, which would at this licentious time occasion disagreeable reflections on the rest of his family as well as on him.

I shall speak more fully to you on this subject on Wednesday, but the time is so short that I did [not] choose to delay opening this affair till then. Besides, I am not fond of taking persons on delicate affairs unprepared. Whatever can be done ought to be done; and I ought as little as possible to appear in so very improper a business.

George, R.

To the king's relief North came to his assistance.

Twelve months later Henry Frederick married – as the only means of obtaining her favours – the Hon. Mrs Horton, a pretty young widow of twenty-four, chiefly remarkable for 'the long length of her eye-lashes, and a pair of most artful eyes'. The king was not informed of the *mésalliance* until a month later, by which time the couple had fled to Calais. As a result of this marriage, and a similar one contracted by the king's other brother, the Duke of Gloucester, about the same time, by the king's express direction Parliament passed the well-known Royal Marriage Act. This Act was subsequently to nullify the union of the king's eldest son, afterwards George IV, with Maria Fitzherbert.

For many years the dukes of Cumberland and Gloucester were rigidly excluded from the court. His brothers, as well as members of his own family, were sources of constant anxiety to the king.

To the Archbishop of Canterbury,[5] *c.* 1780

In personal virtues George III was exceptional. A genuinely religious man, his moral code was high. Unlike the former monarchs of the House of Hanover he strongly disapproved of the vices and debaucheries that were the accepted order of the day among the aristocracy and men of public affairs. The king, furthermore, had the courage to express his opinion on such laxities of conduct whenever and wherever he deemed it expedient.

From the following letter it would appear that illicit revelries were even being indulged within the sanctity of the palace of the Archbishop of Canterbury. This stern reprimand from the king must have given the frisky prelate a shock, and, it is to be assumed, had the desired effect.

(Undated)

My Good Lord Prelate,

I could not delay giving you the notification of the grief and concern with which my breast was affected at receiving authentic information that *routs* have made their way into your Palace. At the same time I must signify to you my sentiments on this subject, which holds those levities and vain dissipations as utterly inexpedient, if not unlawful, to pass in a residence for many centuries devoted to divine studies, religious retirement, and the extensive exercise of charity and benevolence: I add, in a place where so many of your predecessors have led their lives in such sanctity as has thrown lustre on the pure religion they professed and adorned.

From the dissatisfaction with which you must perceive I behold these improprieties – not to speak in harsher terms – and on still more pious principles, I trust you will suppress them immediately, so that I may not have occasion to show any further marks of my displeasure or to interpose in a different manner.

May God take your Grace into his Almighty protection.

I remain, my Lord Prelate,
Your gracious friend, G.R.

Incidentally, there was much corruption in the Church in Georgian times. Hard-living, hard-drinking bishops had become indifferent to the spiritual needs of the people. It had been left to such men as the Wesley brothers and George Whitefield, all ordained in the Church of England, to create a religious revival. This they accomplished by forsaking the stone temples, and expound their message on the hillside, at the pit-head, or on the beaches. At the time that the king wrote the above letter to the archbishop, the aged John Wesley's powerful voice could still command an audience of thirty thousand, congregated in the open air.

To Lord North, 1781

The austere, regulated domestic life maintained by George III and the queen proved unspeakably dull and monotonous for all their family as they reached maturity and particularly for the heir apparent. He had inherited none of his father's fine qualities, and nothing of his uprightness of character.

On the contrary, George junior began kicking over the traces early in his princely career. At nineteen years of age he became seriously entangled with Mrs Robinson, a noted actress, to whom during their liaison the Prince of Wales had written a series of compromising love letters. When their fond attachment came to an end, the heir apparent's 'Perdita' – as he always addressed Mrs Robinson – casting herself in the role of a betrayed woman threatened publication of this correspondence.

The prince had no alternative but to confess his predicament to his father. It must have been a chilling and wintry tale indeed that 'Prince Florisel' poured out to the king on this occasion, and, as will be gathered from the following letter from the king to North, was the cause of further anxiety. Once more the Lord of the Treasury had to step into the breach.

George III's final sentence is somewhat ambiguous. One can only suppose that he meant to infer that he had never had to deal with a case of blackmail before.

Windsor,[6] 40 min. past 9 a.m.

August 28, 1781

I am sorry to be obliged to open a subject to Lord North that has long given me much pain, but I can rather do it on paper than in conversation. It is a subject of which I know he is not quite ignorant.

My eldest son got last year into a very improper connection with an actress and woman of indifferent character.[7] Through the *friendly* assistance of Lord Malden,[8] a multitude of letters passed which she has threatened to publish unless he, in short, bought them of her. He had made her very foolish promises, which undoubtedly, by her conduct to him, she entirely cancelled. I have thought it right to authorize the getting them from her, and have employed Lieut. Col. Hotham, on whose discretion I could depend, to manage this business. He has now brought it to a conclusion, and has her consent to get these letters on her receiving 5,000, undoubtedly an enormous sum; but I wish to get my son out of this shameful scrape.

I desire you will therefore see Lieut. Col. Hotham and settle this with him. I am happy at being able to say that I never was personally' engaged in such a transaction, which perhaps makes me feel this the stronger.

To the Duke of Portland, 1783

As was usual in the case of the Hanoverian heirs apparent, the Prince of Wales set himself up in direct and open opposition to the king. His sole reason was, of course, money.

Early in 1783, on the approach of his twenty-first birthday, the Prince of Wales had chosen Carlton House (purchased by the king's father in 1732) as his residence, and had at once proceeded to enter into heavy commitments in the way of extensive alterations and embellishments to the property in preparation for entertainments there on a most lavish and luxurious scale. His next plan of campaign was to persuade his friends in Parliament to move that the heir apparent's allowance of £50,000 a year should be doubled, and settlement made of all his debts.

In view of the mode of life adopted by his eldest son, the king was infuriated by this suggestion, and also by the deceptive methods followed to put the proposal into execution. This he makes evident in the studiedly formal letter that he wrote to the Duke of Portland, recently appointed leader of a coalition ministry.

> Windsor, 59 min. past 10 a.m.
> June 16, 1783

It is impossible for me to find words expressive enough of my utter indignation and astonishment at the letter I have just received from the Duke of Portland. These words are certainly strong, and would be inexcusable if not authorized by the following facts.

When the Duke of Portland desired I would turn my thoughts to fixing on a sum for the separate establishment of the Prince of Wales, when he arrives at the age of twenty-one years, I desired he would, with the rest of the efficient ministers, consider what proposal should be made to me on that subject. About a fortnight since he acquainted me that it was their unanimous opinion that a sum of one hundred thousand pounds, including the revenue of the Duchy of Cornwall, should be obtained from Parliament. I instantly showed my surprise at so lavish an idea, and the more so when my Subjects are so much loaded with taxes, and said I thought fifty thousand pounds in addition to the revenue of Cornwall, which would nearly exceed twenty-seven thousand per annum of what the late King thought sufficient for me in a similar station, was all that could with reason be granted; and consequently desired that Duke to acquaint the ministers with my opinion, and of my wish that they should reconsider this business.

On the 6th of this month the Duke of Portland told me they continued to think it right to propose that sum to Parliament, from whom they meant the whole sum should come; that the reason of putting it so high arose from a knowledge that the Prince of Wales had debts which must be paid out of his annual income, besides the expense of fitting himself out; and that they meant to acquaint him of this, and that no addition could be made whenever he married. I did not deny that I still thought the sum too large, though I acknowledged if no increase was made whenever he married that I would make no further objection.

I was therefore surprised on the 13th to find the Duke of Portland had not the drafts of the messages, but that they would soon be sent to me, from which time I have been in expectation of them; but this suspense is now fully explained, for the whole proposition is changed. I am to be saddled with the whole odium of this measure, and the expense at the same time ultimately to fall entirely on me who am not, from my numerous progeny, in a situation to bear it, though I had been assured no part was to be paid by me; and in addition I am pressed to take twenty-nine thousand of debt on myself which I have not incurred, that the public may blame me,[9] and the Prince of Wales with so unreasonable an income not be subject to this sum which can alone have arisen from shameful extravagance.

I therefore must declare that unless the proposal is brought back to the mode in which the Duke of Portland first stated it to me, and that all expenses are thrown on the Prince of Wales, I cannot proceed in this business, and shall think myself obliged to let the public know the cause of the delay and my opinion of the whole transaction.

I cannot conclude without saying that when the Duke of Portland came into office I had at least hoped he would have thought himself obliged to have my interest and that of the public at heart, and not have neglected both, to gratify the passions of an ill advised young man.

So furious, in fact, was the king at what he termed, in a second letter he wrote the same day to Portland, 'this shameful squandering of public money, besides an encouragement of extravagance', that he was prepared to dismiss his ministers if the proposal did not go forward along the lines he had originally been asked to approve. His ruling being hastily conceded, the thwarted Prince of Wales proceeded to plunge furiously into still greater debt, possibly on the principle that if his commitments were made sufficiently alarming the king would be forced to see his son's liabilities settled.

Within three years he was in such dire financial straits that he was compelled to apply to his frugal and modest-living parent for assistance. This was peremptorily refused. The Prince of Wales then made a public show of pretended drastic economies – selling his horses, shutting up his handsome apartments at Carlton House, and suspending building and renovations for which he had still further contracted. When this strategic move was supposed to have sufficiently impressed the public, the prince's toadies in Parliament once again raised the question of his allowance. It was finally agreed that he should receive an extra £10,000 annually, £161,000 was issued for payment of his debts, and £20,000 for the work on Carlton House. The heir apparent then settled down happily to his normal way of life, and was speedily more heavily in debt than he had ever been before.

The mental breakdown that the king had suffered five years after coming to the throne had been kept as private as possible, and known only to a select few. In 1788 the malady – accentuated by worries of State affairs combined with the behaviour of his sons, in particular the Prince of Wales – attacked the king more seriously and at greater length.

A moving and an absorbing account of this 'so black period' of George III's madness has been recorded by that fascinating diarist and correspondent, Fanny Burney, as assistant keeper of the robes to Queen Charlotte. In one of her letters she vividly portrays an incident that happened at this time, which in itself sufficiently conveys the fear created by the unhappy king's illness. Fanny, walking in Kew Gardens, had unexpectedly encountered George III accompanied by his medical attendants.

'... I thought I saw the person of his Majesty! Alarmed past all possible expression, I waited not to know more, but turning back, ran with all my might. But what was my terror to hear myself pursued! – to hear the voice of the King himself loudly and hoarsely calling after me "Burney! Miss Burney!" I protest I was ready to die ... Nevertheless, on I ran, too terrified to stop, and in search of some short passage, for the garden is full of little labyrinths, by which I might escape.

'The steps still pursued me, and still the poor hoarse and altered voice rang in my ears more and more footsteps resounded frightfully behind me – the attendants all running to catch their eager master ... Heavens, how I ran. I do not think I should have felt the hot lava from Vesuvius – at least not the hot cinders – had I so run during its eruption. My feet were not sensible that they even touched the ground ...'

It became necessary on this second breakdown to consider the question of a regency should the king fail to recover. After some discussion, this was finally offered to the Prince of Wales, but, to his mortification, in a limited capacity only. Before it could be put into effect, however, the king's condition showed signs of improvement. Ere long he was to be able to go to St Paul's, accompanied by both Houses of Parliament, to return thanksgivings for his restored health. The day was observed throughout the country, and as proof of the king's popularity 'never were illuminations so bright and so general; never was joy more heartfelt and sincere'.

To the Prime Minister, William Pitt, 1789

During his illness, the king's distrust of the Prince of Wales had been so strong that it became a dangerous obsession. In his weakened mental state he had on one occasion even made a violent physical assault on his eldest son, when a fierce hand-to-hand struggle had ensued before the eyes of horrified onlookers. The fracas had ended in Queen Charlotte having hysterics, and the Prince of Wales bursting into tears. The king's suspicions, all the same, were well founded. The conduct of the Prince of Wales and the king's second son, Frederick, Duke of York, at the time of their father's breakdown had been subversive to the king's interests. They had, too, succeeded in bringing their influence to bear on their sailor-brother, Prince William, who, with the connivance of the Prince of Wales, had taken French leave, and returned to England from his station in Jamaica. The elder sons' intentions were to get William created Duke of Clarence, and rope him into their opposition camp. These unseemly happenings at the time of his breakdown are the subject of the following letter that the king wrote on his recovery to William Pitt, who at the age of twenty-four had become Prime Minister six years earlier.

Windsor, 48 mins. past 9 a.m.
May 1, 1789

Mr Pitt cannot be surprised at my being unpleasantly affected by the information of the arrival of my third son from his station in the West Indies at Portsmouth. At the same time it is impossible to have had it communicated with more delicacy than was used by Lord Chatham.[10] I am not surprised as everyone knew the step of sending him leave to return must be disagreeable to me for a variety of reasons that no one chose ever to hint to me, consequently I had not the smallest suspicion that anyone had proposed this measure. I certainly think Lord Chatham could not in my then unfortunate illness take it upon him to refuse the leave; but the quarter from whence the application came has certainly by this given me a proof how little any wish of mine will ever be attended to. It will be now absolutely necessary to give him the same allowance that his brother the Duke of York has, and had my illness not put a stop to my private business, Colonel Hotham could have laid before Mr Pitt the exceeding he has made on his sea allowance. He must also now have his seat in the House of Lords.[11] In truth I have but too much reason to expect no great comfort by an additional member of the opposition faction in my own family.

It would be highly unjust in me not to add that I have every reason to be thankful to Divine Providence for the affectionate conduct of the Queen and of all my daughters; and certainly after having had so strong a warning of their having nearly lost the only protector they can look up to, I must be desirous of having them secured, whenever it shall please the Almighty to end my days, from a total dependence on a successor who does certainly show that their loss would be irreparable; their situation, and the want of a provision that the executive government may go on unmolested should not I entirely recover the vigour of mind and the inclination of taking the same active part I have done for above twenty-eight years, are points that hang heavily on my mind ...

To the Prime Minister, William Pitt, 1794

Nine years prior to the date of the following letter the heir apparent had fallen distractedly in love with Maria Fitzherbert. The story of that lovely young widow survives even to this day to reflect dishonour on the name of George IV. So ardently did the Prince of Wales desire to become the third husband of Mrs Fitzherbert – a Roman Catholic – that on her refusal he staged an attempted suicide. Past coping with the Prince of Wales's erratic behaviour, Mrs Fitzherbert decided to withdraw to the Continent. The infatuated prince, however, pursued her on her travels with his urgent suit of matrimony. In 1785 it became generally known that he had gone through a formal marriage ceremony with her according to the rites of the Roman Catholic Church, and in defiance of the Royal Marriage Act.

For years she lived openly as the wife of the Prince of Wales, highly respected by the society in which she moved. She was compelled into separation, however, when the heir apparent – so hopelessly in debt that he did not know which way to turn – agreed to a State marriage with his cousin, Caroline of Brunswick, as hinted by the king in this letter to Pitt.

Weymouth, August 24

Agreeable to what I mentioned to Mr Pitt before I came here, I have this morning seen the Prince of Wales, who has acquainted me with his having broken off all connection with Mrs Fitzherbert, and his desire of entering into a more creditable line of life by marrying; expressing at the same time that his wish is that my niece, the Princess of Brunswick, may be the person.[12] Undoubtedly she is the person who naturally must be most agreeable to me.

I expressed my approbation of the idea, provided his plan was to lead a life that would make him appear respectable, and consequently render the Princess happy. He assured me that he perfectly coincided with me in opinion. I then said that till Parliament assembled no arrangement could be taken except my sounding my sister[13] that no idea of any other marriage may be encouraged.

To Richard Hurd, Bishop of Worcester, 1803

Napoleon Bonaparte was regarded as England's implacable foe. 'The Little Emperor' was 'The Big Bogy' that threatened her peace. It had appeared for long that nothing could withstand his military genius or satiate his ambition. The kingdoms of Europe simply crumpled before him. Confident of success, Napoleon had already had medals struck commemorating his conquest of England. There was only one thing that lay between 'The Little Emperor' and his fixed purpose: that was England's navy.

The reign of George III if memorable for nothing else would be memorable for the great sea-battles, and for the great sea-fighters who saved the country from invasion at that time. In every coast town men volunteered, drilled, manned defences, and anxiously scanned the horizon for the sails that were intended to fulfil a threat more terrible than the menace of the Armada.

From the following letter, outlining evacuation plans for his womenfolk should Napoleon succeed in landing his forces on England's shores, it will be seen that George III – in the spirit of Elizabeth I – was prepared to place himself at the head of his army and fearlessly go forth to meet the foe. Fortunately, thanks to such admiralship as that of Horatio Nelson – a man whom, incidentally, George III disliked – the king's plans were to prove unnecessary, as the year 1805 disclosed, although the exhausting war continued.

Windsor, November 30, 1803

My good Lord,

... We are here in daily expectation that Buonaparte will attempt his threatened invasion, but the chances against his success seem so many that it is wonderful he persists in it. I own I place that thorough dependence on the protection of Divine Providence, that I cannot help thinking the usurper is encouraged to make the trial that his ill-success may put an end to his wicked purposes.

Should his troops effect a landing, I shall certainly put myself at the head of mine, and my other armed subjects, to repel them; but as it is impossible to foresee the events of such a conflict, should the enemy approach too near Windsor, I shall think it right the Queen and my daughters should cross the Severn, and shall send them to your episcopal palace at Worcester. By this hint I do not in the least mean they shall be any inconvenience to you, and shall send a proper servant and furniture for their accommodation. Should such an event arise, I certainly would rather that what I value most in life should remain during the conflict in your diocese and under your roof, than in any other place in the island.

> Believe me ever, my good Lord,
> Most affectionately yours,
> George R.

To the Earl of Eldon, Lord Chancellor, 1805

The marriage between the Prince of Wales and Caroline of Brunswick had collapsed within twelve months. The truth as to the real cause of their separation was never to come to light, but after the birth of their daughter, Princess Charlotte, the prince declined any further intercourse of any nature with his wife.

George III was exceedingly fond of his granddaughter, and took a keen personal interest in her welfare as heiress-presumptive to the throne. She was nine years of age at the time that he wrote the following letter to his Lord Chancellor. The relationship between himself and his eldest son had become so hostile by this time that the king no longer communicated with the Prince of Wales direct, but only through his ministers. He had been shocked beyond all hope of reconciliation by the prince's treatment of Caroline of Brunswick, and the public scandal created as a consequence.

November, 1805

The king has not thought it necessary, previous to his return to Windsor, to take any further steps for fixing the residence of his Granddaughter, as the apartment is not yet entirely prepared for her reception. It has been His Majesty's earnest wish, from the beginning, in superintending and directing her education, to act in entire concurrence with the wishes of her Father: and it was in full conformity to this principle that he directed a proper place to be prepared at Windsor for her residence, except at such times as she might occasionally visit either of her Parents.

Having since learnt that The Prince is desirous that she should remain under his roof during the time of his usual residence in Town, and that she should remain with His Majesty in the summer (except during the time of occasional visits), His Majesty is disposed to concur in that proposal; and is desirous to fix the period of her residence at Windsor from June to January, and is willing that she should reside at Carlton House the remaining months of the year. And His Majesty would not be desirous of making any alteration in this arrangement, unless it should appear to him to become detrimental to the execution of the plan proposed for the education of The Princess, in which His Majesty can never cease to take the strongest interest, both from personal affection, and from what he feels to be due to the future welfare of his Subjects.

George R.

As a result of the separation of her parents, the little princess was fated to suffer heartache, loneliness of spirit, and endless frustrations. The nation's sympathy went out to her wholeheartedly as her difficulties increased with time. Lord Byron's lines, written on the occasion of her early death in 1817, expressed the country's grief at a tragedy, 'Whose shock was as an earthquake's, and opprest / The land that loved thee so that none could love thee best'.

To the Duke of Portland, 1809

Although he had at no time distinguished himself as a commander in the field during the war with France, in his campaigns with the female sex the king's second son, Frederick, Duke of York, more than distinguished himself, particularly in 1809.

A few years prior to that date he had indulged in a liaison with an extreme commoner by the name of Mrs Mary Anne Clarke, whereby she became established in a mansion off Portman Square, which must have been a refreshing change of outlook from the slums in which she had originated. She was attractive, intelligent, and a witty creature. She was also an excellent businesswoman. While her association with the king's second son lasted, Mrs Clarke had conceived a bright idea of feathering her nest – and presumably that of the duke's – by the sale of promotions to army officers. It is difficult to believe that she could have negotiated such a profitable business without Frederick's connivance. Naturally, however, he denied any knowledge of such dishonest transactions when, after a motion had been raised in the Lower House, an investigation was made into his 'conduct as Commander-in-Chief of the British Army with regard to appointments, promotions, etc.'

Public dismay and indignation ran high at the disclosures which the duke's discarded mistress was only too pleased to make in person before the committee appointed. As an advertisement it probably served her special line of business admirably. She must have made many fresh clients as a consequence. In the end, by a small majority vote the Duke of York was vindicated, but knowing himself dishonoured by such a public enquiry he was faced with no alternative but to resign his appointment.

The formal note that the king wrote to the Duke of Portland at this time gives no indication of the despairing mental state into which he was once again fast sinking.

Windsor Castle, March 18, 1809
The king acquaints the Duke of Portland[14] that he has this day reluctantly accepted the resignation of the Duke of York, which

has been conveyed to His Majesty in a letter of which he has sent a copy to Mr Perceval,[15] and which he will, of course, communicate to his colleagues ...

If the scandal was a severe blow to the Duke of York, it was a still greater blow to his father. Frederick was the only one of his sons of whom the king had held a good opinion. The shame was to prove one of the final straws destined to break the over-burdened back of George III once and for all. More anxieties quickly followed. Perhaps not the least was the gruesome sensation created by the attempted murder at St James's Palace of the king's fifth son – Ernest Augustus, Duke of Cumberland – by the latter's favourite valet, whose prompt 'suicide' left many questions unanswered, and the duke under a cloud of darkest suspicion.

The king's final breakdown came at the close of the year 1810. During a brief lucid interval he was persuaded to sign the Regency Bill. Thereafter he became permanently insane, consigned to a living death for nine tortuous years.

George III died at Windsor Castle on 29 January 1820, in his eighty-second year, and was buried in St George's Chapel. No man within his realm had a more thoroughly English heart, or a more ardent desire to promote the welfare of his people and the interests and honour of the country. Never once, while his reason remained, did he despair of the ultimate triumph of England over all her difficulties.

12

George IV (1762–1830)

On 12th August 1762, 'all the bells of London', so a contemporary scribe informs us, 'rocked the steeples in peals of joy' on the occasion of the birth of a son and heir to George III and Charlotte Sophia of Mecklenburg-Strelitz, at St James's Palace. George Augustus Frederick, Prince of Wales, was described as a 'beautiful buxom baby', and his physical charms as he grew to manhood were to be excessively admired. To such approbation the Prince of Wales himself, it must be assumed, heartily subscribed. Over the years, a writer of the period tells us, he was to be 'pictured in every kind of uniform; in every possible court dress; in every manner of cocked-hat; in Scotch kilt and tartan; in frogged coat with fur collar; in tight breeches and silk stockings; in wig of gold, or brown, or black; with pigtail, without pigtail'. It is said there were more portraits painted of George Augustus Frederick, during the sixty-eight years that he bestrode this narrow world like a colossal cocoon, than of any other human being. He delighted in having his likeness reproduced, for the decoration of palace, hall and cot. In fact, so enamoured was he to be of the portrait of himself in his coronation robes, that he sent a copy to all the courts of Europe and to all the British embassies, as well as presenting it to innumerable town halls, clubs, and private individuals.

Men generally made a great show of their personal appearance in Georgian days. In their attire a group of fops and macaronies could vie successfully with any group of women for magnificence. In such outstandingly gorgeous array the Prince of Wales, from youth up, determined to excel. Because of all the resplendent wrappings and diverse sartorial disguises in which this 'painted, scented and powdered Prince' chose to exhibit himself it is practically impossible to visualise the real man at all.

When Prince of Wales to Charles James Fox, 1785

In the same way, it is difficult to get an accurate view of the character of George IV where his personal letters are concerned, so many of his expressed sentiments proving totally at variance with his actions. The following instance is an example.

Charles Fox – a son of Lord Holland, and a member of the opposition to which the Prince of Wales had closely allied himself and his fortunes – on hearing that the heir apparent was so deeply in love that he contemplated marrying Mrs Fitzherbert, had written advising him against taking this 'very desperate step'. Such a marriage, Fox contended, 'with a Catholic, would throw you out of the succession to the Crown, and could not be legal unless recognised by Parliament'. It appeared to Fox that such a measure, for all parties concerned, was one that only their worst enemies could have devised.

In reply to Fox's counsel, the Prince of Wales wrote the following reassuring letter.

> Carlton House,
> Sunday morning, 2 o'clock,
> December 11, 1785

My dear Charles,

Your letter of last night afforded me more true satisfaction than I can find words to express; as it is an additional proof to me (which I assure you I did not want) of your having that true regard and affection for me, which it is not only the wish but the ambition of my life to merit.

Make yourself easy, my dear friend. Believe me, the world will now soon be convinced that there not only is, but never was, any grounds for these reports which of late have been so malevolently circulated ...

Believe me at all times, my dear Charles, most affectionately yours,

George P.

Yet within ten days of writing the foregoing letter the Prince of Wales had married Mrs Fitzherbert. His infatuation, in fact, amounted to madness. Fox's wife, with whom the prince had more than once discussed the subject, declared that 'he cried by the hour; that he testified the sincerity and violence of his passion by extravagant expressions and actions – rolling on the floor, striking his forehead, tearing his hair, falling into hysterics; and swearing that he would abandon the country, and forgo the Crown.'

Mrs Fitzherbert, who resided on Richmond Hill, had in the meantime become the subject of a popular ballad designating her under the title of the 'Sweet Lass of Richmond Hill', one line of which ran, 'I'd Crowns resign to call you mine!' The song remained popular long after her death in 1837.

When prince regent to his daughter, the Princess Charlotte, 1815

George IV was responsible for bringing heartache – if not tragedy – to many of his womenfolk. Even his own daughter by Caroline of Brunswick was not spared. As unsatisfactory as a father as he had proved as a husband, the prince regent chose to subject Princess Charlotte to severe discipline, against which in the end she openly rebelled.

Towards the close of 1813 he had persuaded her into an engagement with her distant cousin, Frederick, Prince of Orange – a colourless, uninteresting youth, with the reputation of seldom being sober. Charlotte herself was far from being colourless. She was, on the contrary, a lively, sparkling character, with marked courage and independence of mind. It was soon evident to her that the proposed marriage could only end in failure. Along these lines she wrote a frank, clearly expressed letter to her father announcing her 'strong and fixed aversion' to the match.

In reply the prince regent sent his daughter a rambling epistle of some two thousand words in length. It seems to have taken him a long time to draft this screed – probably due to gout in the fingers, to which disability he was fast becoming a martyr – since it is dated 'Between the 20 and 25 February'. Typical of the man himself, it is a pompous document, mainly dressed in flowery language enveloping insincere sentiments.

From the following brief excerpts, it will be noted that the prince regent does not omit the opportunity of casting libellous reflections on the character of Charlotte's frivolous-minded mother.

If your alliance with the Prince of Orange were to be considered only abstractedly with reference to your personal happiness and the welfare of the country, it must appear most desirable that you should conquer your prejudices respecting it, and that you might do so if you were calmly and dispassionately to consider it, I can not doubt. Because if the same tone of mind and temper was to operate now, which prevailed, when you so earnestly and so ardently compelled me, as it were, to betroth you to the Prince of Orange,[1] all these notions which make you consider the whole happiness of your *life*, and *your welldoing*, as you term it, resting upon the abandonment of that union, would be dispelled ... [The Prince of Orange's] character and conduct have been proved through various and subsequent trials, to continue as amiable, as respectable and as unblemished, as they were when you first formed the wise and determined resolution to be united to him ...

You have no reason to apprehend in a union with the Prince of Orange the grievous calamity which I, alas! my dearest child, have experienced from a marriage with a person, whose character, we have had occasion so recently, so fully and so freely to gather, and from the contemplation of which it is so much my wish always to abstain ...

You see and know how much this wretched and unfortunate and cruel matter has placed you, alas! my dear child, by the wicked art and depraved contrivances of your mother, within her power[2] ...

I must here repeat once more that I concur with you in your observation that we can not marry like the rest of the world, for both our elevated rank, and our religious faith limit our choice to few indeed. How fortunate is it then under these circumstances to find youth, character, power, rank, consequence, national interests, and actual national alliance, all united in one, as they now happily are in the Prince of Orange; and how impossible it is even to hope, much less ever to expect to attain so fortunate a combination of circumstances for you, and for the country, in the person of any other ...

To the Princess Charlotte, 1815

To the lengthy epistle that the prince regent had taken five days to indite to his daughter, the impulsive but still determined Charlotte replied by return. 'Could I have bent my mind and my heart', she wrote simply, 'to marriage with the Prince of Orange, I would have done it, but that being quite impossible, I trust you will not think me less, my dearest father'.

The prince regent's answer will be found affectionate enough, but he is clearly chagrined that his daughter should have written so hastily. He had no doubt hoped that he had given her food enough for thought for at least a month before she finally made up her mind.

I begin by assuring you that your mind may be perfectly tranquil, and that you may rest assured that however I may regret what you express in your last letter, there is nothing in the manner of it that gives me the least offence or anything in your determination which shall produce any change of my conduct or of my feelings towards you.

The only thing I have to remark upon, and which gives me no inconsiderable degree of pain, is that (instead of keeping my letter for a reasonable time, before you answered it, by which means the consideration of it might finally have produced some impression in a matter so momentous in all its views) you should have sent the answer before, according to my conceptions, there was time for reason to operate on the representations which I made to you.

With a mind so full of anxiety for you I wished no doubt that the result of my best consideration had been again and again thought over by you. I have, however, the gratification which must always follow upon a conscientious discharge of duty which has been performed by me, in laying the matter before you in all its aspects former and present, formidable as they are.

And I shall only now draw your attention to the concluding part of my letter which must relieve your mind from all uneasiness as to my pressing the matter farther: having thus distinctly stated that its renewal can only flow spontaneously from the parties themselves.[3]

Although the prince regent readily agreed to her marriage with Prince Leopold of Saxe-Coburg, which took place not long afterwards, he never approved of Charlotte's choice of husband. All the same, he was instrumental in arranging for the impecunious Leopold to receive the handsome sum of £50,000 a year, irrespective as to whether Princess Charlotte lived or died.

The public's reaction to the death in 1817 of their idolised princess was that it was a judgment on the prince regent for his tyrannous treatment of her and of her mother. Opinion even went so far as to hint that Charlotte's death had been procured by poison, in which plot the prince regent and 'Old Snuffy' – as his mother was nicknamed owing to her preference for taking her tobacco that way – had played a part. Possibly Princess Charlotte's last words to her medical attendants – 'You make me drunk! Pray leave me quiet. I find it affects my head!' – when they were administering their potions may have given rise to this rumour. In any event, the nation generally was scandalised at what it considered had been neglectful mismanagement of the princess's confinement. Her chief physician, Sir Richard Croft, blew his brains out a few months later.

To his mother, Queen Charlotte, 1817

After the Prince of Wales had been appointed regent, the misunderstandings that had existed between his mother and himself, mainly owing to his callous attitude towards the king's tragic state, were gradually dispelled.

To judge from his letters to her, the prince regent obviously had a genuine affection for Queen Charlotte, as he had also for his sisters – whom he styled 'the dear Sisterhood'. It is said that he needed emotional stimulus to write personal letters, which he frequently obtained by resorting to the decanter. This would appear to be the case in many instances.

The following are excerpts from a letter he wrote to his seventy-two-year-old mother on her approaching official birthday, or, as she herself termed it, her 'sham' birthday.

From the tone of the letter as a whole there is no suggestion that the decanter had been brought to the prince regent's aid on this occasion. The letter, indeed, is not without charm. In spite of his mother's 'glorious stamina', to her eldest son's genuine sorrow she was to die within two years.

> Pavilion, Brighton, 2nd January
>
> I was, my dearest mother, quite overjoyed with the sight of your dear handwriting, as well as with all the good accounts which your letter contained of yourself as well as of all the other dear invalids at Windsor ...
>
> I do not much relish, to tell you the truth, your expressions and your definitions and your nice discriminations about the 2's after the 7's, and the 7's before the 2's. All I know and feel is this, that thank God you are blessed with a better, a sounder and a stronger constitution, than any other person almost now living, my dearest mother, especially for one who has had so enormous a family as you have had ... Therefore you must really forgive me for once, if I scold you a little, when you begin talking to me about the difference between your 7's before your 2's and of the 2's before the 7's ... I will grant you, my dearest mother, that we are not always capable of taking the same liberties with our health and constitutions as one may occasionally and imprudently do in the first bloom and effervescence of youth, but then on the other hand, we are not to allow ourselves to feel either discouraged or hipped when we are blessed with such truly glorious a stamina as it has pleased Providence to bless you with, if because being a few years older we do not, quite so speedily or so rapidly, recover our strength, after so very severe a seizure as that has been, which you have now shaken off. Indeed, indeed, indeed, there are very few persons even of the very youngest who could have done as much ...
>
> I fear I have scribbled too much ... so adieu, my dearest mother, for the present, with every wish and prayer that all

health and every possible blessing may attend you, so long as
his prayers can be offered up or heard, who subscribes himself
Your ever most dutiful and affectionate son,
George P.R.

When in 1820 the prince regent inherited at last the Crown
for which he had long waited with obvious impatience, it
was not to be the triumphal event of the nature that he had
dreamed. He was approaching his sixties in any event, and
was so monstrously fat as to appear grotesque. He was also
still heavily burdened with debt, of course. What was far
worse, however, was the fact that his vulnerable past at once
threatened speedily to overtake him.

The king himself may have had no particular conscience
as to his treatment of his wife, Caroline of Brunswick, but
he knew that the country was determined to have one for
him. It was now all too evident to him that in his vindictive
persecution of the woman whom he had vowed to love and
cherish at the altar, nearly a quarter of a century ago, he had
only succeeded in making her the idol of the public.

Six years previous to the death of George III, the Princess
of Wales had retired, on the advice of her counsellors, to
the Continent. An eccentric, unconventional and amazingly
indiscreet woman, her behaviour while abroad had resulted in
bringing her name into disrepute. Yet such was the country's
sympathy with Caroline of Brunswick in the treatment she
had received at the hands of the prince regent, that the news
shortly after George IV's accession that the queen was on her
way back to England flung the populace into wild speculation
and wilder delight, and flung the king into such distress and
anxiety of mind that he took to his bed. This fortunately
provided a suitable excuse for his not appearing in public
during the crowd's enthusiastic welcome of Queen Caroline.
It was better so. The king was in a far too highly nervous
condition to face the ridicule, the obscenities, and the stone

or so with which the mob was waiting to hail his appearance. They remembered Mrs Fitzherbert. They remembered Princess Charlotte. They also knew all about his various mistresses. The most renowned of these were Lady Jersey, afterwards to be referred to by George IV as 'that infernal Jezebel'; Lady Hertford, to whose husband the prince regent had made a gift of Reynolds's portrait of 'Perdita'; and Lady Conyngham, 'a plump matron with five grown-up children', but still foremost in the king's affections at the time of this crisis.

When king to Sir William Knighton, 1820

In his mental stress and profound self-pity, George IV sent the following hasty note to Sir William Knighton, who as a doctor had entered the king's service when he had been prince regent. Knighton soon became a baronet, and one of George IV's most influential advisers.

> Carlton House, Saty night, May 27
>
> I must implore you, my dear friend, if you have any regard for me to call upon me as soon as possible after your return to London to-morrow morning, as I cannot think of going to Church, nor of stirring out of my home, until I shall have seen you. My mind is in a state that is not to be described, therefore I shall add no more at present than that I am always
>
> Most affectionately yours,
>
> G.R.
>
> PS. Pray do not you also suffer me to linger.

The widespread and friendly spirit, evidenced on all sides, of Caroline of Brunswick's reception by the public on her return to London pressed forward the king's demand for an enquiry into his wife's morals while on the Continent, with a view to his obtaining a divorce. The Bill of Pains and Penalties later introduced by Lord Liverpool, the Prime Minister, following the queen's trial before the House of Lords, accused her of 'guilty and improper conduct since her departure from the kingdom'. It was entitled:

An Act to deprive Her Majesty, Queen Caroline Amelia Elizabeth, of the title, prerogatives, rights, privileges and exemptions as Queen consort of the Realm, and to dissolve the marriage between His Majesty and the said Caroline Amelia Elizabeth.

Considered as an everlasting disgrace to Liverpool's administration, opposition against the Bill became so violent in Parliament and throughout the country that it had to be abandoned.

Whatever may have been Caroline of Brunswick's behaviour during her exile abroad, impartial opinion of the day was emphatically of the belief that she was not guilty of the specific charges that had been brought against her, and that she had been the victim of gross perjury at her farcical trial before the lords.

The queen's spirit was, nevertheless, utterly broken by the strain she had undergone. The newly crowned king was to have the satisfaction of vaunting a black crepe band on his arm within twelve months of his wife's being brought to the bar of the house.

To Sir William Knighton, 1827

With the passing of time the physical deterioration in appearance of the once handsome 'Prince Florisel' determined the king to retire from public gaze to the privacy of Windsor. There, bedecked in highly coloured dressing gowns, or oriental robes, he contented himself as best possible: lying about on couches, and imbibing excessive quantities of cherry brandy. Only in Ascot week did the king venture forth in semi-state, playing off his winks and nods to the gaping crowd, and kissing his hand, just as he had done in his gay and youthful days.

His distress at his increasing physical girth will be gathered from the following letter he wrote to his old friend, Sir William Knighton.

Royal Lodge, June 18, 1827

... As to myself, I am pretty well bodily; but I have little or no use of my poor limbs, for I can neither walk up nor down stairs, and am obliged to be carried, and in general to be wheeled about everywhere. For my powers of walking, or even of crawling about on crutches, or with the aid of a strong stick are not in the smallest respect improved since you last saw me, – at the same time my knees, legs, ankles and feet swell more formidably and terribly than ever. This, I am sure you will agree with me, ought now to be seriously attended to without delay, by some plan devised and steadily acted upon, in order to stop the further progress, and to remedy it effectually and finally; for there is no question it is an increasing and progressive evil (at least, so I fear) unless steps are found, and that speedily too, of averting it.

You must now have had enough of my epistolary quality; I shall therefore, dear friend, hasten to a conclusion, with the assurance that I am always

Your sincere and affectionate friend,

G.R.

Whatever methods Knighton adopted to curb this 'increasing and progressive evil', as George IV rightly termed it, they were to prove unavailing. The king was, in fact, beyond the aid of medical science, and his end was fast approaching. It came at three o'clock in the morning on 26th June 1830, at Windsor Castle, a few weeks before his sixty-eighth year.

Those whose duty it was to investigate the contents of their late king's crammed wardrobes, cabinets and desks, were confronted with an astonishing array of 'treasure' which he had hoarded for over fifty years. Outmoded apparel – boots, coats, pantaloons. A host of trifling keepsakes – locks of hair, ladies' gloves, love letters, faded flowers. Perhaps the most surprising discovery among this royal magpie's personalty, however, was five hundred pocket-books, laid by or forgotten, each containing sums of money. The total cash that came to light amounted to £10,000.

In the opinion of one of his many biographers,[4] the reign of George IV 'saw great deeds and great men; it could have seen few men in all the realm less deserving a word of praise than George IV. Even the most courtly historian would be hard put to it if he were set to find out any passage in the whole of his matured life which compels admiration.'

On the other hand, there is the view of the Duke of Wellington, who had close personal association with George IV, which gives a shrewd and perhaps a fairer estimate of the king's character. 'He was indeed', the duke declared, 'the most extra-ordinary compound of talent, wit, buffoonery, obstinacy, and good feeling – in short, a medley of the most opposite qualities, with a great preponderance of good – that I ever saw in any character in my life'.

George IV was buried in St George's Chapel, Windsor.

13

William IV (1765–1837)

In 1762 George III had purchased Buckingham House – later to be known as Buckingham Palace – as a residence for Queen Charlotte, and there on an August morning three years later their third son, William Henry, was born. The infant's prospects of becoming King of England being remote, the London steeples on this occasion appear to have remained firmly at the perpendicular, their bells making no exceptional clamour.

By no means an attractive baby, William grew no more prepossessing in appearance as he passed from youth to manhood. He was, on the contrary, definitely ugly: thick-set, red-faced, and possessing a head shaped like a pineapple. Further, as to character, he early showed resentment of any kind of restraint. As his father grimly remarked more than once, 'William was ever violent when controlled'. The disciplinary life of the Navy suggested itself to the king as the most suitable profession for his third son, in the circumstances.

Becoming a midshipman at the age of fourteen, William was to see service in America and in the West Indies. His superiors, however, quickly learned that what the king had said about William was all too true. He proved insubordinate even before he had seen sufficient service to command a ship of his own. Once this occurred, he drove the Admiralty frantic with his mad-cap pranks. On the first occasion that he sailed away from a foreign station without leave, William had done so for the simple reason that he was 'sick of nigger faces'. He did, however, subsequently bring back to England with him a black mistress by the name of 'Wowski'.

When Prince William to Henry Martin, Naval Commissioner, 1786

During his coat-of-navy-blue days William was, of course, frequently in and out of love. One such affair was serious. At the age of twenty-one he proposed marriage to Sarah, the attractive and only daughter of Henry Martin, Naval Commissioner at Portsmouth. When the news reached George III he wrote agitatedly to the British Naval Commander, Richard Howe, 'I find it indispensably necessary to remove him [William] from the Commissioner's house at Portsmouth. And therefore desire that either the *Hebe* may be removed to the Plymouth station or William placed on board the 32 Gun frigate that is there. I merely throw out what occurs to me on a very unpleasant and unexpected event ...'

The heartbroken William was forced to say goodbye for ever to Sarah, and forbidden to write to her. Once aboard the *Hebe* he wrote instead to her father the following honest letter.

Hebe, Feb. 6th, 1786

Dearest Sir,

We are thus far on our way to Plymouth. Our cruise has been full of events ...

In a heavy squall as we were standing off, the main yard gave way, and we found it badly sprung. The only thing we then had to do was to bear up for Guernsey, where we anchored on Thursday at noon, and lay all the next day to repair our damage. We sailed again Saturday morning, and found it necessary to take shelter here from the badness of the weather. We shall remain in Torbay till the wind shifts.

I hope a certain person is in good health and spirits. As for myself ... God knows I have suffered enough in my own mind and do still. To my lovely girl, I leave it to you, sir, to say to her what you think proper. I love her from the bottom of my heart, and only wish I had been in the situation of life to have married her. My best wishes and prayers shall be always offered up to heaven for her welfare.

I once more beg your forgiveness, and hope you will ever consider that I am, sir,

> Your most affectionate but unfortunate friend,
> William

A short while later he was to add:

I find absence has increased my passion. What I feel on this unhappy subject is not to be expressed ... Nothing has yet transpired of my future destination. The *Pegasus* is ordered to be commissioned, most probably she intends to take me to America. The sooner the better ... Do pray give my best wishes to the dear object of my heart, and tell her what you think proper. Love her I do, and hope to do so all my lifetime[1] ...

William's seafaring career reached its climax in 1788, at the time of George III's serious breakdown, when 'the Sailor Prince', encouraged by the Prince of Wales, as already mentioned, more or less took French leave once more. 'What in heaven's name might he not do next?' the despairing Admiralty enquired (presumably of the wild waves, since William himself would have been the last to know). The problem of how best to deal with his total disregard of naval discipline was solved by withdrawing him from active service. 'The Sailor Prince' was thereafter compelled to kick his heels about on shore. His promotion in rank came merely as a matter of routine. (Incidentally, in her *Diary* Fanny Burney describes a characteristic anecdote relating to William when he was an enforced landlubber. Her amusing pen-picture of, as she terms him, 'a Royal sailor' will be found in Appendix D.)

As a member of the House of Lords the young Duke of Clarence soon made himself conspicuous. He was for ever leaping to his feet to expound his views on any and every subject under debate. True, his reasons were more often than not as two grains of wheat hid in two bushels of chaff – the chaff being provided by his listeners – but there were flashes of sound common sense in his diatribes. If muddle-headed, he was of honest intent always. (For example, the Duke of Clarence bore no personal animosity towards Caroline of Brunswick, but during her trial he took the side of his brother, not out of respect for the latter but for the sole reason that he had the deepest sympathy for Mrs Fitzherbert as a discarded wife.)

Within a short while Dorothea Jordan – 'a fine comedy actress who won the hearts even of Methodists' – sailed into the life of 'the Sailor Prince'. At the time she was playing 'Little Pickle' in *The Spoil'd Child* at Richmond, and was the mistress of Richard Ford, afterwards a police magistrate and to be knighted, who was responsible for four of her offspring. Mr Ford demanded a cash settlement for forfeiting her favours to the Duke of Clarence. Mrs Jordan's fifth child had been 'a little accident' that had occurred when she was in her mid-teens.

For the next twenty years William and Mrs Jordan settled down to a life of blameless irregularity, without even 'the semblance of a quarrel', as Mrs Jordan herself said in later times. As a sailor William was handy about the house, and fortunately loved children. To Mrs Jordan's five illegitimate offspring together the devoted couple added ten more before their separation in 1811.[2] William, like his father, was a home-lover, and had the makings of an excellent husband. Mrs Jordan, too, with her great maternal instinct, was more suited to be a wife than a mistress. The fact that she continued her stage career in between the intervals of child-bearing was due to financial reasons, and to keeping her growing brood in every comfort, William having generously taken her first five bastards under his roof. If it had not been for the Royal Marriage Act, there is small doubt but that 'the Sailor Prince' and 'Little Pickle' would have sailed to the altar together, 'Mr Jordan' having been a birth only of the productive Mrs Jordan's imagination.

When Duke of Clarence to the Lords of the Admiralty, 1794

When towards the close of 1792 war with France was threatening, 'the Sailor Prince' grew exceedingly restless. He ardently desired to take an active part, because, before all else, William was a patriot. At no time was he interested in party politics as such, but only concerned with what, according to his lights, was for the good of the country. Here again he was like his father. The Admiralty ignored his existence; however, the disappointed William sent the following emphatic letter to their lordships. They did not deign to reply. Such treatment seems extraordinary. Even had they feared that the unpredictable William might once again jeopardise naval discipline, the lordly admirals might, in the circumstances, have had the courtesy to offer some explanation.

Clarence Lodge,[3] March 15, 1794

My Lords,

At a time when this country is engaged in war with a powerful and active enemy, whose great aim appears to be the subversion of all the ancient monarchies of Europe, it becomes every man who values the Constitution under which he enjoys so many blessings, to rally round the throne, and protect it from the dangers by which it is so imminently threatened.

Conscious that during my naval career I never committed an act which could tarnish the honour of the flag under which it was my pride and glory to fight, I solicit in this hour of peril to my country that employment in her service which every subject is bound to seek, and particularly myself, considering the exalted rank which I hold in the country, and the cause which it is my duty to maintain and defend.

I regard a refusal of that employment as a tacit acknowledgment of my incapacity, and which cannot fail to degrade me in the opinion of the public, who, from the conduct which has been pursued towards me, are justified in drawing a conclusion unfavourable to my professional character, on account of the very marked neglect which has been shown towards every application on my part which has been transmitted to your lordships to be employed in the service of my country.

If the rank which I hold in the navy operates as an impediment to my obtaining the command of a ship without that of a squadron being attached to it, I will willingly relinquish that rank, under which I had formerly the command of a ship, and serve as a volunteer on board any ship to which it may please your lordships to appoint me.

All I require is active service, and that when my gallant countrymen are fighting the cause of their country and their sovereign, I may not have the imputation thrown upon me of living a life of inglorious ease, when I ought to be in the front of danger.

William

To Admiral Collingwood, 1805

In the course of his professional life at home and abroad, 'the Sailor Prince' had become acquainted with many leading officers and distinguished admirals, and with the majority of these he continued on terms of fast friendship through life.

His intimacy with Nelson dated from William's early days

at sea. He had come under the former's command during the time he was stationed in the West Indies. William owed much of his nautical knowledge to the instruction of Nelson, for whom he entertained boundless admiration. In aftertimes he was pleased to boast that he had been the friend and pupil 'of the greatest naval hero the world has seen'. When in 1787 Nelson had married Mrs Nisbet, the widow of a physician at Nevis, William consented to give the bride away. He could not resist remarking to the bridegroom, however, that he 'never saw a lover so easy, or say so little of the object of his regard'. Nelson's feelings were, in the emotional William's opinion, 'not what is vulgarly called love'. The news of the death of his hero, with whom, as it were, he had held hands across the sea for so many years, came as a severe blow.

Collingwood, too, stood high in the affection and esteem of 'the Sailor Prince', and not surprisingly so in view of Collingwood's fine character and naval record. At the Battle of Trafalgar – Nelson's plan of attack being to bear down upon the enemy in two columns, thus breaking their line in separate places – Collingwood, in the *Royal sovereign*, had led the first column. Nelson himself, in the *Victory*, had headed the second column.

Shortly after the news of Nelson's death on this great naval occasion, the following letter – as from one admiral to another – was written by William to the friend known always to him personally as 'dear Collingwood'.

St James's, November 9th, 1805

Dear Sir,

As a brother admiral, and as a sincere well-wisher to my King and my country, permit me to congratulate you on the most important victory, gained on the 21st of October, by your gallant self, and the brave officers, seamen, and royal marines, under your command, and formerly under my lamented and invaluable friend, Lord Nelson.

The country laments the hero, and you and I the loss of our departed friend.

Five-and-twenty years had I lived on the most intimate terms with Nelson, and must ever, both publicly and privately, regret his loss.

Earl St Vincent[4] and Lord Nelson, both in the hour of victory, accepted from me a sword, and I hope you will now confer on me the same pleasure. I have, accordingly, sent a sword, with which I trust you will accept my sincere wishes for your welfare.

I must request you to let me have the details of the death of our departed friend; and I will ever remain, dear sir,

Yours unalterably,

William

Two months later 'the Sailor Prince' attended the State funeral of Nelson at St Paul's with tears pouring unashamedly down his ruddy cheeks.

To Lady de Crespigny, 1811

Although the Duke of Clarence was publicly reviled for separating from Mrs Jordan after so prolonged an association, she herself could not at any time have regarded the liaison as being 'till death us do part'. From her letters it does not appear that she was completely taken by surprise, and certainly she bore no malice. She never reproached the action of her lover of twenty years' standing. In fact, she protested to a friend that the parting had only occurred because the duke was so pressed financially that he was forced, in the interests of his large family, to seek a wealthy wife.

This William proceeded to do with all speed. His first attempt was as imbecilic as others of a later date, as the following entertaining excerpts from a long letter he wrote to Lady de Crespigny reveal. She was the aunt of Catherine Tylney-Long, who was one of the wealthiest heiresses in the country, and only twenty-one years old. The elderly William, despite his ducal coronet, must have appeared to her as a pathetic and an unwittingly amusing old bore. In any event, her heart was given elsewhere – to William Pole Wellesley – whom she married shortly after the date of this letter, having had six proposals from the Duke of Clarence in the meantime.

Ramsgate,
Saturday morning, One O'clock
[19th October 1811]

Dear Lady Sarah,

I write at this singular moment because I have just left your Ladyship's lovely and truly amiable niece after having had the happiness of dancing with Miss Long the whole evening. I told her I was going to write to your Ladyship and asked her if I should deliver any message. The bewitching Catherine at first hesitated, and then said, '*Give my aunt my best compliments.*' I went on by venturing to know whether she had spent a pleasant evening: she smiled and said, '*You may add to my aunt I have had an agreeable evening.*' This message made me take up my pen to your Ladyship, tho' there is not any post tomorrow ... Of course my attentions are clearly pointed to Miss Long, and I really flatter myself the lovely little nice angel does not positively hate me. I walk with her and of course never leave her, and she does not dislike my devoting my public attendance on her.

This morning I found Miss Long walking with her mother and Emma followed by Pole. I joined them immediately, and the fascinating Catherine gave me her hand before him most heartily, and we walked near two hours together. She listened to me, paid no attention to anything else and was delighted with some remarks I made upon Pole. I went to Lady Catherine's[5] in the evening and escorted over to the library Miss Long: she had promised to dance two dances with him. I had previously obtained Lady Catherine's consent for the whole night and made her promise in future whilst we remain here to dance with me, and, to cut the matter short, I told Pole civilly I would not give her up to any man, and danced on with her. She hurt one of her beautiful little feet and gave up dancing, and I had an opportunity of conversing with her the remainder of the night ...

Miss Long knows my propositions for the marriage articles, of which she has kindly approved. Her dear consent is all that is wanted: it is a fair question. Miss Long can now be a judge if she hates me: if not, what time will she require to make up her mind before she will give me her hand and heart. Her relations wish it and so do mine.[6] Mrs Jordan has behaved like an angel and is equally anxious for the marriage. Miss Long cannot therefore be afraid of any *éclat* from that quarter ... Miss Long must be quite sure I love her and adore her. My two elder brothers are married, and I am therefore at this moment the first unmarried man in the Kingdom. Good God, to be kept six months on the rack is cruel. She has approved of my conduct and therefore knows me to be a man of honour. Besides, the character of the third son of the King cannot be a secret, and I know she likes what she has heard of me; the whole, therefore, must turn on whether Miss Long can like me or not ... In short, can Catherine Long love the Duke of Clarence?

She looked and danced like an angel and was the envy of the whole room. I have written a very long letter, and my only excuse to your Ladyship is my real and constant affection for the lovely and fascinating Catherine ...

Ever believe me, Dearest Lady Sarah,

Yours most affectionately

To his mother, Queen Charlotte, 1817

Shortly after the death of Princess Charlotte the prince regent asked his mother to persuade the Duke of Clarence, in the interests of the succession and as prospective heirs to the throne were at a premium, definitely to make up his mind to a suitable marriage. It was, of course, common knowledge that William had been attempting to tie himself up in lawful wedlock with one wealthy lady or another ever since his separation from Mrs Jordan, but he had been flatly turned down on each occasion. Few heiresses, despite the great attraction of becoming a royal duchess, were likely to be enthralled at the prospect of such an alliance. William may have been 'the first unmarried man in the kingdom', as he phrased his state, but on the other hand, he was no longer young, he had £60,000 worth of debts, and was suspected of being off his head.

The Duke of Clarence listened to his mother's counsel with, as she wrote to the prince regent, 'most careful attention'. His explanations, however, regarding his difficulties, personal and financial, became so involved that the puzzled Queen Charlotte appealed to William to make his views clear on paper. This he did, as will be seen from the following letter that he wrote to her – in its ingenuousness a little masterpiece – and which she passed on to the prince regent.

Bath, December 18, 1817

Dear Madam,

Your Majesty having requested me to put my thoughts in writing on the subject of the letter of the Prince Regent, I take up my pen to state as clearly as I can my sentiments and real situation.

I acknowledge a private and *public* duty and only wish to reconcile the two together: if the *Cabinet* consider the measure of my marrying one of consequence they *ought* to state to me what they can and *will* propose for my establishment. For *without previously* being acquainted with *their* intentions as to *money* matters I *cannot* and *will not* make any positive offer to any Princess.

I have *ten* children *totally* and *entirely* dependent on *myself*:

I owe *forty thousand pounds* of *funded* debt, for which of course I pay interest, and I have a *floating* debt of *sixteen thousand pounds*. In addition *to all which* if I *marry* I must have a *town* house and my house at Bushy completely repaired and *entirely* new furnished. *Thus* situated, and turned *fifty*, it would be madness in me to marry without *previously* knowing what my income *would be*.

If *that* settlement is made which I consider *adequate*, I shall *only* have to explain my *real* situation as the *fond* and *attached* father of *ten* children to the Princess whom I am to marry; for without a *complete* understanding of my *full* determination to see *when* and *where* I please *my daughters* I *cannot* and *will not* marry.

As for the Princess I think under *all* consideration the Princess of Denmark is probably the most proper provided her character is that which I should trust will bear investigation.

I hope I have expressed myself to your Majesty's satisfaction. One comfort at *least* I have that I have *opened* my heart most *fully* and *entirely*, and shall therefore leave in your Majesty's hands these lines as the complete sentiments that *must ever* dictate my line of conduct on a measure in which both my *public* and *private* duty is concerned.

I remain, Dearest Madam,

> Your Majesty's most affectionate and most dutiful son,
>
> William

Unfortunately for the Duke of Clarence his stipulations to the cabinet were barely at the committee stage before he was to learn that the Princess of Denmark had rejected his proposal. His disappointed mother was a few months later prostrated to hear from a triumphant William that he had proposed – and been accepted! – by an Oxfordshire heiress, Miss Wykeham, who had inherited Thame Park estates from her grandmother, the Hon. Sophia Wenham. This was too much for Queen Charlotte, the king, and the privy council.

They combined to compel William to withdraw his suit, to his consternation and dismay. He demanded that Miss Wykeham should be compensated by being given a barony. This was refused, since it would obviously have established a precedent where any further matrimonial indiscretions on William's part were concerned. William, all the same, never forgot his moral obligation to Miss Wykeham. When he became king he created her Baroness Wenham.

Finally Queen Charlotte selected as her third son's wife the twenty-five-year-old Adelaide, eldest daughter of the late Duke of Saxe-Meiningen, and William found himself in possession of an excellent helpmeet. Adelaide had inherited her father's good judgment and sense of duty. She was, too – like William himself – a home-lover.

Following an essentially economical wedding, the Duke of Clarence immediately took his young bride to Hanover. The reason for his hurried departure abroad was the importunity of his inconsiderate creditors, which decided William to remain out of England indefinitely. In due course splendid reports were received from members of the duchess's suite as to the astonishing change in the character and habits of the Duke of Clarence. 'You would be surprised at the Duke, if you could see him', wrote his equerry, Colonel Wilbraham. 'His wife has entirely reformed him, and instead of that *polisson* manner of which he used to be celebrated, he is now quiet and well-behaved as any-body else'. Wrote Gabriele von Humboldt, Adelaide's lady-in-waiting, 'I would not have believed that he [the duke] could show so much delicacy and restraint. I think she is not insensible to his consideration. It is evident to all of us that he is falling in love with his wife. What an agreeable surprise to find him so amenable and gracious! I did indeed misdoubt this marriage which now I think will prove happier than I had ever hoped ...' which was to be the case. The only occurrence that marred William's new-found matrimonial bliss was the death of Adelaide's first child within a few hours of birth.

To the Prime Minister, Lord Liverpool, 1819

With the passage of time the happy, if agitated, Duke of Clarence took up his pen and wrote the following news to Lord Liverpool.

Liechtenstein, August 2nd, 1819

My dear Lord,

Though it is with real satisfaction yet it is also with an anxious mind I now address your Lordship to request you to inform the Regent that there is every reason to believe the Duchess once more with child: it is now a fortnight since Halliday[7] and myself had our suspicions; but within the last three days the symptoms that attended the Duchess in her last pregnancy have so fully appeared that Halliday thinks it is his duty to write by tomorrow's post to Sir Henry Halford[8] on this most interesting event. Things being thus I should be uneasy if I did not address these lines to your Lordship for the information of the Regent; my anxiety to see the Duchess safe landed in England must be and is very great ...

I trust and hope to arrive with this excellent and admirable Princess at St James's on the tenth [of September]. I make no doubt the yacht will be on the fourth at Calais. Your Lordship can easily imagine the feelings I must have on this interesting state of the Duchess, and the anxiety I shall undergo till the happy moment arrives which I trust in God will make her a mother. Having every wish to comply with the desires of this superior minded Princess, I shall be most happy ... to see the Duchess at St James's under the able care of Sir Henry Halford, which will also relieve the mind of Dr Halliday.

I shall of course write occasionally till my arrival in England, and trust I shall have nothing but what is favourable to communicate. Adieu and ever believe me,

My dear Lord,
Yours sincerely,
William

Once again William's hopes and those of his 'admirable Princess' were doomed to disappointment. Adelaide's second child – Princess Elizabeth – died within three months, and with her died any further possibility of Adelaide's producing a prospective heir to the Crown.

On the death of Frederick, Duke of York, some six years later, the Duke of Clarence became the next in direct line of succession. The prospect of his being king was imminent, as George IV, in monastic seclusion at Windsor, was causing himself and his physicians deep concern.

To Sir George Cockburn, 1828

George Canning, appointed head of the administration on the sudden illness of Lord Liverpool, took a kindly and an understanding view of the Duke of Clarence. He was of the opinion that the elderly heir to the throne would make a good monarch, provided he went into strict training at once. Canning accordingly revived the position of Lord High Admiral – which had been in abeyance since the death of Queen Anne's husband, George of Denmark – for William's benefit. The office was more decorative than active. The Duke of Clarence was to have the title and certain ornamental duties, but the work was to be directed by an Admiralty board under Sir George Cockburn. (Cockburn had been one of the admirals who had taken part in the attack on Washington in 1814, during the American War of Independence, and had been criticised for 'disgraceful conduct' on that occasion.)

'The Sailor Prince' was enchanted with his appointment, with Canning, and with himself. Within a matter of days, however, he was seriously at cross-purposes with Cockburn over the question of pensions and promotions for naval officers which the Lord High Admiral wished to introduce. Dissension in this connection had barely died down before, to the distraction of the Admiralty board, the Lord High Admiral had hoisted his flag on the royal sovereign yacht, and sailed merrily to sea without a by-your-leave to anyone. He was forced to return owing to the unexpected death of Canning, but it was not long before he hoisted his flag once more and sailed away o'er the dashing spray. On Cockburn's strong protest the Lord High Admiral sent the following message from the *Royal Sovereign*.

Sir,

Your letter does not give me *displeasure* but *concern*, to see *one* I had *kept* when appointed to this situation of Lord High Admiral, *constantly* opposing what I consider good for the King's service.

In this free country everyone has a *right* to have *his* opinion and I have therefore to have *mine*, which differs totally from *yours*. The *only* part of *your* letter which I *can* approve is where *you* mention *expense*, and being now under weigh I have only to say I shall *for the present* leave the order *you so properly object to* in your hands till I return, when I shall talk the matter over with you deliberately. But I cannot conclude without repeating *my* Council is not to *dictate* but to give *advice*.

Faced with this main-top challenge, as it were, the Admiralty board helplessly appealed to the presiding Prime Minister, the Duke of Wellington. Wellington appealed to the king. George IV appealed to the Lord High Admiral, who, the king protested, had placed himself in a most embarrassing position, and was 'in error from beginning to end'. The Lord High Admiral stoutly refused to haul down his flag, and in the end decided to resign rather than be subordinated to Cockburn's decrees. William certainly was 'ever violent when controlled'. Nevertheless, one has a sneaking sympathy for him in thus attempting to break through red tape.

Before departing from the Admiralty, after only a couple of months as Lord High Admiral, William did not omit a

Parthian shot where the board was concerned. He distributed promotions galore, and in addition, silver ink-stands and invitations to his home at Bushey Park to all and sundry taking his fancy. Despite his anger with his colleagues at the time, however, when he became king two years later he bore no malice for the treatment he had received.

It was not to be expected that the nation as a whole would go into transports of enthusiasm when the Duke of Clarence ascended the throne at the age of sixty-five. Apart from none too reassuring newspaper gossip as to his private life, the country knew practically nothing about the new monarch save that he had been their 'Sailor Prince'. England loved sailors, however, and was pleased, despite his aged and somewhat grotesque appearance,[9] to have a 'Sailor King' on the throne. William Henry was pleased to be there, too. His only regret was that his desire that he should be crowned as Henry IX had met with no approval. He had always preferred his second Christian name.

It was soon evident that King William IV was eccentric to a degree that sometimes seemed to suggest a lurking tendency to insanity, or so his ministers considered. He was fussy, garrulous, excitable, noisy, overbearing, apt to take strong likes and dislikes, and to express his feelings with total disregard for the accepted conventionalities of social life. 'Altogether', says Charles Greville, the clerk of the council both to George IV and William, writing shortly after the king's accession, 'he seems a kind-hearted, well-meaning, not stupid, burlesque, bustling old fellow, and if he doesn't go mad may make a very decent king; but he exhibits oddities'.

Certain of these oddities were embarrassingly apparent to his guests during the king's State-dinner speeches. It was his habit to ramble along on all manner of subjects in the same oration, and seldom did he fail to give vent to some startlingly indiscreet remarks. For example, when the French ambassador was present on one occasion the king recounted his recollections of the days when Napoleon held the imperial throne of France, and closed his speech with an exultant reference to the glorious triumphs England had obtained over her enemies the French. *'Bien remarquable! Bien remarquable!'* as the renowned French diplomat, de Talleyrand, himself was heard to exclaim when William IV had once proposed a toast which those present afterwards declared had 'scorched their ears'. He could be equally upsetting to guests at his private dinner parties.

One of the king's foremost pet aversions was 'that baggage Kent!' as he styled his brother Edward, Duke of Kent's German-born widow, mother of the direct heir to the throne, Princess Victoria. William IV rightly considered that his little successor should spend some months of each year at his court, but this the duchess declined to allow, evidently in fear that Victoria's wicked uncle William might influence her child from the so straight and narrow way that the duchess had ordained for her. The duchess had been appointed to act as regent in the event of William IV's demise before Victoria reached her majority, and was so puffed up with pride at this prospect – which she hoped might occur as reality any day – that she considered it an obligation to the nation ceremoniously to parade the young Victoria about the country as Queen of Tomorrow, to the king's unspeakable indignation. Further, she insisted upon being received with a royal salute of guns wherever and whenever possible. The king's dislike of 'that baggage Kent, with her pop-gun mania' was not surprising, especially as she missed no opportunity to upset him. Such public performances were unpardonable enough, but her insulting attitude towards 'those *dreadful* Fitzclarences!' was something that the old king – who adored his family – could never forgive. He sensibly considered that it was no fault of his children that they were illegitimate, and he always treated them – expecting everyone else so to do – as if they had been born in holy wedlock. When he ascended the throne he had conferred on members of the Fitzclarence family who were not already holding higher titles the social status of children of a marquis.

When king to Princess Victoria, 1832

The opening paragraph of the following letter that King William wrote to his niece in his own hand, with its fine flourishing signature, suggests that once again the Duchess of Kent had proved a successful obstructionist. It will be noted that William IV entrusts his letter to his sister, Princess Sophia. This was to ensure that the child received his message. It was well known that Victoria was never permitted by her mother to receive an unopened letter.

> St James's Palace, May 26th, 1832
>
> Dear no longer little but growing Woman tho' equally beloved Niece,
>
> I regret exceedingly you were prevented spending last Saturday and Sunday with me.[10] I have now therefore to invite you to dine with *all* your Relations *here* on *my* Birthday as you are now really quite old enough to appear at my Table on particular occasions.
>
> Your dear and good Aunt Sophia will deliver this to you and can assure you how happily I look forward to drinking your health next Wednesday.
>
> God bless you, and ever believe me,
>
> > My dearest little Friend and Niece,
> > Yours most affectionately,
> > William R.

Five years later, on Tuesday 10 June 1837 the flag on Windsor Castle flew half-mast. 'The Sailor King' had received his final sailing orders in the small hours, at twelve minutes past two. After several weeks of severe asthmatic trouble, William IV died calmly, with resignation and dignity. 'Believe me', he said to the Archbishop of Canterbury shortly before the end, 'I have always been a religious man'. He had also always been a true democrat.

The old king had been genuinely attached to his niece, and in his final hours had requested that she might be brought to visit him. This her mother refused to permit. Nevertheless, the dying king's thoughts were greatly preoccupied with his successor. He was sure, he said, repeatedly and prophetically, that 'she will make a good woman and a good queen. It will touch every sailor's heart to have a girl queen to fight for. They'll be tattoo-ing her face on their arms, and I'll be bound they'll think she was christened after Nelson's ship.'

In estimating the character of William IV, the English historian, Harriet Martineau,[11] remarks, 'There was no comparison between the comfort of intercourse with him and with the two preceding sovereigns. He was too harebrained to be relied on with regard to particular measures and opinions; but his benevolent concern for his people, his confiding courtesy to the ministers who were with him (whatever they might be), and his absence of self-regard, except where his timidity came into play, made him truly respectable and dear, in comparison with his predecessors. When his weakness was made conspicuous by incidents of the time, it seemed a pity that he should have been accidentally made a king; but then again some trait of benignity, or patience, or native humility, would change the aspect of the case, and make it a subject for rejoicing that virtues of that class were seen upon the throne, to convince such of the people as might well doubt it that a king may have a heart, and that some of its overflow might be for them.'

William IV's funeral took place at night in St George's Chapel, Windsor, and for the last time the Royal Crown of Hanover – which passed on his death to his brother, Ernest Augustus, Duke of Cumberland – was placed beside the Imperial Crown on the coffin of a King of England.

Epilogue

Considered as a whole, these one-time Kings of England constitute an interesting study in human nature. Regarded individually, there is a marked contrast to be observed in their characters, and from the evidence offered by their private correspondence, each displays something of the quality of his true essence – its strength, its weakness, its greatness or its paucity.

As the founder of a dynasty[1] Henry VII stands out pre-eminently and with impressive clearness against the background of those kings that followed in his train. He was determined not only to reign but to govern, as was later his granddaughter, Elizabeth I, who was surprisingly similar to him in temperament. Although hated for his avarice, Henry VII was nevertheless reverenced by his subjects. He was a religious-minded man, and, while never appearing desirous of avoiding war, was a great lover of peace. The admiration his memory evokes cannot, unfortunately, be transferred to his successor.

By his father's arduous labours Henry VIII had inherited a quiet and prosperous kingdom. Perhaps his own history is the best judge and most descriptive proof of this second Tudor king's strength and abilities as a ruler. It is certainly difficult to form a clear conception of his personal character, since Henry VIII changed at different periods of his reign. All the same, it can be said with truth that his finer qualities were almost completely submerged by his voluptuous nature. There is little in his private life, in any event, that claims respect for Henry VIII as a man.

It is puzzling to conceive the devout little Edward VI as anything but a changeling. There appears to be no relationship between his actively conscientious temperament and that of his amoral father or slavish-minded, dissembling mother, Jane Seymour.

James I, wittily termed 'the wisest fool in Christendom', was obviously on occasion the most unwise fool in his private correspondence. This curious and in some ways pathetic character had exceptional abilities and intellectual acquirements, but he himself and events of his reign were at times so wholly ludicrous, while also being tragic, that it would require the dramatic pen of a Thomas Carlyle to do justice to the subject.

Within a span of three and a half centuries, from the accession of Henry VII to that of the last monarch of the House of Hanover – Queen Victoria – thirteen kings and five queens regnant reigned over England. If rumour is to be discountenanced, with one exception all of them died natural deaths. As a ruler Charles I had grave faults. Nevertheless, surely few can read his private letters without a feeling of esteem for the endearing qualities he discloses as a son, brother, husband and father. His judicial murder – that 'so glorious action' as Milton phrased it – in its open daring and despotism was an unprecedented event in the whole history of the country. It was as well a tactical blunder on the part of the perpetrators. By their illegal and unconstitutional act they had inadvertently made Charles I a martyr in the eyes of the people and the nations at large, and had thereby simultaneously laid the executioner's axe to the foundation of that high ideal – the English Commonwealth.

The personal characters of Charles II and James II suffer

something in the nature of eclipse in the light of that of their father. They were both profligate, and by comparison would appear as spiritless monarchs, and perhaps even less suited than Charles I to reign over a great and freedom-loving people. This fact is particularly to be deplored in the case of Charles II. He had been endowed with marked capacities. It must be conceded that during his reign valuable reforms were introduced, national institutions founded, and encouragement given to science, literature, the arts and architecture, in which progressions Charles II himself played no minor part. Had he only been capable of governing himself he might have appeared in the annals of history as an able sovereign. His real tragedy, however, was that he had not the gift of choosing wise counsellors or appreciating sound advice, as was unfortunately the case with all the Stuart monarchs. In the possession of this faculty, and the skill to use it to advantage, the Tudors had been supreme.

Although each, of course, had his individual merits or de-merits as a ruler, no further comment is necessary here as to the personal characters of William III and the four Georges, these having been sufficiently outlined already to serve as reasonably accurate thumbnail portraits. Where William IV is concerned, however, it should be said that it is pleasing to end this compilation with the unwittingly in-lighter-vein correspondence of that big-hearted and lovable King Comic and Great Patriot withal.

And yet, in conclusion, whatever personal preference may be entertained for any one of these rulers of bygone centuries, to the memory of most of whom handsome monuments were to be erected, perhaps the name of none – for all time – will have greater emotional appeal to the majority of lovers of England's history than that of the humbly interred

Charles, *Rex*.

Extracts from the *Eikon Basilike*

Although I have much cause to be troubled at my wife's departure from me, yet her absence grieves me not so much as the scandal of that necessity which drives her away doth afflict me; – that she should be compelled by my own subjects to with-draw for her safety. I fear such conduct (so little adorning the Protestant profession) may occasion a further alienation of her mind and divorce of affection in her from that religion, which is the only thing in which my wife and I differ ... I am sorry that my relation and connection with so deserving a lady should be an occasion of her danger and affliction. Her personal merits would have served her as a protection amongst savage Indians, since their rudeness and uncivilised state knows not to hate all virtue, as some men's cruelty doth, among whom I yet think there be few so malicious as to hate her for herself; the fault is, *she is my wife*.

I ought then to study her security, who is in danger only for my sake. I am content to be tossed, weather-beaten, and ship-wrecked, so that she be safe in harbour. I enjoy this comfort, by her safety in the midst of my personal dangers. I can perish but half, if she be preserved. In her memory, and in her children, I may yet survive the malice of my enemies, although they should at last be satiate with my blood. I must leave her then to the love and loyalty of my good subjects. Neither of us but can easily forgive, since we blame not the unkindness of our common people in general. But we see that God is pleased to try the patience of us both by ingratitude of those who, having eaten of our bread, and being enriched by our bounty, have scornfully lifted up themselves against us. Those of our own household have become our enemies. I pray God lay not their sin to their charge, who think to satisfy all obligations to duty by their Corban of religion, and can less endure to see than to sin against their benefactors, as well as their sovereigns ... But this policy of my enemies is necessary to their designs. They sought to drive her out of my kingdom, lest, by the influence of her example, eminent as she is for love as a wife and loyalty as a subject, she should have converted or retained in love and loyalty all those whom they had a purpose to pervert. Pity it is that so noble and peaceful a soul should see, much more suffer from, the wrongs of those who must make up their want of justice by violence and inhumanity ... Her sympathy with my afflictions makes her virtues shine with greater lustre, as stars in the darkest night. Thus may the envious world be assured that she loves me, not my fortunes. The less I may be blest with her company, the more will I retire to God and to my own heart, whence no malice can banish her. My enemies may envy me; they can never deprive me of the enjoyment of her virtues while I am myself.

Princess Elizabeth's Narrative Endorsed: *what the king said to me on the 29th of January, 1648, the last time I had the happiness to see him*[1]

He told me that he was glad I was come, for, though he had not time to say much, yet somewhat he wished to say to me which he could not to another, and he feared 'the cruelty' was too great to permit his writing. 'But sweetheart,' he added, 'thou wilt forget what I tell thee.' Then shedding abundance of tears, I told him that I would write down all he said to me. He wished me, he said, 'not to grieve and torment myself for him, for it was a glorious death he should die, it being for the laws and religion of the land.' He told me what books to read against popery. He said 'that he had forgiven all his enemies, and he hoped God would forgive them also; and he commanded us, and all the rest of my brothers and sisters, to forgive them also.' Above all, he bade me tell my mother 'that his thoughts had never strayed from her, and that his love for her would be the same to the last'; withal he commanded me (and my brother) to love her, and be obedient to her. He desired me 'not to grieve for him, for he should die a martyr, and that he doubted not but that God would restore the throne to his son; and that then we should be all happier than we could possibly have been if he had lived.' Then, taking my brother Gloucester on his knee, he said, 'Sweetheart, now will they cut off thy father's head.' Upon which the child looked very steadfastly upon him. 'Heed, my child, what I say; they will cut off my head, and perhaps make thee a king. But mark what I say; you must not be a king as long as your brothers Charles and James live; therefore, I charge you, do not be made a king by them.' At which the child, sighing deeply, replied, 'I will be torn to pieces first.' And these words, coming so unexpectedly from so young a child, rejoiced my father exceedingly. And his majesty spoke to him of the welfare of his soul, and to keep his religion, commanding him to fear God, and He would provide for him. All which the young child earnestly promised.

Mary Bellenden to Mrs Howard

The following undated letter was written by Mary Bellenden to Mrs Howard after the former had ceased to be a maid-of-honour, and had retired into the Weald of Kent. In its curiously elusive charm it is reminiscent of Shelley's lines, 'I am gone into the fields / To take what this sweet hour yields', and comes like a breath of fresh air. Obviously Mary Bellenden was enjoying her wholesome freedom from the artificial and scandal-mongering life at court. Mrs Howard also could write equally delightful letters to her friends.

How do you do, Mrs Howard? that is all I have to say. This after-noon I am taken with a fit of writing; but as to matter, I have nothing better to entertain you than news of my farm.

I therefore give you the following list of the stock of eatables that I am fatting for my private tooth. It is well known to the whole county of Kent that I have four fat calves, two fat hogs, fit for killing, twelve promising black pigs, two young chickens, three fine geese, with thirteen eggs under each (several being duck-eggs, else the others do not come to maturity); all this, with rabbits, and pigeons, and carp in plenty, beef and mutton at reasonable rates.

Now, Howard, if you have a mind to stick a knife into anything I have named, say so!

Extracts from Fanny Burney's *Diary*

The following scene described in her *Diary* by Fanny Burney was enacted in a private dining room at St James's Palace, the occasion being in celebration of George III's birthday, 4 June.

Mrs Schwellenberg, Queen Charlotte's keeper of the robes, had come over to England with Charlotte Sophia of Mecklenberg-Strelitz at the time of Charlotte's marriage to George III, and had been in the queen's service for over a quarter of a century. As assistant keeper of the robes, Fanny Burney – who was in her late thirties – found working under Mrs Schwellenberg a most exacting experience. The others mentioned were members of Queen Charlotte's suite. De Luc, a Swiss, had the honour of reading Fanny Burney's *Cecilia* to Queen Charlotte although, as Dr Johnson's 'dear little Burney' herself declared – one suspects not without exaggeration – 'he couldn't speak four words of English'. Incidentally, Fanny was in the queen's service for five years, and at the time that she wrote the following account had already asked Queen Charlotte's permission to retire, as her health could no longer stand her arduous duties.

This occurrence recounted by Fanny took place in 1791, when the Duke of Clarence was twenty-six years of age. Perhaps William Henry's high spirits were in part due to the fact that he had recently fallen in love with Mrs Jordan, who was to remain 'Queen of his heart' for the next twenty years.

At dinner Mrs Schwellenberg presided, attired magnificently. Miss Goldsworthy, Mrs Stainforth, Messrs. de Luc and Stanhope dined with us; and, while we were still eating fruit, the Duke of Clarence entered.

He had just risen from the King's table, and was waiting for his equipage to go home and prepare for the ball. To give you an idea of the energy of his Royal Highness's language, I ought to set apart a general objection to writing, or rather intimating, certain forcible words, and beg leave to show you, in genuine colours, a Royal sailor.

We all rose, of course, upon his entrance, and the two gentlemen placed themselves behind their chairs, while the footmen left the room; but he ordered us all to sit down, and called the men back to hand about some wine. He was in exceeding high spirits and in the utmost good humour. He placed himself at the head of the table, next to Mrs Schwellenberg, and looking remarkably well, gay, and full of sport and mischief, yet clever withal as well as comical.

'Well, this is the first day I have ever dined with the King at St James's on his birthday. Pray, have you all drunk his Majesty's health?'

'No, your Roy'l Highness: your Roy'l Highness might make dem do dat,' said Mrs Schwellenberg.

'Oh, by — will I! Here, you (to the footman); bring champagne! I'll drink the King's health again, if I die for it! Yet, I have done pretty well already: so has the King, I promise you! I believe his Majesty was never taken such good care of before. We have kept his spirits up, I promise you; we have enabled him to go through his fatigues; and I should have done more still, but for the ball and Mary – I have promised to dance with Mary!'

Princess Mary made her first appearance at court to-day; she looked most interesting and unaffectedly lovely: she is a sweet creature, and perhaps, in point of beauty, the first of this truly beautiful race, of which Princess Mary may be called *pendant* to the Prince of Wales.[1]

Champagne now being brought for the Duke, he ordered it all round. When it came to me I whispered to Westerhaults to carry it on: the Duke slapped his hand violently on the table and called out, 'Oh, by — you shall drink it!'

There was no resisting this. We all stood up, and the Duke sonorously gave the Royal toast.

'And now,' cried he, making us all sit down again, 'where are my rascals of servants? I shan't be in time for the ball; besides, I've got a deuced tailor waiting to fix on my epaulette! Here, you, go and see for my servants! d'ye hear? Scamper off!'

Off ran William.

'Come, let's have the King's health again. De Luc, drink it. Here, champagne to de Luc!'

I wish you could have seen Mr de Luc's mixed simper – half pleased, half alarmed. However, the wine came and he drank it, the Duke taking a bumper for himself at the same time.

'Poor Stanhope!' cried he: 'Stanhope shall have a glass, too! Here, champagne! what are you all about? Why don't you give champagne to poor Stanhope?'

Mr Stanhope, with great pleasure, complied, and the Duke again accompanied him.

'Come hither, do you hear?' cried the Duke to the servants, and on the approach, slow and submissive, of Mrs Stainforth's man, he hit him a violent slap on the back, calling out: 'Hang you! Why don't you see for my rascals?'

Away flew the man, and then he called out to Westerhaults: 'Hark 'ee! Bring another glass of champagne for Mr de Luc!'

Mr de Luc knows these Royal youths too well to venture at so vain an experiment as disputing with them; so he only shrugged his shoulders and drank the wine. The Duke did the same.

'And now, poor Stanhope,' cried the Duke; 'give another glass to poor Stanhope, d'ye hear?'

'Is not your Royal Highness afraid,' cried Mr Stanhope, displaying the full circle of his borrowed teeth, 'I shall be apt to be rather up in the world, as the folks say, if I tope on at this rate?'

'Not at all! You can't get drunk in a better cause. I'd get drunk myself if it was not for the ball. Here, champagne! Another glass for the philosopher! I keep sober for Mary.'

'Oh, your Royal Highness!' cried Mr de Luc, gaining courage as he drank, 'you will make me quite droll of it if you make me go on – quite droll!'

'So much the better! so much the better! it will do you a monstrous deal of good. Here, another glass of champagne for the Queen's philosopher!'

Mr de Luc obeyed …

[The duke] then said it was necessary to drink the Queen's health.

The gentlemen here made no demur, though Mr de Luc arched his eyebrows in expressive fear of consequences.

'A bumper,' cried the Duke, 'to the Queen's gentleman usher.' They all stood up and drank the Queen's health.

'Here are three of us,' cried the Duke, 'all belonging to the Queen: the Queen's philosopher, the Queen's gentleman usher, and the Queen's son; but, thank heaven, I'm nearest!'

'Sir,' cried Mr Stanhope, a little affronted, 'I am not now the Queen's gentleman usher; I am the Queen's equerry, sir.'

'A glass more of champagne here! What are you all so slow for? Where are all my rascals gone? They've put me in one passion already this morning. Come, a glass of champagne for the Queen's gentleman usher!' laughing heartily.

'No, sir,' repeated Mr Stanhope; 'I am equerry now, sir.'

'And another glass for the Queen's philosopher!'

Neither gentleman objected; but Mrs Schwellenberg, who

had sat laughing and happy all this time, now grew alarmed, and said: 'Your Roy'l Highness, I'm afraid for the ball!'

'Hold your potato-jaw, my dear,' cried the Duke, patting her; but, recollecting himself, he took her hand and pretty abruptly kissed it, and then, flinging it hastily away, laughed aloud, and called out: 'There, that will make amends for anything, so now I may say what I will. So here! a glass of champagne for the Queen's philosopher and the Queen's gentleman usher! Hang me if it will not do them a monstrous deal of good!'

Here news was brought that the equipage was in order. He started up, calling out: 'Now, then, for my deuced tailor!'

'Oh, your Royal Highness!' cried Mr de Luc, in a tone of expostulation, 'now you have made us droll, you go!'

Off, however, he went. And is it not a curious scene? All my amaze is, how any of their heads bore such libations.

In the evening I had by no means strength to encounter the ball room. I gave my tickets to Mrs and Miss Douglas ...

Notes

1 Henry VII

1. Lord Lovell's body not being found among the dead after the Battle of Stoke, it was supposed he had fled to safe hiding. At the beginning of the eighteenth century when the viscount's seat at Minster Lovell, in Oxfordshire, was undergoing reconstruction, workmen discovered a secret underground chamber. There they found the skeleton of a man, with head resting on the arms, seated before a crumbling writing-table. It was assumed that the fugitive Lovell had sought refuge in this subterraneous chamber where he had perhaps died from starvation or neglect.
2. Germans.
3. 'forthwith'.
4. 'subjects'.
5. 'prepared'.
6. attendant squires.
7. Men armed with bills or halberts, i.e. combined spear and battle-axe. The demi-lances were horsemen who carried light lances.
8. This early twelfth-century castle was made famous in literature by Sir Walter Scott's novel of that name.
9. Sir John Chenie, or Cheney, one of the victors of Bosworth Field. Although remarkable for his strength and prowess, he was unhorsed by Richard III himself in that battle.
10. Cistercian abbey in Hampshire founded by King John, and to be suppressed in Henry VIII's reign.
11. Perkin Warbeck was afterwards compelled to read this confession openly in the stocks in London, one day before Westminster Hall and the next at Cheapside.
12. 'perversion of truth'.
13. 'sorrow' or 'grief'. Warbeck had sent his young wife for safety to St Michael's Mount in Cornwall, where a monastery fortress had been

established since the time of William the Conqueror. She was brought before Henry VII as a prisoner shortly after her husband's arrest, and he was so moved by her loveliness and distress that he appointed her to the service of his queen. The Lady Catherine was thereafter always known as 'The White Rose', but as a tribute only to her beauty.

14. 'punishment'.
15. 'obedience' or 'submission'.
16. Seemingly Louis XII, who came to the throne in 1498, and to whom Henry VII was distantly related. Henry's paternal grandmother – Katherine of Valois, who, as the widow of Henry V, had married Sir Owen Tudor – had been a daughter of Charles VI of France. Margaret Beaufort herself had very wide and influential family connexions on the Continent.
17. Fisher became Bishop of Rochester. Condemned as a traitor in Henry VIII's reign, he was to be beheaded on Tower Hill in his eightieth year.
18. Greenwich Palace, built in 1433 for Humphrey Plantagenet, second Duke of Gloucester, became a favourite residence of all the Tudor monarchs.
19. 'get worse' or 'weaken'.

2 Henry VIII

1. Said by his enemies to have been the son of a butcher, Wolsey had been Henry VII's chaplain. He was Dean of Lincoln on Henry VIII's accession, and the new king was 'wholly taken in by his smooth tongue and pliable behaviour'. Wolsey's rise thereafter to the chancellorship was as swift and spectacular as was to be his fall.
2. Anne's stepmother, reputed to have been a Norfolk woman of humble origin. Anne herself is alleged to have been born in that county, at Blickling Hall. It was said that it was at the hall that her secret marriage to Henry VIII took place in 1533.
3. 'loneliness' or 'dreariness'. As late as the mid-nineteenth century the term was still used in some parts of Kent, as 'It is an ellinge house', meaning lonely or remote.
4. The king's schemes for divorce were known as 'The king's secret matter'. Far from being secret, however, it was known to all who did not choose to shut their eyes to the signs of the times.
5. 'Either there or nowhere'.
6. One or two of Henry's letters to Anne Boleyn have a fanciful heart as signature, with the inscription in French signifying, 'Henry seeks Anne Boleyn, no other', on each side of the heart.
7. One-time steward of the royal household.
8. Meaning 'the headship of the Convent'.
9. This probably refers to Anne's decision to retire to Hever Castle during the epidemic.
10. This descriptive reference to Anne Boleyn was made contemptuously by

'Meg' Roper, eldest and favourite daughter of Sir Thomas More who was to be beheaded in 1535 because he refused to accept the lawfulness of the king's marriage to Anne Boleyn. It is said that when she came to the throne Elizabeth I offered a ducal coronet to Margaret Roper, which the inconsolable daughter of More declined, 'lest it should be considered as a compromise for the judicial murder of her father'.

11. Hunsdon, one of the Boleyn residences.
12. i.e., 'while at Court'.
13. Evidently refers to some French ditty sung by Anne.
14. Sir Walter Welche, one of the king's privy chamber.
15. Anne's father, created Earl of Wiltshire in 1527.
16. By 'natural daughter' the king means the earl's lawful daughter by his first wife, as opposed to stepdaughter of the present Lady Boleyn.
17. Dr Butts.
18. York House had been the London residence of the northern archbishops since 1298. After Henry VIII had converted the property into his royal palace, Whitehall remained for over a century and a half the London residence of the court. In 1698 it was burned to the ground, and the court transferred to St James's.
19. Alludes to Suffolk House.
20. i.e., for Anne's return to London.
21. It is a pity that no information as to the nature of this particular ballad is available. All the same, it is clear that an attempt has been made, in Henry's view, 'to pick out mine eyes with a ballad-maker's pen', as Shakespeare puts it.
22. The king's niece, Lady Margaret Douglas. Henry VIII's elder sister, Margaret Tudor, had been married to James IV of Scotland in 1503. Not long after his death on Flodden Field, Margaret Tudor had taken as her second husband the Earl of Angus, and 'Marget' Douglas was the issue of this marriage. As Countess of Lennox she became the mother of Lord Henry Darnley, second husband of Mary Stuart.

3 Edward VI

1. Seemingly Henry VIII did not confer on Edward the title of Prince of Wales, as Edward never signs himself as such. This honour was first bestowed on English princes in 1301, when Edward I conferred it on his son, afterwards Edward II.
2. London's Castle, built in the eleventh century, was in its day to serve as a fortress, a royal residence, and a State prison. James I was to be the last monarch to reside there.
3. Refers to the Protector who, despite Edward's assurance, was loudly to condemn Thomas Seymour's marriage with the queen dowager without licence of those exercising the authority of the Crown. Somerset refused all aid to his brother when Thomas Seymour was sentenced to death for high treason some six months later.

4. Originally a leper hospital, mentioned as early as 1100, Henry VIII had acquired this property and grounds in 1532 for the purpose of erecting a hunting lodge.

5. The following account of this unusual tide is taken from an early MS. of London (Bodleian Library), 'This year, likewise, there fortuned a wonderful tide of the Thames, which came nearly as far as Gravesend, and overflew the banks, doing great hurt, especially in the parts opposite Greenwich; and many poor people were nigh ruined, and all their goods lost. About the same time a great fish, called a dolphin, was taken at Queenborough, and was carried to London, and shown as a great marvel to many. Some say the winds made the tides contrarious all over the world. Certain it is that many marvels happened by reason thereof.'

4 James I

1. Sir William Keith, the Scottish ambassador. James VI had instructed him to combine with the French ambassador in using every effort to avert his mother's execution.

2. *Nihil utile quod non sit honestum*, 'Nothing is really to our interest that is not honest and honourable'.

3. James's fear of a 'dagger-stroke', or any form of cold steel, was pre-natal in origin. Mary Queen of Scots, it may be remembered, had witnessed the murder of her favourite, Rizzio, shortly before James's birth. Incidentally, Sir Theodore Mayerne, famous royal physician of that time, said of James I that 'he had a drunkard for a wet-nurse, to whose vitiated milk he was indebted for so considerable injury that, although weaned within twelve months, he could not walk till his sixth year'.

4. The succession to the English throne.

5. i.e., 'without ostentation'.

6. Probably Sir Robert Carey, a relative of Elizabeth I, through her aunt, Mary Carey.

7. The *Basilicon Doron*, or His Majesty's *Instructions to His dearest Son, the Prince*. The book at a later date was to be highly approved by men of learning.

8. Anne of Denmark was a daughter of Frederick II, King of Denmark and Norway, and had obviously urged her regal birth as the reason why she should have preferential consideration.

9. Edmund Peacham, a Somerset clergyman, condemned for high treason on a manuscript-sermon censuring the king's extravagances. He died after torture in 1615 before sentence of death could be executed.

10. Hay, afterwards Earl of Carlisle, one of James I's favourites, took advantage of his visits to the Tower to entice Lucy Percy, daughter of the ninth Earl of Northumberland, to elope with him. In this escapade Hay engaged the assistance of the Countess of Somerset. Lady Percy had ostensibly been visiting her father, who was also a prisoner in the Tower at the time and powerless to prevent the runaway match. As the wife

of Carlisle, Lucy Percy was to prove in the next reign one of Henrietta Maria's most treacherous associates (p. 101).

11. One of the king's numerous pet-names for his favourite.
12. Villier's wife.
13. Royal residence in Essex.
14. i.e., 'godchild'.
15. Bristol, who acted as interpreter for 'the boy adventurers', loathed Buckingham. On Charles's accession, Bristol brought serious accusations against Buckingham, and was accused of high treason in consequence. This charge he victoriously defeated, however.
16. The Infanta.
17. Peter Bayne, *The Chief Actors in the Puritan Revolution*.

5 Charles I

1. i.e., 'personal possessions'.
2. Adam Newton, Dean of Durham, Prince Henry's tutor. He was later tutor to Charles.
3. Louis XIII, brother of Henrietta Maria.
4. Marie de' Medici, second wife of Henry IV of France who had been assassinated in 1610.
5. The young queen, Anne of Austria; her sister-in-law, Henrietta Maria; and Jean Baptiste Gaston, Duke of Orleans, younger son of Henry IV. The title of 'Monsieur' always reverted to the second son or brother of the reigning King of France.
6. Refers to Maria, Infanta of Spain and sister of Anne of Austria.
7. Cardinal Wolsey had leased this old Saxon manor of Hamntone, then a priory, in 1514, with the intention of converting it into a private residence of unequalled splendour. He had, however, to surrender it to Henry VIII in 1525, and it thereafter became one of the royal residences until the death of George II.
8. Henrietta Maria's principal lady had found no favour with Charles since their first encounter.
9. The queen's chamberlain.
10. i.e., 'use as an intermediary'.
11. There is no evidence to substantiate this. The queen herself indignantly denied it. She asserted that she had never approached within fifty paces of the gibbet and then only in the company of her husband. The accusation made against Henrietta Maria of having walked barefoot as a penitent to Tyburn Tree must have been recalled with some poignancy when, at the Restoration, the bodies of Cromwell, Bradshaw and Ireton – disinterred from Westminster Abbey – were to swing at Tyburn for 'the butchery of a King whom they could not degrade'.
12. Sir Richard Graham, who had been one of Charles's *cortège* on the Spanish expedition, and had proved an adept as a Scot at foraging when fare at the Continental inns was meagre.

13. The king's private correspondence was in his cabinet that was taken by the victorious Sir Thomas Fairfax at Naseby Field on 14 June 1645. Later it was published by special order of Parliament under the title of *The king's Cabinet Opened, or Certain Packages of Secret Letters and Papers written by the King's Own Hand.* Some writers have endeavoured to throw doubt on the authenticity of the letters, but if the documents had been forged they would probably have reflected more internal evidence against the character of the king. Moreover Charles I himself admitted their genuineness. Referring to their publication he says, 'The taking of my letters was an opportunity, which as the malice of my enemies could hardly have expected it, so they knew not how with honour and civility to use. Nor do I think, with sober or worthy minds, anything in them could tend so much to my reproach as the odious divulging of them did to the infamy of the divulgers ... nor is there anything more inhumane than to expose them to public view.'

14. Henrietta Maria had written, 'For the love of God, trust not yourself in the lands of these people. If ever you go to London before the Parliament be ended, or without a good army, you are lost.'

15. Claude de Lorraine, the Duke of Chevreuse, who had stood proxy for the king at Henrietta Maria's marriage at Nôtre Dame. He was the second husband of the wealthy and famous beauty at the French Court, Mme de Motteville, a close confidante of Henrietta Maria's both in the latter's prosperity and adversity.

16. Selsey, on the Sussex coast.

17. In the opinion of the English historian Gardiner, in his *History of the Great Civil War*, the Scots would gladly have protected Charles I 'had he been willing to comply with what they felt to be just and due to their creed'. As is evident from his letters, however, the king had no intention of deviating one inch from the course on which he had determined.

18. 'This day [10 November 1647] will be made famous in aftertimes', declared *The Moderate Intelligencer*, 'because, towards the end of it His Majesty escaped a kind of restraint under which he was at Hampton Court, and according to the best relation, thus: He, as was usual, went to be private a little before evening prayer; staying somewhat longer than usual, it was taken notice of, yet at first without suspicion; but he not coming forth, suddenly there were fears, which increased by the crying of a greyhound ['Gypsey'] again and again within, and upon search it was found the King was gone, and by way of Paradise [a room so called] into the garden, in probability suddenly after his going in, and about twilight.'

19. Lady Catherine Stanhope, a lifelong friend of Henrietta Maria's, was appointed State governess to the princess royal, and had accompanied the child-bride to Holland. She later had the personal care of Mary's son – afterwards William III – until his tenth year.

20. Husband of Mary Villiers – daughter of the Duke of Buckingham

– whom Charles I had adopted after her father's assassination. Richmond was to be among the faithful few permitted to inter the king's body 'when falling snow covered the pall with the colour of innocency ... So the white King went to his grave'.

21. The appended list of the children of Charles I and Henrietta Maria was made by Elizabeth in her own hand, probably during the time she was held prisoner:

Prince Charles James, born at Greenwich, May 15, 1628 [d. at birth].
Prince Charles, born at St James's, May 29, 1630.
Princess Mary, born at St James's, November 4, 1631.
James, Duke of York, born at St James's, October 14, 1633.
Princess Elizabeth, born at St James's, December 29, 1635.
Princess Anne, born at St James's, March 17, 1637 [d. 1640].
Princess Katharine, born at Whitehall, January 29, 1639 [d. within a few hours].
Henry, Duke of Gloucester, born at Otlands [Oatlands Park, a royal palace in Surrey], July 18, 1640.
Princess Henrietta Anne, born at Exeter, June 16, 1644.
Ellis, Harl. MS.

22. In this parenthetical remark the king was probably referring to his own unwise favouritism of Buckingham in the early years of his reign.

6 Charles II

1. The trouble in Ireland which Charles mentions refers to the Irish rebellion of 1641. The general rising was determined upon by some Irish chieftains, and was intended as an insurrection to redress the civil wrongs and remove religious disabilities in that country. It developed, however, into a massacre of the Protestants in which reputedly some twelve thousand men, women and children were either murdered outright or died of ill-usage and exposure.

2. One of the royal palaces in Hertfordshire.

3. Sir Gabriel Sylvius, who later married a daughter of the ancient Howard family.

4. Theobald, Viscount Taafe, an Irish Royalist.

5. i.e., a 'running dance'.

6. One of Elizabeth of Bohemia's five daughters. She also had eight sons, the third being Prince Rupert who became famous during the Civil War as a Royalist general. Pepys termed him 'the boldest attaquer in the world for personal courage'. Elizabeth of Bohemia came over to England at the Restoration, but died two years later.

7. Montague was a naturalised Frenchman, long immersed in political intrigue. He had recently become the dowager queen's confessor on the death of Father Philip, who had been Henrietta Maria's confessor since her marriage. Father Philip had had great influence for good on the

queen's character, and had he been alive the differences between herself and her youngest son would probably never have arisen. Montague was really at the root of the trouble

8. The queen regent.
9. Portuguese ambassador and Catherine of Braganza's godfather, later created Marquez de Sande by the queen regent as a mark of her approval of his successful completion of the marriage treaty.
10. Richard Russell was Bishop of Portalegre in Portugal and Catherine of Braganza's almoner. He seems to have acted as a secret agent in the marriage.
11. James Butler, first Duke of Ormonde and Lord-Lieutenant of Ireland.
12. James, Duke of York.
13. Sir Alan Broderick, one of the household.
14. The Duke of Ormonde.
15. Refers to Anne of Austria, who was incurably ill. She died three years later.
16. Refers to his mother, Henrietta Maria, with whom Charles was not on the best of terms.
17. The royal physician's prescriptions were still regarded as unrivalled, although he had been dead for a number of years.
18. The Duke of Monmouth, who had just returned from a visit to Henrietta Anne.
19. Newmarket had definitely entered upon its racing career in the reign of Charles I, although there had been racing there before his father's time. Charles II erected a stand about 1667, and built a royal palace in High Street. Nell Gwynne also had a house at Newmarket.

7 James II

1. On 31 December of this same year (1662) Pepys notes in his *Diary*, 'The Duke of Monmouth is in so great splendour at Court, and so dandled by the King, that some doubt that, if the King should have no child by the Queene (which there is yet no appearance of), whether he would not be acknowledged for a lawful son; and that there will be a difference follow between the Duke of York and him; which God prevent!'
2. Peterborough stood proxy for the duke at the State ceremony in Modena.
3. Louis XIV.
4. James was under the impression that his daughter was pregnant.
5. i.e., escort. Ossory, son of the Duke of Ormonde and Catherine of Bradganza's chamberlain, had married into a Dutch family.
6. This disinherited prince of the House of Stuart was in course of time to assume the name of the Chevalier de St George, although he was always called by his enemies 'The Prentender'.
7. A hunting palace belonging to William.
8. The king is here alluding to Mary's oft-repeated assertions that William's preparations were only to defend himself against attack from France.

9. Among the Jacobite songs and poems that went into circulation at this time, one opened with the following lines:

> Oh, we have heard that impious sons before
> Rebelled for crowns their royal parents wore;
> But of unnatural daughters rarely hear,
> Save those of hapless James, and those of ancient Lear.

10. Refers to the king's attempt to come to terms with William of Orange.
11. James II's natural son by an early mistress, Arabella Churchill, lady-in-waiting to his first duchess, Anne Hyde. Berwick proved a distinguished soldier, and lost his life at the siege of Philippsburg in 1734, when 'as he mounted the trenches the batteries on each side went into simultaneous action, and a ball cut him in two'. He was one of the last great generals of Louis XIV's reign.

8 William III

1. Clear proof of William's duplicity was found in his private correspondence at Kensington Palace after his death, from which it was evident that his agents had been actively intriguing to depose James II while he himself and his wife were diplomatically carrying on a friendly correspondence with the king and queen.
2. As Mary Worth, a maid-of-honour to Princess Mary, she had compromised herself with Zulestein, and the latter had been persuaded into marriage with her by Princess Mary and Doctor Ken, to the intense fury of William of Orange, who had been absent in Amsterdam at the time. He had a peculiar possessiveness where his favourites were concerned.
3. Skelton perseveringly warned the king of the machinations of the Prince of Orange, but nothing at that time would induce James seriously to credit the truth of such suggestions. In fact, on his daughter's protesting that Skelton was working in the interests of France against her husband, James had his ambassador sent to the Tower.
4. Refers to the Battle of the Boyne.
5. When William's signature was doubly affixed, as in this case, it indicated that the execution of the warrant was to be regarded as urgent.
6. William III had had this new brick palace built at Loo shortly after his marriage to Mary, who had laid the first stone. The decorations and the layout of the expensive gardens there had given her some pleasure in her loneliness, but Mary had never returned to Loo after she came to the throne.

9 George I

1. Chamberlain to George of Hanover.
2. Refers to his uncle, Prince Rupert, his mother's brother.
3. Sir Charles Cottrell, master of court ceremonies.

4. The Duke of Hamilton.
5. Catherine of Braganza.
6. i.e., Princess Anne.
7. William Howard, Viscount Stafford, had been accused of complicity in the alleged 'Popish Plot' of 1678, and on the evidence of false witnesses was convicted of high treason. 'He has been condemned', says Evelyn, 'on testimony that ought not to be taken on the life of a dog'.
8. The king poured gold and jewels on his mistresses. To the aloof Caroline, however, he once made the oddest gift. We read in *Brice's Weekly Journal* of 8 April 1725, 'The wild boy whom the King has presented to the Princess of Wales, taken last winter in the forest of Hamelin, walking on all fours, running up trees like a squirrel, feeding on twigs and moss, was last night carried into the presence of the King, the Royal Family, and many of the Nobility ... He is committed to the care of Dr Arbuthnot in order to try whether he can be brought to use speech and made a sociable creature'. Dr John Arbuthnot, great physician, scientific scholar, and gentle-natured man, came to the conclusion, however, that 'Peter, the Wild Boy' – as he was thereafter known – was a 'confirmed idiot'. Poor 'Peter', wearing a leather dog-collar for some sixty years, was boarded out on a Hertfordshire farm. He died in 1785. A brass plaque was put up to his memory in the church of St Mary at Northchurch in the same county.

10 George II

1. i.e., including his household.

11 George III

1. i.e., Kew House, which had been the residence of George's father and mother for many years. On his mother's death in 1772 George III and his family occupied Kew House as their summer residence.
2. The prince is apparently referring to George II's mistress, Lady Yarmouth, who was assumed to be an active agent in State affairs. She once bet a clergyman that he would be made a bishop, the stakes being 5,000. She saw to it that her gamble was successful, and collected her winnings from the astonished parson.
3. Refers to the Peace of Fontainebleau between Great Britain, France, Spain and Portugal, 1762: an honourable termination of a war that had added £75 million to the national debt of the country. In the king's view, war was 'bloody and expensive'.
4. Richmond Lodge was pulled down in 1772, and its grounds became part of Kew Gardens.
5. The Hon. Frederick Cornwallis, uncle of Charles Cornwallis, first marquis, and Governor-General of India.
6. Principal home and State residence of English sovereigns from as early as the twelfth century.

7. The reader may perhaps be familiar with Sir Joshua Reynolds's famous painting of Mrs Robinson as 'Perdita'. Later, in her memoirs, 'Perdita' recorded most intimate details of her relationship with the Prince of Wales.

8. George Capell Viscount Malden, later fifth Earl of Essex.

9. The king had reason to anticipate such censure. Public-spirited people were not only concerned with the Prince of Wales's spendthrift way of life but, by contrast, with the conditions of the humbler classes. The work of Elizabeth Fry, the prison reformer, was thus not surprisingly satirised by Lord Byron:

> Oh, Mrs. Fry! Why go to Newgate? Why
> Preach to poor rogues? And wherefore not begin
> With Carlton, or with other houses? Try
> Your hand at harden'd and imperial sin.

The poor rogues, however, had their consolation. They could get drunk for a penny, and dead drunk for twopence, for gin at least was cheap.

10. First Lord of the Admiralty.

11. William – afterwards William IV – was created Duke of Clarence this same year, and took his seat in the Lords.

12. Even Caroline of Brunswick herself spoke highly of Mrs Fitzherbert. 'Dat is de Prince's true wife', she remarked to Lady Charlotte Campbell, one of her ladies-in-waiting, not long after her marriage. 'She is an excellent woman; it is a great pity for him dat he ever broke vid her'.

13. The 'toothpick' Augusta, who, it will be remembered, had married the Duke of Brunswick-Wolfenbüttel.

14. William Pitt had died in 1806, at the age of forty-seven, having worn himself out by the long stress of expected invasion, and Portland had formed a new ministry in 1807.

15. Spencer Perceval, Chancellor of the Exchequer and leader of the House of Commons. He was shot dead in 1812, when he was Prime Minister, in the lobby of the house by a half-demented merchant named Bellingham supposedly labouring under some personal grievance.

12 George IV

1. An unpardonable overstatement!

2. The prince regent is here referring to an indiscreet attachment Charlotte had formed for one of her mother's friends, a Captain Hesse of the Light Dragoons, which had occurred the previous year. It was probably little more than a girlish infatuation, but Caroline of Brunswick's encouragement had created a compromising situation for her daughter. Charlotte was persuaded by her father that her mother's influence threatened moral danger to herself, and she had been made to promise never to write to her mother – who by now had left the country – without her father's permission.

3. Meaning, renewal of her engagement to Frederick of Orange.
4. Justin Macarthy, *History of the Four Georges*.

13 William IV

1. Sarah, for her part, was to remain faithful to William's memory. She died unmarried in 1826.
2. The following is a list of the children (known as the Fitzclarence family) of the Duke of Clarence and Mrs Jordan:

   George Augustus Frederick (1794–1842), created Earl of Munster, 1831. (Committed suicide.)

   Henry (1795–1817). Died as a captain in India.

   Sophia (1796–1837). Married the first Lord de Lisle and Dudley.

   Mary (1798–1864). Married General Fox.

   Frederick (1799–1854). Lieutenant-General in the army.

   Elizabeth (1801–56). Married the sixteenth Earl of Errol.

   Adolphus (1802–63). Rear-Admiral: Naval *aide-de-camp* to Queen Victoria.

   Augusta (1803–65). Married (i) the Hon. John Kennedy Erksine, and (ii) Lord John Frederick Gordon.

   Augustus (1805–54). Rector of Mapledurham, Oxfordshire.

   Amelia (1807–58). Married the tenth Viscount Falkland.
3. Clarence Lodge, Richmond, had been given to William as a country residence when he became Duke of Clarence. It stood on the edge of the Old Deer Park. For town accommodation he had been allotted quarters at St James's Palace, 'with a table and covers, the number of courses to be limited, and £2,000 a year'.
4. As Admiral Jervis, Earl St Vincent – with only fourteen ships to the Spaniards' twenty-seven – had in 1797 beaten the latter off Cape St Vincent, thus preventing the loss of England's command of the Channel.
5. Catherine's mother, Lady Catherine Tylney-Long.
6. This was wishful thinking on William's part. They were either flabbergasted or convulsed with laughter.
7. Andrew Halliday, an army surgeon who had distinguished himself at Waterloo. This may have given him recommendation in the eyes of William, but seems hardly a suitable qualification for a maternity specialist. The births of both Adelaide's babies had been premature, Halliday on the first occasion having bled the duchess during an attack of pleurisy.
8. The king's physician.
9. The following description of William IV and Queen Adelaide was given by an eyewitness of the arrival of their majesties to inspect the Tower of London shortly after their coronation, 'The king is a little, old, red-nosed, weather-beaten, jolly-looking person … The queen … a little insignificant person as ever I saw. She was dressed, as perhaps you will see by the papers, 'exceeding plain' in bombazine with a little shabby muslin collar, dyed Leghorn hat, and leather shoes.'

10. Evidently the king had invited Victoria to stay with him over her birthday, which was 24 May. By '*my* Birthday' he means, of course, his official birthday.
11. *History of England during the Thirty Years' Peace.*

Epilogue

1. It is interesting that the three dynasties here reviewed should each have owed its succession to the female line: the House of Tudor to Margaret Beaufort; the House of Stuart to Margaret Tudor; and the House of Hanover to Sophia Stuart, via her mother, Elizabeth Stuart, daughter of James I. Further, the Houses of Saxe-Coburg and Windsor descended from the last monarch of the House of Hanover – Queen Victoria.

Appendix B: Princess Elizabeth's Narrative

1. The year in England at that time began on 24 March, and not on 1 January, as was later arranged in the eighteenth century. The year of Charles's death, old-style calendar, was therefore 1648, although it is usually given as 1649, according to the reformed calendar.

Appendix D: Extracts from Fanny Burney's Diary

1. Mary was the king's fourth daughter.

Acknowledgements

I have to acknowledge the gracious permission of Her Majesty the Queen to make use of the letter written by King William IV to Princess Victoria which appears on p. 253.

I express my thanks and acknowledge my indebtedness to the following authors and publishers:

Sir Arthur Bryant and Cassell & Co. for granting the use of letters from *Letters of Charles II*.

Professor Bonamy Dobree, M.A., and Cassell & Co. for permission to use letters from *Letters of George III*.

Professor Aspinall and University Press, Cambridge, for use of letters from *Letters of George IV* (Crown copyright), and also to the same author and Arthur Barker, Limited, for permission to use letters from *Mrs Jordan and Her Family*.

To the Navy Records Society (Admiralty) for use of a letter from *The Correspondence of Lord Collingwood* (1837), and to the same Society for permission to use excerpts from two letters from *Letters of Sir Byam Martin*, quoted from Miss Doris Leslie's delightful book *Royal William*, in which the letters first appeared in print.

Mr Roger Fulford for his kind permission to use letters from *Royal Dukes* and *George IV*. I am under further obligation to the author of these two admirable books for many useful facts in my sections on George IV and William IV.

Miss Grace Thompson and the Hutchinson Group for permission to use a letter from *The Patriot King*.

Longmans, Green & Co. for the use of letters from Wilkins's *Caroline the Illustrious*.

In compiling this correspondence I am again obliged to public and private libraries for ready facilities offered, in particular the manuscript department and reading room of the British Museum, and Guildhall and Marylebone Public Libraries.

I have also to express my gratitude to Sunday Wilshin for reading the book in manuscript, and making valuable suggestions, and my sincere thanks to Selene Moxon for assistance in proof-reading.

Margaret Sanders

Bibliography

Aspinall, A., *Letters of George IV* (Cambridge: Cambridge University Press, 1938)

Aspinall, A., *Mrs Jordan and her Family* (London: Arthur Baker Ltd, 1951)

Bryant, A., *Letters of Charles II* (London: Cassell & Co., 1935)

Cartwright, J., *Madame* (London: Seeley & Co., 1894)

Dobrée, B., *Letters of George III* (London: Cassell & Co., 1935)

Ellis, H., *Historical Letters* (London)

Ellis, H., *Original Letters Illustrative of England's History*, vol. 4 (London: Richard Bentley, 1846)

Fitzgerald, P., *Life and Times of William IVI* (London: Tinsley Brothers, 1884)

Fulford, R., *George IV* (London: Duckworth, 1935)

Fulford, R., *Royal Dukes* (London: Pan Books, 1933)

Halliwell-Phillipps, J., *Letters of England's Kings* (London: Henry Colburn, 1846)

Jesse, J., *Memoirs of the Life and Reign of George III* (London: Tinsley Brothers, 1867)

Langdale, C., *Memoirs of Mrs Fizherbert* (London: Richard Bentley, 1856)

Leslie, D., *Royal William* (London: Hutchinson & Co. Ltd, 1940)

Strickland, A., *Lives of the Queens of England,* vols 2, 4, 5, 6 (London: Colburn & Co., 1840–1852)

Thompson, G., *The Patriot King: William IV* (Boston: E. P. Dutton & Co., 1933)

Wilkins, H., *Caroline the Illustrious* (London: Longmans & Company, 1904)

Books Suggested for Further Reading

Bryant, A., *Charles II* (London: Collins, 1955).

Chapman, Hester, W., *The Last Tudor King: A Study of Edward VI* (London: J. Cape, 1958).

Hartman, C., *Charles II and Madame* (1950).

Huish, R., *Life and Reign of William IV* (London: William Emans, 1850).

Ogg, D., *William III* (London: Collins, 1956).

Pickthorn, K. W. M., *Henry VII*, vol. 1 (Cambridge: Cambridge University Press 1934).

Pickthorn, K. W. M., *Henry VIII*, vol. 2 (Cambridge: Cambridge University Press, 1934).

Plumb, J. H., *The First Four Georges* (Franklin Watts, Incorporated, 1956).

Pollard, A. F., *Henry VIII* (London: Longman Green & Co., 1951).

Turner, F. C., *James II* (London: Eyre & Spottiswoode, 1948).

Wilson, D. H., *James VI & I* (London: Jonathon Cape, 1956).

Young, G. M., *Charles I* (London: Hart-Davis, 1950).

CONCRETE

NETTA B.

CONCRETE

Copyright © 2019 Netta B.